50 FACTS
THAT SHOULD
CHANGE
THE
WORLD

2.0

Jessica Williams

disinformation®

© 2007 Jessica Williams

Published by The Disinformation Company Ltd.
163 Third Avenue, Suite 108
New York, NY 10003
Tel.: +1.212.691.1605
Fax: +1.212.691.1606
www.disinfo.com

An earlier edition of this book was published in Great Britain by Icon Books Ltd.
This edition is fully revised and updated for the United States.

Library of Congress Control Number: 2007937480

ISBN: 978-1932857-90-0

Cover Illustration: Rebecca Meek . thecreativeshop

Printed in USA

10 9 8 7 6 5 4 3 2 1

Distributed by:
Consortium Book Sales and Distribution
Toll Free: +1.800.283.3572
Fax: +1.612.746.2606
www.cbsd.com

To my aunt, Rosemary Williams,
a tireless activist for animal rights
whose memory inspired me as I wrote this book

Contents

...THAT SHOULD CHANGE THE WORLD

Acknowledgements

I had always believed that writing a book would be a solitary process, but I believed wrong. Numerous people have helped, inspired and contributed, and I am incredibly grateful to all of them.

Extra-special thanks go to Neil Durkin of Amnesty International and Steve Crawshaw of Human Rights Watch; to Jacqui Hunt of Equality Now!; to Gladwell Otieno at Transparency International Kenya; and to Barry Hugill of Liberty, Neera Sharma at Barnardo's and Simon Davies at Privacy International. Thanks also to the people who took time to talk to me, to those who contributed or inspired the arguments herein, and to all the groups, large andsmall, working to make the world a better and fairer place.

There are two people without whom this book would not have happened, and I mean that without the slightest exaggeration: Professor Ziauddin Sardar, whose generous recommendation and encouragement really did set this all in motion, and Andrew Furlow at Icon Books, who dealt with an apprehensive and doubt-stricken author with true aplomb.

To my colleagues at HardTalk – Carey, Tim, Sola, Ali, Bridget, Tanya, Sian, Tama, Nick and Dougal – thank you for your inspiration and enthusiasm. Thanks also to my family and friends for their kindness, unstinting support and understanding in the face of a suddenly silent telephone. My best friend Callum managed to cheer me on from 12,000 miles away – an impressive feat by anyone's standards. And then, there is John – who has been my first sub, my sounding board and a wonderful and patient partner in crime. He will be truly embarrassed to be in any list like this, which just makes me more determined to thank him.

About the Author

Jessica Williams is a journalist and television producer for the BBC, where she has researched and produced interviews with such disparate figures as the political philosopher Noam Chomsky, President Paul Kagame of Rwanda, Sir David Attenborough, Northern Ireland First Minister David Trimble, and the late American academic Edward Said.

Introduction: Why should these 50 facts change the world?

Setting out to change the world is a pretty difficult task. At first, it's hard to see how a fact, a simple piece of information, can do that. But I firmly believe that each one of the 50 facts in this book is capable of changing the way we think – and when it comes to changing the world, that's the most important step we can take.

Each fact in this book tells us something important we need to know about modern life in the modern world. Each is accompanied by a short essay which aims to give a bit of context, looking at the story behind the statistic: what the scope of the problem is, how we got here, and what we can do now. At the end of the book there's a full list of where the 50 facts are sourced from; you'll also find a glossary which will explain any unfamiliar terms, and a guide to how you can get involved.

This is the second edition of *50 Facts That Should Change The World* (hence, the 2.0); the first edition came out in 2004. This edition has had a fairly major overhaul – updating some of the facts, completely replacing others. And there's one major reason for this: the world *is* changing.

Some of the original 50 facts are just simply not true any more. The first edition contained a fact about how 70 percent of the world's population had never heard a dial tone. That's no longer true, thanks almost entirely to mobile phones. It made me so happy to draw a big line through that fact, thinking that maybe with this mushrooming of technology we might be making some serious progress in eroding the "digital divide," the huge gaps that used to exist between the information-saturated rich world and the countries where you might face a year-long wait to have a telephone connected. There's quite a long way to go yet, but the momentum is there.

Another fact that's missing from this edition is the one about the US spending about the same amount of money on pornography as it does on foreign aid. America is now spending far more than it did on overseas development assistance: some $27 billion, according to the OECD's figures, helpfully broken down by the website globalpolicy.org. The porn industry hasn't grown at the same rate – if anything, it's deflated slightly. It's heartening that the US is giving so much more development aid, although globalpolicy.org notes that nearly $7 billion of that figure is going to Iraq.

Obviously, this book can't take the credit for those advances (I wish it could!). But there is one overriding force that can take credit: the desire of people in the world that they should happen. People speaking out, making their voices heard, influencing the debate, making politicians listen to them. And this trend is growing every day.

Since the original *50 Facts* book was released, there's been a huge surge in what I guess you could call everyday activism. One of the ideas behind *50 Facts* was that if you didn't like what you read – if the facts made you angry, sad, upset or keen for change – then you could go out and do something about them. In some cases there are real, definite actions you can take: for example, if you're concerned about food miles, start embracing locally-grown and seasonal produce, get inspired by the slow food movement and take a real interest in where your food comes from. In others, it's more about joining groups that are pushing for change, keeping certain issues in mind when you vote, that sort of thing. Those courses of action feel somewhat less direct, perhaps, but they're just as good a way to effect change.

There's now so much emphasis on this kind of activism. The high profile given to climate change has given a particular urgency to the idea that we're all able to do our bit: there are prime-time ads on television, huge features in newspapers, encouraging everyone to switch to energy-efficient light bulbs, turning appliances off rather than putting them on standby, and a host of other tiny acts that, added together, make a big difference.

And if you want to take it further, there are now whole websites dedicated to this kind of thing: We Are What We Do (http://www. wearewhatwedo.org) sets out 100 everyday actions that will help change the world, from using a pen all the way from start to finish, to calling your IT helpdesk just to ask how their day's going. As I was writing this new edition, the hottest it-bag of spring 2007 was We Are What We Do's collaboration with the handbag designer Anya Hindmarch, a reusable canvas shopping bag. Price: a hefty $10. The model Lily Cole carried one at London Fashion Week and demand for the bag ran so high that We Are What We Do's web server collapsed under the strain and the bags were soon changing hands on eBay for more than $400. You wouldn't have seen that kind of madness about a shopping bag five years ago.

It's been fascinating to watch this change sweep over Britain, and there's every sign it's happening overseas too. In the US, we've seen individual states challenging the federal government (most recently, over climate change) and winning, forcing the Bush administration to change its ways. Websites are springing up everywhere, for every conceivable issue. Tech-savvy activists are harnessing new technologies like podcasting and video-sharing websites to get their point across. This is true in developing countries, too: one woman told the BBC that she believes mobile phones have done as much for Kenyan democracy as a change in the government.

So there's a lot that has changed, but there's still so much to be done. It's still true that many of the facts in this book have at their core the issue of inequality. Whether we're talking about an unfair distribution of income, of opportunity or of power, it's still the biggest problem that the world faces. And it's one of the toughest ones to solve.

Globalization – which, in its most basic form, merely refers to the increasing interconnection of the world through trade, communications and investment – still could do much to address the inequalities the world faces. But this will happen only if it's applied in the right way. Rich nations have been able to use globalization as a further tool of exploitation, imposing tough barriers on developing countries while lavishly propping up their own economies. Corporations have used the abundance of cheap labor and natural resources in poorer countries to increase their profits. Using globalization as a force for good is still the biggest challenge we face.

It was really interesting to gauge the reactions of people I encountered while I was promoting *50 Facts*. I was derided as a chunky-cardigan-clad, sandal-wearing twenty-something by one prominent Australian newspaper – which made me laugh, because only one of those things is true, and only then if you class flip-flops as sandals. Reviews on the internet were mostly really positive, though I was tickled by a supporter of the National Rifle Association telling one website that I'd got it all wrong about gun control.

One of the more eye-opening experiences I had was a trip to Japan. *50 Facts* was released in Japanese by Soshisha, and it turned out to be something of a success over there. I was invited over to Tokyo by Nihon TV who wanted me to present a segment of their show *The Most Useful School in the World* – I would be playing the part of a guest teacher, lecturing a "classroom" of Japanese celebrities.

To the immense amusement of my colleagues, Nihon TV asked for me to send video footage of my office at the BBC, which was cut together into a montage that featured me at the end as a Facts-busting superheroine. It was all as surreal as you might expect – and then I gave my prepared lecture, and suddenly everything got very serious. I was told after the show that a couple of the celebrities had been in tears during the segment because they were so strongly affected by what they'd heard. After the show had aired, Soshisha were contacted by many readers urging them to publish a version for school children so that their kids could learn about these issues – and set about changing the world. I can only imagine what will happen when the next generation puts all its energy into making the world a fairer, better place.

When I started writing *50 Facts*, I became convinced that individual actions could make a real difference. Now it seems that many other people are starting to embrace this idea. It really does prove that the eminent anthropologist Margaret Mead was right when she said "never doubt that a small group of thoughtful, committed people can change the world. Indeed, it is the only thing that ever has."

I am convinced these 50 facts should change the world, because the world *is* changing. And after you read this book, I hope you will be convinced too.

The average Japanese woman can expect to live to be 84. The average Botswanan will reach just 39

If you were born in the developed world, there is a good chance you will look forward to a longer life than your parents – and your children will live longer still. The average human lifespan has doubled over the past 200 years, and in most countries the trend continues. In the developed and wealthy world, science has managed to eradicate previously devastating diseases and deliver us a quality of life that our ancestors – living the life Thomas Hobbes famously described as "nasty, brutish and short" – would never have dared to hope for. We may not yet have the key to immortality, but we can have a damned good shot.

It's only in very recent history that we've been able to dream of living long, active lives. During the Roman Empire, life expectancy was just 22 years. By the Middle Ages in England, some 1,500 years later, there was only a little improvement – people could expect to live about 33 years, and not necessarily healthy years either.[1] The threat of famine was ever-present, and medicine was limited to a few brutal surgical techniques. Epidemics of typhoid and leprosy were common, and the Black Death, which swept through Europe between 1347 and 1351, killed a quarter of the population.

The dramatic improvement in human life expectancy didn't start until the Industrial Revolution, which began in England in the 19th century and spread quickly throughout Europe. Since 1840, the average life expectancy in the longest-lived countries has improved steadily – rising by three months every year. And that growth continues to this day.

So what's behind this sudden surge in our life expectancy?

Certainly, the massive social changes in the early 19th century contributed a great deal. The growth of industry meant a huge boom in urban centers, and whole suburbs had to be built to accommodate the streams of workers leaving behind a harsh rural existence for a new life in the city. Those already in the cities no longer needed to live in cramped conditions where diseases spread quickly. There was access to clean water and proper sanitation, facilities we take for granted today which had a remarkable impact on public health. Tuberculosis and cholera, which previously would lay waste to whole communities, became far less common.

When people did become ill, the advancement of medical treatment meant leeches and trepanation were cast aside. The discovery of antibiotics was another huge step forward, dramatically reducing the number of women who died during childbirth. It's telling that the concept of "quality of life" is such a recent invention. Until recently, life itself was enough of a blessing.

So how much longer will this growth continue? Does the body have a finite lifespan, or could we continue to prolong life indefinitely? One assumption is that despite advances in science and medicine, we will reach a point where our bodies just cannot continue to function. Established wisdom has it that our lifespan is determined by evolution. If we continue to give birth to babies that live longer and longer, the delicate balance between survival and reproduction could be lost: the average age of populations will grow steadily older, and this could have far-reaching impacts on the ability of governments to provide basic services. Indeed, developed nations may already be reaching this point.

The group with the longest life expectancy, Japanese women, currently reach 84.6 years on average, and they're showing no signs of slowing down. At the time of writing, Japan boasts the oldest living person (Mrs. Yone Minagawa, who turned 114 on January 4, 2007) and the world's oldest man (Mr. Tomoji Tanabe, a comparatively youthful 111). As remarkable as these "super-centenarians" are, some believe that in the future this kind of extreme longevity could become commonplace. *Science* predicted that in six decades the average Japanese baby girl could expect to live to 100.[2] No longer an occasion for a telegram from the Queen, reaching your century could become just another birthday – albeit one with a very large cake.

For those living in Central and Southern Africa, though, there is little cause for celebration. Life expectancies here are not growing. In fact, due to the ravages of the HIV/AIDS pandemic, they're declining rapidly. The US Census Bureau predicts that 51 countries will see a fall in the average life expectancy as the virus continues to claim millions of lives.

In Botswana, for example, a baby born in 2002 could expect to live an average of 39 years. That's 30 years less than the average would have been without AIDS. By 2010, Botswanans are predicted to live just 27 years.[3] It's a sobering thought, and one that makes the developed world's centenary aspirations seem like a dreadful vanity.

AIDS is the starkest reason for the lower life expectancies in the developing world, but there are many others. Infant mortality rates in many countries remain high. In Sierra Leone, 157 babies out of every thousand will die before their first birthday. Contrast that with Iceland's 2.6 babies, and it's easy to see why the infant mortality rate is considered such a sensitive measure of a country's public health.[4] Access to clean water, nutrition and healthcare are crucial during pregnancy. In the West, those are a given – but that's still not the case in many countries. Young children who don't get enough food are far more likely to die from diseases like flu and diarrhea, and around the world UNICEF estimates that 150 million children are malnourished.

Poverty also greatly reduces life expectancy. Lack of access to safe drinking water is still a major cause of death in many countries. Polluted air or soil can cause disease, and it also makes food production more difficult. As rapidly growing populations put the land and natural resources under increasing strain, more and more land is turning to desert as local ecosystems are destroyed.

It's clear, then, that life expectancy poses very different challenges to the developed and developing worlds. Higher-income countries must come to terms with their aging populations and start to provide for the stresses that will be placed on health and welfare systems. Governments and corporations are already being forced to look at the way they provide for people in retirement. If the average British man now lives to 75, he will spend his last decade drawing a pension from the state. It's a pleasant prospect, certainly, but one that will become harder and harder to sustain. Some European governments are already discussing raising the age for compulsory retirement, and as the population gradually grows older there will be fewer people working to put the necessary money back into the welfare system. Governments are already facing vociferous criticism from people who feel they're being short-changed – the long-held belief that a productive working life should be rewarded by a comfortable retirement is proving hard to shake.

In the developing world, meanwhile, tackling the AIDS pandemic is the biggest priority for many countries. African nations are worst hit at present, but there is every indication that China, India and the countries of the former Soviet Union will lose millions of their people to AIDS in the next ten years. The World Bank highlights the need to prevent illness through better public health, but it's hard to do that when literacy and access to education are limited.[5] AIDS is still a source of great stigma in most countries, and many governments have shown reluctance to acknowledge the problem. In June 2003 the Global Fund to Fight AIDS, Tuberculosis and Malaria had signed grant agreements worth $5.3 billion by the end of 2006, but it warned that it needs another $8–10 billion a year to reach the Millennium Development Goals.[6]

The World Bank also points to hard choices ahead for many governments. Treating people suffering from AIDS is very expen-sive: it's estimated that Britain's National Health Service spends an average of £15,000 a year on each AIDS patient. These costs create a great strain on health systems in the developed world – but in developing countries where funding is limited and resources scarce, it's simply impossible to cater properly to all those who need treatment. The World Bank suggests that funding might best be spent on education and prevention – in short, concentrating on those who are still healthy rather than on those who are certain to die. But when hospitals are full and infection rates are still high, that seems like a very calculating decision and one that governments will almost certainly find hard to take.

A third of the world's obese people live in the developing world

It seems like the cruellest irony of all: the world that is fighting hunger is also battling an epidemic of obesity. For the first time, the number of overweight people is starting to rival the number who are underweight. And the epidemic is not confined to the rich countries of the world. More than 300 million people in the world are obese, and headlines about the current crisis of "globesity" are common. But perhaps more worryingly, 115 million of the world's obese people live in developing countries. It seems that along with the consumer trappings that come with increasing wealth, people in poorer countries are adopting some of the West's most dangerous habits – with almost certainly devastating consequences. The World Health Organization (WHO) says obesity rates across the globe have risen three-fold or more in the past twenty years, but often faster in developing countries.

Never in the history of the world have we had so much to eat, but it seems that in a culture of plenty, the choices we make become even more important. As the world's population becomes increasingly urban, eating habits across the globe are changing substantially. Public health experts refer to this as "nutrition transition." Farmers who once grew a range of crops on a subsistence basis begin to concentrate on single cash crops. Countries begin to import more food from the industrialised world. Rather than eating fresh fruit and vegetables, people opt for highly processed, energy-dense foods, heavy in fat, sugar and salt. Combine this with increasingly sedentary lifestyles – where people drive rather than walk, work in offices rather than fields, watch sports rather than play them – and it's a lethal prescription.

Obesity and excess weight increase the likelihood of serious chronic diseases. Cardiovascular disease, hypertension, strokes and certain forms of cancer are all more common in overweight people – as is the form of diabetes once known as "adult onset," but now seen in children as young as ten. This in itself creates an increased risk of heart attacks and strokes, and can cause blindness, kidney failure and nerve damage. The financial and social burden is already placing a strain on health budgets in developed countries: obesity-related conditions cost the US 12 percent of its health budget in the 1990s, some $118 billion – more than double the $47 billion attributable to smoking.[1] According to the WHO, the majority of chronic disease cases are occurring in the developing world.[2] And in countries where health systems are already sorely challenged, the strain could become intolerable.

In China, 5 percent of the population as a whole is classified as obese – but look at the cities, and that figure increases to 20 percent. Many of those are children, the "little emperors" created by China's one-child policy. Across Asia, it's the same story. Obesity among Thai children between five and twelve years of age rose from 12 percent to 15–16 percent in just two years. Nearly 10 percent of Japanese nine-year-old boys are overweight now – compared with 3 percent in 1970.[3]

Rates of obesity are soaring in Latin America too, almost rivalling those in its neighbor to the north. Sixty-four percent of Mexican women are overweight, and 60 percent of men. It's a familiar story here too: people moving to cities, working very hard in sedentary jobs, fuelling up on cheap industrially produced food. The *Guardian* notes that in some remote villages in Mexico it is easier to buy a bag of potato chips than a banana.[4]

Over all, though, the world's fattest people live in the Pacific Islands. In Nauru, 77 percent of the adult population is obese – twice the rate of the wealthy European Union countries. Pacific cultures traditionally revere size as a sign of wealth and power. Once, you would have had to be very rich to eat enough to get fat.

But now, a flood of cheap imported foodstuffs puts dangerous obesity within the reach of most people.

Where once local diets would have consisted of fish and tropical fruit, markets are full of meat rejected by richer overseas markets. Turkey tails from the US, lamb and mutton flaps from Australia and New Zealand – once these high-fat meats would have been used as pet food or fertiliser, now they are delicacies. In Tonga, healthier protein options such as locally caught fish were between 15 and 50 percent more expensive than mutton flaps or imported chicken.[5] Some have blamed the countries exporting these meats for "dietary genocide." Samoa's health minister, Mulitalo Siafausa Vui, described the imported meat as "junk food dumped by richer countries on poorer countries."[6] Fiji went further, announcing a ban on the import of lamb and mutton flaps – New Zealand threatened to lodge a complaint with the World Trade Organization (WTO).[7]

Obviously, the world's aid organizations make a priority of alleviating hunger. But they also acknowledge that obesity, and all its related health problems, is reaching a crisis point.

Part of the solution seems to be getting better information out to areas where obesity levels are soaring. The United Nations' Food and Agriculture Organization (FAO) talks of the need to get food production experts (who decide how to grow more crops and where) in touch with nutritionists. The WHO is also striving to set down guidelines about what constitutes a good diet. National governments can do more to promote healthy eating and exercise in schools – Singapore's Trim and Fit scheme has reduced obesity among children by nearly a half through changes in school catering and increasing the amount of exercise and nutritional education.

But there is a clear danger that criticising certain food types too harshly could spark a huge backlash from the food industry. In April 2003 the WHO and the FAO were poised to issue a report on diet which suggested that sugar should make up no more than 10 percent of a balanced diet. The US Sugar Association launched a stinging attack, calling the report "misguided [and] non-science-based."[8] The

Association said 25 percent was a far more realistic safe level, and it also wrote to the US Health Secretary calling for the report to be withdrawn. It also threatened to put pressure on the American administration to scrap the WHO's funding. Defiant, the WHO and FAO report was launched, in what was seen as a victory for non-governmental organizations over the lobbyists – but the message was clear, and far from palatable.

Nutritional education is part of the solution, but it's clear that economics have a major role to play. In Tonga, a WHO report suggested that development of sustainable farming and fishing industries would help to make healthier traditional foods available at a reduced cost. Banning the importation of unhealthy food, as Fiji did, is another possibility. But options like this may incense the wealthier countries, who have much to gain from exporting cheap food to developing countries, and the consequence could be a complaint to the WTO. As the Tonga report concludes, "it behoves national policy-makers to be aware of the health impact of 'commodities of doubtful benefit,'" and of the role of trade in health of the population."[9]

In the developed world, newspaper articles and television reports constantly discuss the merits of one miracle diet after another. But as most dieters know, the answers to overweight are seldom found in a glass of diet soda. And in the developing world, where obesity is as much to do with trade and globalization as anything else, it's a bitter draught indeed.

If you stand at the junction of Oxford Street and Regent Street in central London, there are 161 branches of Starbucks within a five-mile radius

Fancy a coffee? If you live in almost any major city in the West, there will be more than a dozen chain stores that will be happy to oblige you. In Britain we each consume 1.2 kilograms of coffee every year[1] and last year we spent £730 million on it.[2] As substantial a sum as that is, we still consume far less coffee than the international average of 4.6 kilos a year – and those coffee retailers obviously believe there's still plenty of room for growth.

If you're standing on our street corner above – just outside one of the exits to Oxford Circus underground station – there are 86 branches of Starbucks within a half-hour walk.[3] In fact, there are now more branches of Starbucks in London than there are on Manhattan Island in New York City – the archetypal caffeine-fuelled metropolis.[4] And even then, that's not enough. In January 2007 Starbucks announced that it aims to open a new store in London every fortnight for the next decade.

At the time of writing, Starbucks had 13,168 company-operated or licensed stores around the world.[5] Its goal is to have 40,000 stores worldwide – which would make it bigger than McDonald's.[6] And right now, business is good. In the last quarter of 2006, the company opened more than eight new stores *every day* around the world, to boast a net revenue of $2.35 billion and an 18 percent surge in profits.[7]

So far, this sounds like just another business success story. A company that started with a single outlet in Seattle 35 years ago has grown to become one of modern retail's biggest success stories. There are outlets in some of the most conservative countries in the Middle East; the eighteen branches in Riyadh display the same décor and ambience as you would expect in any outlet around the world, except for the curtained areas where the female customers must sit, shielded from male eyes. There is even a Starbucks in the Forbidden City in Beijing, the site of the former Imperial Palace – although maybe not for much longer. The administrators for the UNESCO World Heritage Site are considering closing the store after half a million Chinese signed an online petition protesting against its presence in such a culturally important site.[8]

But sometimes it pays to look behind the headlines. Fuelling this boom in coffee is a commodity trade in which there are clear winners and clear losers. On the winning side are the coffee retailers who charge high prices for their beverages. The losers are the farmers who grow the raw beans.

The cup of coffee that you buy in a chain retailer might cost you £1.80 in Britain, perhaps $3 in the US; of that price, the farmers in Ethiopia who grew the beans for that cup get about 3 cents, or less than 2 pence. Or let's do the math another way. After deducting their costs, coffee farmers receive about $1.10 for a pound of coffee. A retailer selling espressos could get up to $160 for that same pound of coffee.[9]

This point is made with great force in a documentary called *Black Gold*, made by English brothers Nick and Marc Francis. The film follows Tadesse Meskela, a spokesman for Ethiopia's impoverished coffee growers, as he tries to get a better deal for his people. Meskela runs a coffee farmers' cooperative, and one moving scene from the film shows him explaining to the farmers how much their crop is sold for in rich countries. The farmers don't make enough to live on and are dependent on food aid, while the fruits of their toil are sold for high prices. The film has certainly drawn attention to his country's plight; Meskela has since met former British Prime Minister Tony

Blair and the film may well do for fair trade what Al Gore's film *An Inconvenient Truth* has done for climate change.[10]

The film-makers are adamant that they didn't single out Starbucks for criticism – in fact, they say, they tried to contact the company many times during the making of the film. All the same, the coffee giant has swung into a charm offensive. Starbucks says the film doesn't represent a full picture of what the company's doing in Ethiopia: it has called the film "inaccurate" and "incomplete" and pointed to the company's commitment to paying fair prices for coffee, as well as its humanitarian projects.[11]

But while this debate was raging, a somewhat more sinister story was unfolding. In 2005 the Ethiopian government filed applications to trademark three of its most famous coffee bean names: Sidamo, Harar and Yirgacheffe. Trademarking the names would allow farmers to negotiate better prices for these sought-after speciality beans and could add as much as $88 million in annual income for Ethiopia's coffee industry. But according to Oxfam, Starbucks asked the US National Coffee Association to block the trademark bid.[12]

As Professor Douglas Holt of the Said Business School at Oxford University puts it, these actions are not surprising for a large multinational company. They have aggressive profit targets to meet and a market position to defend. But Starbucks has gone out of its way to convince its customers that it is no ordinary multinational and that it sells "coffee that cares."[13] In February 2007, Starbucks and the Ethiopian government issued a joint press release stating that the company would no longer stand in the way of the trademark applications. But Starbucks has since refused to engage in discussions on the issue and has also not signed a voluntary licensing agreement which would help increase the farmers' bargaining power.[14] Instead, the company promised to double purchases of East African coffee by 2009 and pledged $1 million in micro-finance to farmers in the region. This is, of course, better than nothing. But Starbucks had a real chance to lead the way in promoting fair trade, and that chance may have been missed.

As Starbucks continues its march towards its target of more stores than McDonald's, it's sobering to think too about what that might mean for the face of our towns and cities. Not so long ago, the best you could hope for on the English high street was that your local greasy spoon might have an Italian coffee machine. Sure, in the big cities there were cafés that might serve a decent cup, but they were by no means everywhere. Growing up in New Zealand, I don't think I tasted an espresso until I was in my late teens. Coffee was either instant or (at best) drip-filtered, and it almost universally wasn't great.

Now, every shopping street in Britain (and in New Zealand, and much of the rest of the world) will have at least one chain coffee shop, complete with "baristas" and staggeringly complex menus. No longer will your only coffee options be black or white, with sugar or without – you can order a drink as complicated as you like, in the style of 90s supermodel Linda Evangelista, whose coffee order became legendary: a half-caf, double-tall, non-fat, whole-milk foam, bone-dry, half-pump mocha, half sugar in the raw, double cup, no lid, capp to go.

But there is another side to this blossoming of choice. Chain coffee shops, chain restaurants, chain boutiques are all leading to a strange new phenomenon: the Clone Town. The term was invented by think tank the New Economics Foundation (NEF) to describe a phenomenon it saw happening in Britain. Smaller commercial centers, among them many ancient market towns, have started to lose many of the features that made them representative of the areas they served. The NEF pointed out that between 1997 and 2002, specialist stores like butchers, bakers and fishmongers were shutting up shop at the rate of 50 stores a week. Twenty traditional pubs closed their doors every month.[15] In their place: supermarkets, catalogue stores, chain pubs. The commentator Nick Foulkes paints the picture: "The homogenization of our high streets is a crime against our culture. The smart ones get the international clones – Ralph Lauren, DKNY, Starbucks and Gap; while those lower down the socio-economic hierarchy end up with Nando's, McDonald's, Blockbuster and Ladbrokes."[16]

When yet another national or international chain comes to our high street, we get the illusion that we have more choice. In fact, we get no choice. Smaller, independent retailers get pushed out and are replaced by national and multi-national operators whose huge economies of scale mean they wield enormous power over us. Consider the often-quoted statistic that for every £7 of retail spending in the UK, £1 is spent in Tesco supermarkets. Do you really want to give one business that much power in your life?

Of course, Starbucks is by no means the only retailer implicated in this trend, and it would be wrong to place too much blame at their door. But it seems that even the company itself is starting to wonder if it's gone too far. In a recent memo leaked to the internet, Starbucks founder and Chairman Howard Schultz mused to his Chief Executive, James Donald, that he was worried about where the brand he'd built was heading. He wrote that the company's massive expansion had led to the "watering down of the Starbucks experience" and the "commoditization" of the brand. "One of the results has been stores that no longer have the soul of the past and reflect a chain of stores vs the warm feeling of a neighborhood store ... some people even call our stores sterile, cookie cutter, no longer reflecting the passion our partners [employees] feel about our coffee."[17]

It's too early to tell if Schultz's concerns will translate into a change of emphasis for Starbucks. But it should certainly make us think. I wouldn't want to suggest you never visit Starbucks: from time to time, I go there too. It's an almost-inevitable force in modern life. But when you do go there, make sure you go for the fair trade coffee. Pick up their literature in-store and don't be afraid to write in to tell them what you'd like them to do. Then do the same thing in every chain coffee store you visit.

And don't stop going to your local independent café just because there's a new place down the road. It may not offer the same bizarrely-flavored syrups or those ice-blended confections that are so tempting on a hot day – but chances are it's a lot more precious to your community.

China has 44 million missing women

The official news reports had a faint but clear undertone of alarm. China's state news agency reported in October 2002 that the latest national census showed something very concerning about the sex ratios in the world's biggest nation. For every 100 baby girls born in China in 2000, there were 116.8 baby boys. And comparison with the past two censuses showed things were getting worse. If the gap continued to widen, said the *Shanghai Star*, some 50 million men in China might find themselves unable to meet a suitable wife. That would then cause problems for families, the economy and social services. One expert even predicted a rise in the kidnapping of women as desperate men sought to find a bride.[1]

The imbalance is the chilling result of a preference for sons which is widespread in China, India and other parts of South and East Asia. Parents anxious not to have a baby girl may have scans to determine the unborn child's sex, and if the fetus is shown to be female, they will seek an abortion. Many baby girls are killed in the first few days or weeks of their life, parents finding ways to outfox police and health workers by making the deaths seem like natural events. If the girl is lucky enough to survive babyhood, her birth may never be registered – leading to a life on the margins, where education, healthcare and even getting enough food to eat will be denied her.

Even though birth rates in India, China and Taiwan are falling steadily and are now coming close to those in the Western world, the long-standing bias against baby girls is not disappearing. The increasingly wide availability of ultrasound technology is making it easier for parents to choose not to give birth to a female child. Dr. V. Parameshvara, a former president of the Indian Medical Association, estimated that 2 million sex-selective abortions are performed in India every year[2] and a UNICEF study published in December

2006 said 7,000 fewer girls were born in India every day.[3] In an effort to stem the tide, both India and China have made sex-selective abortions illegal. Doctors in both countries who perform routine scans on pregnant women are not allowed to tell them the sex of the baby. But some clinics don't always obey the rules. The *Shanghai Star* reported that illegal ultrasound scans can be obtained for around $60–120,[4] while doctors in India will find other ways to communicate the result: giving families a pink-wrapped candy if a fetus is a girl, blue if it's a boy.[5]

In India, as post-mortem techniques become more sophisticated, parents are resorting to more gruesome ways to kill their daughters. Radha Venkatesar in the *Hindu* newspaper detailed some of the techniques described to her by mothers in the Salem district of Tamil Nadu.

One such "novel" method is feeding hot, spicy chicken soup to the babies. "They writhe and scream in pain for a few hours and then die" [according to one woman]. When NGO activists get wind of infanticide, the villagers promptly counter that "the child was suffering from bloated tummy and had to be given chicken soup." Another ruthless elimination method catching up in Salem villages is to over-feed babies and tightly wrap them in wet cloth. After an hour of breathless agony they die ... but the latest technique of asphyxiating the baby by placing beneath a pedestal fan at full blast has stumped the police who have managed to register just five cases of female infanticide in Salem in the past year."[4]

For a baby girl who manages to survive her first weeks, there may be other more insidious perils still ahead. Boys may often be given preference in healthcare. One study in India showed no gender gap in deaths from severe and non-preventable diseases, but girls were twice as likely to die from diarrhoea – which is treatable.[5] Boys may often have more money spent on their clothes, and be fed more nutritious food. Right from the start, their chances of survival are better. The girl child has a difficult life.

In China, the famous "one child" policy has meant that many births go unreported. In rural areas especially, larger families are becoming more common. The Chinese government appears to be relaxing its strictly coercive approach to family planning, and as women move around the country to work, it becomes harder to monitor pregnancies. Chinese demographers say that spot checks by the State Statistics Bureau have yielded under-counts of up to 40 percent in some villages. It's hard to say what proportion of those "invisible" children are girls. But the State Family Planning Commission says that some rural families are larger because the parents want a son.[6]

But what happens to these unregistered children? In the eyes of the law, they simply don't exist. These children will not be able to go to school or receive state-funded healthcare. Their opportunities in life will be severely affected.

In order to give these baby girls a chance, governments need to tackle the problem of female infanticide decisively. But what may be more difficult is tackling the deeply entrenched social attitudes that make people think it's okay to kill baby girls. The problem is that infanticide – of both boys and girls – has a long and bloody history. The Society for the Prevention of Infanticide concludes: "Infanticide has been practiced on every continent and by people on every level of cultural complexity ... [it] has pervaded almost every society of mankind from the Golden Age of Greece to the splendor of the Persian Empire."[7] In times when food was scarce, one way to control the effects of starvation was to restrict the number of children allowed to survive to adulthood.

In East and South Asia, the proverbs that enshrine the preference for boys are many. "Daughters are like water that splashes out of the family and cannot be got back after marriage." "Eighteen goddess-like daughters are not equal to one son with a hump."

In patriarchal societies, the question of whose responsibility it is to care for one's parents is particularly important. In these societies, a daughter's role largely ends at marriage, while the son's lasts for life. And where there is little in the way of social support for older people, that counts for a lot. According to Monica Das Gupta, a demographer at the World Bank, "the grown woman can be useful ... she can work in the fields and be a good mother, but the fact that she's educated and employed doesn't change her value to her parents, who won't benefit from all that." In societies where daughters and sons share the job of caring for aging parents, sex ratios don't display the same preference for boys.

As well as their role as good providers, sons are the ones who carry on the family name and inherit ancestral lands, and in some religions they are the only ones who can perform particular rites of passage on behalf of their parents. There is a lot of pressure, then, for women to give birth to sons. A woman's value and standing in a community will go up if she bears sons, down if she bears daughters.

In India, parents of daughters dread the point at which their girls reach marriageable age and become enmeshed in the traditions of dowry. In the majority of communities in India, a groom's family will demand some kind of payment from the bride's family – cash, precious metals, real estate or some other valuable item. Sometimes, the demands don't stop after the marriage, and parents may feel they have to give in to the requests to ensure the safety of their daughter. And with good reason: India's National Bureau of Investigation believes that violence related to dowry claims sixteen women's lives every day.[8] Aid agencies believe that dowry is directly linked to the issue of female infanticide. One writer reported seeing signs in the Indian state of Haryana reading: "Make your choice – spend a few hundred rupees now [on aborting a female fetus] and save a few hundred thousand rupees later [in dowries]."[9]

It would be bad enough if this bias against the girl child were merely a matter of tradition – once the grisly reality of these traditions is laid bare, then they're not impossible to change. But, sickeningly, the problem of the "missing women" seems to be rooted in economics. Female children cost money, and when they marry these living pieces of property become part of their new husband's family. It's a simple, chilling fact.

There are signs that things are changing. Many previously

agrarian societies are becoming more urbanised, and that is having an effect on these traditions – and their bloody outcomes. In South Korea, the sex ratios are starting to even out: whereas in 1990 there were 117 boys for every 100 girls, by 1999 that had declined to 110. Younger generations are becoming more economically independent of their families, and so the perceptions of sons as providers and daughters as burdens are slowly being worn away.[10]

In more agrarian societies, though, it may prove harder to convince parents of the worth of a female child. Census figures in India and China have drawn public attention to the growing imbalance between the sexes, and both governments have outlawed sex-selective abortions. Aid agencies and women's groups descend on private clinics and lobby the government to close down those which are flouting the law. But it may take a generation of brideless men to kick-start a widespread social change.

Brazil has more Avon ladies than members of its armed services

It's a strange mental picture – hundreds of thousands of smartly dressed women, marching through the streets of Brazil, hands not saluting but extended, ready to press a doorbell. While Brazil's armed forces have 454,000 personnel on active service,[1] Avon has 700,000 "revendadoras" – or, as we would put it in English, Avon ladies.[2] Working all over the country from the inner cities to the Amazon jungle, they've helped to make Brazil Avon's second-biggest market by volume after the US.

Spurred on by growing discretionary incomes in the West, and expanding middle classes in the developing world, the beauty industry is enjoying a boom time. The global market is worth $95 billion and is growing at up to 7 percent a year, more than twice as fast as the developed world's GDP.[3] Women, and increasingly men, are lining up to purchase what industry pioneer Charles Revson famously called "hope in a jar."

What exactly does the beauty industry sell? A cynic might say it pushes expensive containers filled with colored, scented potions of dubious effectiveness. But there's obviously a lot more to it than that. What are the forces at work that can make a grown woman delight in buying a brand new lipstick, when she has five others at home in exactly the same shade?

Far more than what's in the pretty glass jars, the beauty industry sells a potent mixture of self-esteem, empowerment and evolution-ary advantage. The desire to adorn ourselves is as old as the human race itself, and in every culture in the world, physical beauty confers many benefits. Unattractive men earn 15 percent less than their more aesthetically appealing colleagues, while fat women earn 5 percent less.[4] A study of more than 10,000 people in 37 cultures by the American psychologist David Buss found that men consistently value attractiveness and youth in a potential mate, whereas women value ambition, status and resources. The uniformity of these preferences across so many cultures led Buss to conclude that they are a fundamental part of human psychology: "Youth is a cue to fertility, the physical appearance of the woman provides a wealth of information about her fertility, and then women want a good provider, someone who will be there through lean times."[5]

But there's more to the allure of "lipstick, powder and paint" than just the possibility of ensnaring a mate. More recently, advertising for cosmetics and other beauty products has focused on the desire – no, more than that, the *responsibility* – that every woman has to pamper herself. We're not doing this to attract men; we're doing this to make ourselves feel better, to be the best person we can be.

All of this might have seemed dazzling to the founder of Avon, David McConnell. A door-to-door salesman in New York State in the late 19th century, he started giving away perfume with the books he was selling. The perfume began to be more in demand than the books, and the business was born. He named the company in honor of his hero, William Shakespeare.

The bard himself may have had a few words to say about beauty in his time, but it's hard to imagine that he would have put as much time and care into crafting a line as today's cosmetics companies. A skim through a high-profile American glossy magazine yields a mass of girl-power messages. "Because you're worth it." "Love the skin you're in." "It's a fact. With [our brand], life's more beautiful." We're not just smoothing on moisturizer, we're making ourselves, and the world around us, better. And that's a very potent prescription.

Brazil prizes physical beauty exceptionally highly. In the land of bikinis so tiny that they are sometimes nicknamed "dental floss," calling someone vain can be considered a compliment, because it implies they try hard to make themselves more attractive. Avon's own research shows that 90 percent of Brazilian women consider beauty products to be a necessity, not a luxury – compared with an average of 77 percent worldwide.[6] Small wonder, then, that the sector has largely managed to ride out the country's many economic upheavals: In 2005 Brazil's beauty products market grew by 34 percent, reaching sales of $13.8 billion and becoming the world's fourth-biggest beauty market.[7]

Brazil's battalions of Avon ladies are not just beautifying their customers, they are making their own lives better. Brazil's economic crises have drawn many women to direct selling companies to supplement their family's income. In a country where business and politics are closely entwined with personal relationships, this makes for a perfect arrangement. Some 60 percent of perfume and 80 percent of lipstick sales are made face-to-face rather than at a cosmetics counter.[8] Many people say they would prefer to pay a little more to buy from someone they know: as one anthropologist put it, "personal relations count more than economic logic in Brazil."[9] With unemployment high and economic reversals an established fact of life, economists estimate that at least a third of Brazil's economy is "off the books."[10]

Direct sales work also allows women to break away from some of the more traditional forms of employment in Brazil. For many of these women, who lack education or qualifications, the only real option is becoming a cook or a maid to a richer household – which may mean moving away from their family and relinquishing any sense of independence. Selling products like Avon allows some flexibility, a sense of control, independence. As their businesses become successful, the *revendadoras* take on extra sellers to help them, taking a cut of their profits.

While Avon has been good for Brazil, there's no doubt that Brazil has been good for Avon. Avon has made significant investments in Brazil – a center for research and development, a new range targeting beauty professionals from hairdressers to cosmetic surgeons.[11] Lessons learned in markets like Brazil have helped the corporation to strike out into other uncharted markets. Eastern Europe and Russia have proved particularly profitable countries for

Avon, with operating margins more than double the company's worldwide average.[12] And other retailers are flocking to Latin America with the hope of replicating Avon's successes: Nestlé trialled a door-to-door strategy to promote health yogurt products, while General Motors used Brazil as a test market for direct sales of small cars over the Internet. In 2002, Brazil became the world's third-biggest market for direct sales, behind the US and Japan.[13]

While Avon has cachet in the developing world as a successful Western manufacturer, the company is attempting to reinvent itself as a global symbol of aspiration. In Britain and the US, however, it's having to fight hard to keep up with the times without throwing away its heritage. Celebrities like the tennis sensations Venus and Serena Williams have been called in to help update Avon's image. It's all part of appealing to younger women, the generation that grew up with "girl power." But the best role models could be right within the company itself. The Avon ladies of the Amazon, paddling canoes to sell deodorant and lipstick in the jungle – it doesn't get much more "girl-power" than that.

Ninety-four percent of the world's executions in 2005 took place in just four countries: China, Iran, Saudi Arabia and the USA

At 6:17 PM on May 28, 2003, Napoleon Beazley was pronounced dead at the penitentiary in Huntsville, Texas. The Texas Board of Pardons and Paroles refused to commute his death sentence to a life prison term. Before his execution, Beazley declared: "The act I committed to put me here was not just heinous, it was senseless. Tonight, we declare to the world that justice does not allow for a second chance...tonight, we tell our children that in some instances, killing is right."[1]

The desire for vengeance is probably as old as human nature itself. The biblical concept of "an eye for an eye" informed justice systems for many hundreds of years. One who takes a life should have his own life taken in return. It seems that many people still hold that view dear.

Napoleon Beazley was just seventeen years old the night he killed John Luttig during a car-jacking. He had owned up to the killing and apologized to Luttig's family, although he never did explain just quite what drove him to murder that night. The crime shocked Beazley's home town of Grapeland. Beazley was president of his senior class, son of the town's first black city councilman. He hoped to attend Stanford Law School one day. Those who campaigned for him not to be put to death cited a wealth of reasons why he should be spared: Beazley was a minor at the time of the murder, he had no prior arrests and he was sentenced to death by an all-white jury.[2] All appeals were unsuccessful, and Beazley was executed by lethal injection.

President George W. Bush's support for the death penalty is well known: Texas led the US execution stakes while he was Governor, and he made his position clear during his presidential campaign in 2000, telling a meeting of Catholic journalists that he felt capital punishment "sends a chilling message that there is a consequence to your actions." In the same speech he spoke of his belief in the "sacredness of human life."[3] If you kill another person, it seems, in the President's eyes, your life is no longer sacred. In America, there is a continued high level of support for the death penalty – a Gallup poll conducted in May 2003 found that 74 percent of Americans support capital punishment for those convicted of murder.[4]

The human rights group Amnesty International reports great progress in its efforts to abolish the death penalty once and for all. More than half the countries in the world have abolished it in law or in practice. Amnesty notes that every year in the past decade, three countries on average have abolished the death penalty. And once abolished, the death penalty has seldom been reintroduced.[5]

But Amnesty goes on to note that in 2005 just four countries carried out 94 percent of all known executions: China, Iran, Saudi Arabia and the USA. In China, at least 1,770 people were executed, and Amnesty notes that this figure was based on limited and incomplete records – the Chinese government keeps its executions quiet and seldom publicises them, so the true figure is believed to be far higher. At least 94 executions were carried out in Iran, at least 86 in Saudi Arabia, and 60 people were executed in the USA.[6]

China's use of the death penalty has been widespread and unrepentant. In the three months between April and July 2001, at least 1,781 people were executed – more than the rest of the world put together for the preceding three years. As part of a "Strike Hard" campaign against crime, police and prosecutors were urged not to hold up the judicial process, as China aimed to "tackle the serious economic crime situation before entry to the WTO [World Trade Organization] and the challenge of globalization."[7] Courts boasted of their speed and special procedures. Many minor offences became capital crimes: bribery, pimping, stealing gas and selling unsafe food among them. Most executions take place after rallies in front of massive crowds, and prisoners are often paraded through the streets on their way to their final destination.

China's government has consistently defended its use of the death penalty, calling human rights groups "irresponsible."[8] In 1997 the government introduced death by lethal injection as an alternative means of execution, and there are signs that this is proving popular among the provincial authorities as well. Amnesty reported the advent of "mobile execution vans," which were being distributed to courts in Yunnan province. The vans were approved on March 6, 2003, and were put straight into commission, with two convicted drug traffickers being executed in a van later that day.[9] Indeed, there are reports that the number of executions continues to rise. The NGO Hands Off Cain quotes a "judicial source" as saying that China carried out 5,000 executions in 2003, and a member of the People's National Congress, Cheng Zhonglin, told the state-published *China Youth Daily* in March 2004 that 10,000 people were executed each year.[10]

In Iran, human rights groups have noted a sharp rise in public executions, and other forms of corporal punishment like amputations and floggings being carried out in front of members of the public. In October 2002, five men were convicted of a series of attacks on women in Tehran. Their bodies were hoisted on mobile cranes and paraded through the city.[11] One woman who had travelled 125 miles to see the execution told Reuters, "I feel relieved when I see this. It's good for the men to see it too, so that they stop harassing women."[12] Many of the crowd applauded when the men were killed. Despite an official moratorium from the government, a man and a woman were stoned to death at Mashhad in Iran in May 2006, and seven women and a man currently face the same punishment.[13]

Many of us would like to think that such barbarism couldn't happen in the Western world. But it can, and it does.

Until March 2005, when the Supreme Court declared it unconstitutional, the USA was one of a tiny handful of countries that executed prisoners who were under eighteen at the time of their crime. Between 1990 and 2005 it executed seventeen child offenders – more than any other country.[14]

The US Supreme Court halted executions in 1972, concerned that the death penalty was being handed out too haphazardly. In 1977, the killing began again, after the court ruled that new laws would rid the system of bias. But 25 years after the death penalty was reinstated, Amnesty International said the US system was close to a "lethal lottery." Its report, *Arbitrary, Discriminatory and Cruel: An Aide-memoire to 25 Years of Judicial Killing*, lists case upon case where the defendants have been executed in circumstances which should raise serious questions for any legal system.[15]

According to Amnesty, "scores" of prisoners suffering mental retardation or illness had been put to death. In 80 percent of executions since 1977, the original murder victims were white. The report lists 50 cases where African-Americans were convicted by all-white juries, each one showing a pattern of black juror exclusion by government prosecutors.

It also details the brutalising effect the death penalty has on those affected by crime. Many activists for capital punishment justify their views on the basis of the rights of the victims. The death penalty, they argue, gives a sense of "closure" to the families, a form of emotional relief that makes up for the massive loss they have suffered. But some of the behavior seen at executions speaks of a baser desire. At the 1985 execution of James Raulerson, convicted of killing a police officer, more than 70 police attended, some wearing T-shirts reading "Crank up old Sparky." They celebrated with champagne and applause outside the prison. A volunteer witness at the 2000 execution of Steve Roach reportedly said it was her third time, and that she kept volunteering because she found them "interesting." Another witness reportedly came to watch Roach die as a way of avenging the killing of his own son – for which no one had ever been convicted.[16]

One of the most effective ways to force countries to recognise their human rights obligations is international pressure. That makes it even more galling for campaigners that the world's most powerful nation is endorsing capital punishment. Iran's membership of President Bush's famous "axis of evil" may not be based on its enthusiasm for the death penalty, but the President has also made subtler statements which may well influence those who are blocking reform. In a written statement after clashes between students and police in Tehran in July 2002, the President expressed his sympathies for the students, saying that "their government should listen to their hopes...the vast majority of the Iranian people voted for political and economic reform. Yet their voices are not being listened to by the unelected people who are the real rulers of Iran."[17] According to Human Rights Watch, singling out the unelected leaders for criticism made the US government's statements an important influence on human rights conditions in the country for the first time in many years.[18] The European Union has adopted a policy of engagement towards Iran, but has made it clear that it wants to see improvements in human rights.

In China's case, the award of the 2008 Olympics to Beijing may provide more opportunities to pressure the regime to reform its human rights policies. The decision was announced with great fanfare in July 2001 – in the midst of the massive executions of the "strike hard" campaign. Human Rights Watch had written to the then president of the International Olympic Committee, Juan Antonio Samaranch, urging the IOC to require guarantees on human rights from Beijing before awarding the games to the city. The IOC declined to do this. But the new president, Jacques Rogge, said he had made it clear to the Chinese government that he expected its human rights record to improve, and that the IOC "will act."[19] Human

Rights Watch has instigated letter writing campaigns to major sponsors of the Olympics to urge them to use their corporate might to the same ends. And there are signs that high-ranking officials within China are tiring of the rate of executions. In March 2007, the Supreme People's Court, the Ministry of Public Security, the Ministry of Justice and the country's top prosecutor said that while China could not abolish capital punishment altogether, the number of death sentences should be reduced. The statement also suggested that condemned prisoners should not be paraded through the streets and suspects should not be tortured.[20] Fairly fundamental stuff, you might think – but if the warnings are heeded, this could be a major step forward.

And there are signs that even the US is susceptible to pressure. There may be a change coming in America, too. In May 2001, the US was voted off the UN Human Rights Commission. It was the first time since the Commission's 1947 inception that the US had not been represented. America's ambassador to the UN at the time called the vote "very disappointing."[21] The US has since been voted back on to the Commission, but there was little doubt that the episode was a stinging rebuke – and a great embarrassment. The US Supreme Court has also acknowledged the importance of international opinion in its decisions on the death penalty. In its March 2005 decision which declared the execution of minors to be unconstitutional, the Court's majority opinion mentioned "the overwhelming weight of international opinion against the juvenile death penalty." It's thought that the ruling could save up to 70 lives.

And pressure can also come from within the US. In January 2003 Illinois Governor George Ryan decided to commute the sentences of all 167 inmates on death row to life imprisonment. Governor Ryan, a Republican, said he had decided he would no longer "tinker with the machinery of death."[22] At a White House press briefing, communications director Ari Fleischer said the President believed this was a matter for the state to review under state laws, but said "the President does believe the death penalty does serve as a deterrent to crime. He believes that for violent and heinous crimes that the death penalty ultimately saves lives."[21]

As confused as the President's view might seem from that statement, he's made it clear that pressing states to abolish the death penalty is not something he considers is his role – and not something he would ever do. So it's clear that pressure needs to be brought to bear on individual state governors. Because if America continues executing offenders at its current rate, it will not be saving lives. By continuing a barbarous and unfair punishment, it makes all our lives a little poorer.

Supermarkets know more about their customers than the government does

It seems like a reasonable enough proposition: you visit a particular chain of shops regularly, so you decide to sign up for their loyalty scheme. Each time you shop, you show your card, and accumulate points – which you can then redeem for vouchers or gifts. Fair enough. The shop gets your guaranteed custom, and you get rewarded for shopping with them. It seems like a win-win situation. That is, until you figure out what else the retailer might be getting from the deal.

As well as trying to get you to spend more money in their stores, loyalty programs are a way for retailers to collect information about their customers. Let's say you visit your local supermarket twice a week, handing over your loyalty card each time. Every single item you buy is recorded and the data is saved – perhaps for several years. The UK's biggest loyalty scheme is the Nectar card, which claims to have some 13 million cardholders. When you look at their range of "sponsors" – Sainsbury's supermarkets, Debenhams department stores, BP, Vodafone, Threshers wine merchants, to name but a few – the amount of information that's held about each cardholder is "stunning," according to an industry source. It's estimated that in Britain, on average, loyalty card schemes hold more centralised information about their customers than the government does.[1]

In the US, the sheer size of some retailers means the amount of information they hold is even more staggering. The Wal-Mart chain admits that it holds 460 terabytes of data on its computers – that's the number 460 followed by 12 zeros.[2] That's more than twice the amount of information on the entire Internet – or 23 times the information held in all the 128 million books in the US Library of Congress.

So rather than a friendly piece of plastic that helps you save money, the loyalty card may be more like a spy, watching what you spend and drawing conclusions from your purchases. It's not just a question of figuring out if you're a vegetarian, or if you have a cat: companies use sophisticated socio-demographic software to determine your stage of life, the size of your household, your income, what your interests are. You will then be assigned into one of a number of pigeonholes which have been designed to identify certain segments of British society. Are you a young couple about to set up in your first home, a family with teenage children, an older couple who are likely to take lots of overseas holidays? Your shopping basket will give you away. According to a customer forecaster at a British supermarket, "data can come even from things that are not immediately obvious. How much toilet paper, how many lightbulbs, how many steaks you buy. We can tell not just your likely house size but your household size. So if you're buying a Britney Spears CD and you've got no one else registered on your card, you've either got young kids or you're a gay man."

So when we moved house recently, and my partner called up to change the address of his loyalty card, the marketing machine kicked in. Within days of arriving at our new house, there was a package from the loyalty card promoters, with a welcome bar of chocolate, a bunch of vouchers for cleaning products, and a handy phone number so we could find our nearest store. Okay, so there wasn't much detective work involved there: we had told them we were moving, they responded. But according to the data analysts, your shopping basket can give just as clear a message. When a couple is expecting their first child, their shopping basket always changes; and the information can even disclose who's thinking of "defecting" to a competitor's store, triggering a series of tempting offers to encourage the cardholder to stay.

So what's the problem? Who cares if your supermarket knows a bit about you? After all, you're getting something out of it too, aren't you? The promoters of loyalty card schemes say they're just trying to offer a better service to their customers. But in the US, people have seen the potential in the huge reservoirs of information held by the card companies – and they're doing their best to get their hands on it.

The US-based Caspian group, which campaigns against loyalty card schemes, says that card data has already been used in American courts. In one case, a supermarket wanted to use register receipts to defend a personal injury action: the plaintiff claimed he fell on some spilt yogurt, the store proposed to prove he was an alcoholic by showing purchases of wine and spirits.[3] And there are other, more sinister ways in which this data could be used against you. In the wake of September 11, one US grocery chain voluntarily delivered its loyalty card records to the FBI. A lawyer working for the chain contacted Larry Ponemon of the consulting group Privacy Council. Ponemon says the chain offered up the information because it was trying to help: "It wasn't a case of law enforcement being egregiously intrusive or an evil agency planting a bug or wiretap. It was a marketing person saying, 'maybe this will help you catch a bad guy.'"[4] Customers were never told that their information had been shared with the government. Ponemon claims that federal agencies have created an algorithm that maps the terrorist potential of nearly every citizen of the US. Federal agents reportedly reviewed loyalty card transactions for the 9/11 hijackers to create a profile of their shopping preferences.[5]

There is no guarantee this might not happen in other countries. Privacy advocates talk about the idea of "function creep" – information systems that have been set up for one reason can end up being used for other purposes. This is one of the biggest concerns about the introduction of Radio Frequency Identification (RFID) tags.

RFID is a tracking system that uses a tiny transmitter chip joined to an antenna. The chip can "talk" to scanning devices within a certain range. So, at its most benign, it would operate like a barcode, sending information to cashier machines. It would help track goods from manufacturer to warehouse to checkout. It would alert retailers if goods had been shelved in the wrong place, or if something was being stolen. Once our household appliances catch up with the technology, the benefits could be the stuff of science fiction: a frozen chicken that tells the oven how it needs to be cooked, a fridge that tells you when your milk has gone sour.

But there are other, more worrying uses for the technology. Stores might "notice" that you were wearing expensive clothes, and surreptitiously raise their prices. And potentially, RFID would allow a particular person's movements and habits to be tracked at every moment of the day. US food manufacturers and retailers are already banding together to push RFID as an anti-terrorism strategy: proponents approached the Homeland Security secretary Tom Ridge to demonstrate how RFID could help the government recall food supplies contaminated by a terrorist attack,[6] but it doesn't take a lot of imagination to see how else it could be used.

In Britain, experiments with RFID have been partly funded by the Home Office. Tesco has trialled the tags in packs of razors, while Marks and Spencer announced that it would trial the tags by embedding them into packaging.[7] While the European Central Bank's reported plans to embed the tags in all Euro has yet to come to pass, Japanese manufacturer Hitachi announced in February 2007 that it had produced an RFID tag which measured just 0.05 mm.[8] The British government has announced that it will experiment with implanting RFID tags in car lisence plates[9] and there are plans for all cars in Britain to be fitted with tracking devices. Mobile phone companies are already offering a service whereby you can register a phone number and then track the user. And in London, users of the Oyster smart travelcard have their every journey monitored. Each smart-card has a unique number linked to the owner's name, and that information is recorded every time the card is swiped past a ticket gate. Transport for London says it plans to retain the information for "a number of years."[10]

Businesses assure us that these methods of collecting information are not really about monitoring individuals. But all the same, controls need to be put in place to ensure that people are able to opt out of schemes they don't like – and that there is some degree of protection of the information that's collected. The British human rights group Liberty notes that the regulation of the information shouldn't be left up to companies.[11] Privacy legislation needs an urgent overhaul if our information is to be given proper protection.

Even then, though, we need to ask ourselves if the minor benefits we get from loyalty schemes and smart-cards are worth the risks of being spied on. Contact retailers to let them know you're concerned about privacy, and demand more information about what they're doing to secure it. Don't be tempted by the offers of ten cents off dishwashing liquid and extra points with your cornflakes, and get rid of your loyalty cards. Maybe it is paranoia, and maybe a lot of this technology will be implemented no matter what we do about it, but that doesn't mean we should just stand by and let businesses snoop into our shopping baskets – and our lives.

Every cow in the European Union is subsidised by $2.50 a day. That's more than what 75 percent of Africans have to live on

It's unlikely that Europe's cows know how lucky they are – cows are, after all, not known for their intellect. But the generous subsidies paid to their farmer owners make them among the most fortunate beings alive. The European Union's cows come under the Common Agricultural Policy, or CAP, as it's more commonly known. Each one of them attracts $2.50 per day in subsidies.

Put another way, the Catholic aid agency CAFOD calculated that for the money the EU spends protecting its farmers, each of the EU's 21 million cows could go on a round-the-world trip once a year. The cows could touch down in London, Shanghai, Hong Kong, Singapore, Hanoi, Siem Reap, Brisbane, Rarotonga, Los Angeles and San Francisco – with $800 spending money to help them along.[1] What makes this even more remarkable is that the EU's cows aren't the most heavily subsidized in the world. According to the World Bank, that prize goes to Japanese cows, which receive $7.50 every day.[2] Presumably, when the Japanese cows join their European friends on their round-the-world trip, they fly business class.

CAP lies at the very heart of the modern European Union. Agriculture was a key element of its precursor, the Common Market, when it launched in 1958, and in a post-war environment it was thought crucial to guarantee food supplies at affordable prices – as well as securing a fair standard of living for farmers. But Europe's landscape has changed a lot since then. The EU says that in the early 1960s, one in five people in the then six member states worked on the land. By 1998, that had declined to fewer than one in twenty people across the then fifteen member states.[3]

The policy is complex, sometimes illogical and incredibly politically charged. The *Economist* described it as "the single most idiotic system of economic mismanagement that the rich Western countries have ever devised."[4] The eminent economist Jeffrey Sachs once remarked, "I have never mastered EU agricultural policy, because I figured if I did so it would drive me into such a surrealistic world that I would never climb out of that twilight zone again."[5]

Due partly to this complexity, CAP has become a very expensive way to secure cheap food and fair wages. In 2007 agriculture payments ate up 56 billion euros (about $76 billion), 49 percent of the overall budget.[6] With the EU's membership expanding to 27 states in 2007, the way that CAP is administered is a key issue. Many of the new member states, like Poland and Slovakia, are still largely dependent on agriculture. Bringing them into the system of subsidies has serious implications for the EU's budget.

The cost to governments is, of course, passed on to consumers. The system, which was designed initially to secure affordable food, has now, perversely, made our weekly shopping bills far larger. According to calculations by the Organization for Economic Cooperation and Development (OECD), food prices are 44 percent higher in the EU than they would be without CAP. Milk costs 70 percent more, beef 221 percent more and sugar 94 percent more.[7] Yet average yearly incomes in Britain's farming sector are falling, and in 2002, 52,000 farmers left their land – more than double the figures for the previous year.[8]

The long-awaited reforms of CAP, unveiled in June 2003, represented a massive compromise between the competing interests of the member states. The link between subsidies and production was removed, so that there would no longer be an incentive to overproduce – but even this had to be made subject to exceptions. Agriculture Commissioner Franz Fischler called it "the start of a new era." But critics noted that Europe would still spend about the same amount in subsidies; all that had been achieved was to make the system even more complicated.

The issue that concerns aid agencies is that Europe's lavish farm subsidies are seriously hurting the developing world. Farmers produce more food than European markets really need, so they sell their subsidized excesses to the developing world at a cost far below that of production. Local producers can't possibly match the prices, with devastating effects for farmers who don't enjoy the extravagant subsidies of the rich world.

According to Oxfam, the EU's sugar regime provided "one of the most powerful and unambiguous examples of dumping."[9] The World Bank estimates that the EU sugar regime has caused world prices to fall by 17 percent.[10] In late 2005, after the World Trade Organization demanded that the EU take action, sugar subsidies were cut by 36 percent. But Oxfam called the reforms a "betrayal" and said they did not go nearly far enough.[11]

At the same time, "escalating tariffs" – duties that are low on raw or unprocessed materials, and rise sharply with each step of value added – stop countries developing their manufacturing and export sectors. The World Bank quotes the example of US tariffs on Chilean tomatoes. The tariff on fresh tomatoes is 2.2 percent – but if they are processed into sauce, the tariff leaps to nearly 12 percent. In this way, African coffee growers are effectively confined to exporting raw beans, and Mali and Burkina Faso in West Africa to the export of raw cotton. The World Bank's chief economist, Nicholas Stern, called these measures "taxes on development."[12]

Europe isn't the only offender, of course. America massively increased its subsidies and other aid to farmers in May 2002 – the administration will spend an additional $180 billion over the next decade. President Bush called it a "safety net for farmers." The subsidies will now follow a "counter-cyclical" pattern – meaning that it will cancel out signals given from the market, encouraging farmers to continue to produce in times of surplus, leading to yet further overproduction. America's subsidies have become more distorted over time: most of the direct cash payments are made to farmers who grow crops, like wheat, corn and cotton. Six out of ten American farmers get no money from the government.[13]

The EU is trenchantly critical of the US subsidies, claiming that the US had "lost any claim to be a credible force for farm policy reform in the WTO agriculture negotiations."[14] The relationship between the two, already sorely tested by the US decision to impose tariffs on imported steel, threatened to deteriorate into a trade war.

By August 2003 Europe and America appeared to have settled their differences, as the two prepared their arsenals for the Cancún meeting of the World Trade Organization (WTO) in September 2003. Agriculture was expected to be a major topic of discussion, and a number of powerful and populous nations (among them China, Brazil and India) agreed to join forces to push for change. They called themselves the G21 – a disparate group of nations with one common aim – and the EU and the US both knew that they would be under pressure. At the Doha round in 2001, the two had made promises to eliminate export subsidies – and it was clear that neither had kept their word. By the fourth day of meetings at Cancún, the talks had collapsed, with the main sticking point being – you guessed it – agricultural subsidies. The lasting image of Cancún summed up the desperation felt by the developing world. Lee Kyang-Hae, a former head of South Korea's federation of farmers, stabbed himself to death during protests. A statement from South Korean farmers confirmed that Mr. Lee killed himself "after seeing how the WTO was killing peasants around the world."

At the time of writing, the Doha trade round is suspended; the WTO made the decision in July 2006 after the US and Europe were unable to reach agreement on farm subsidies. Europe accused the US of a lack of flexibility, while the US said Europe and the developing world had not done enough to open up their markets. The Indian trade minister Kamal Nath described the round as "between intensive care and the crematorium," while the head of the WTO, Pascal Lamy, spoke of the need for all parties to reflect on a "serious situation."

In early 2007, the US and EU were talking again, but time is running out. President Bush's mandate from Congress to negotiate "fast track" trade deals expires in the middle of 2007, and without some progress a new mandate may be difficult to secure. Without it, any deal that the President agrees may be undone by Congress – a prospect which would make many countries reluctant to agree anything.

Meanwhile, some developing nations are opting instead to sign more bilateral trade agreements. But these are even more prone to arm-twisting and pressure politics, with the big trade powers only too willing to threaten to close markets. And when one trade route is freed up through a new bilateral agreement, it often has adverse effects on others. Brazil's foreign minister Celso Amorim admitted that for developing countries, the WTO is irreplaceable.[15]

For the Doha round to be resuscitated, the US and Europe must be prepared to act on their promises to help the developing world. But large emerging economies like Brazil, India and China also need to do their part, to counter the critics who claim they're asking for better access to rich country markets while refusing to lower tariffs at home. It's within the gift of all of these countries to bring the trade round back from the brink – if they don't, the grave injustices of the developed world's agriculture policies will continue.

In more than 70 countries, same-sex relationships are illegal. In nine countries, the penalty is death

On January 1, 2002, three men were beheaded in the city of Abha in southwestern Saudi Arabia. Ali bin Hatan bin Saad, Mohammad bin Suleiman bin Mohammad and Mohammad bin Khalil bin Abdullah were executed after being found guilty of "engaging in the extreme obscenity and ugly acts of homosexuality, marrying among themselves and molesting the young."[1] Amnesty International noted that, as is customary, the trial proceedings were shrouded in secrecy. It seems likely that the three men were executed primarily because of their sexual orientation.[2]

According to the International Lesbian and Gay Association, which carries out a comprehensive survey of laws around the world, there are nine countries where homosexual acts are punishable by death: Mauritania, Sudan, Afghanistan, Pakistan, the Chechen Republic, Iran, Saudi Arabia, the United Arab Emirates and Yemen. Of those nine, three are known to have executed homosexuals in the past decade: Afghanistan, Iran and Saudi Arabia. It has been estimated that since the Islamic revolution in Iran in 1979, more than 4,000 homosexuals have been executed.

Such barbaric treatment for gays and lesbians is, according to traditional Islamic thinking, justified under Sharia Law. The Qur'an is clear on its prohibition of same-sex intercourse: one often-quoted source is Qur'an 7:80–81: "We also sent Lut: he said to his people: do ye commit lewdness such as no people in creation ever committed before you? For ye practice your lusts on men in preference to women: ye are indeed a people transgressing beyond bounds."[3]

Islamic schools of thought differ on how severe the punishment for homosexual acts should be – but it's clear that some governments consider the death penalty to be an appropriate punishment, even if it is only infrequently applied. Critics say the practice reflects poorly on levels of tolerance in the Muslim world. The Al-Fatiha Foundation, a group dedicated to gay and lesbian Muslims, claims that there is "a growing movement of progressive-minded Muslims, especially in the Western world, who see Islam as an evolving religion that must adapt to modern-day society."[4] But it's clear that there is some way to go before traditionalist governments can be convinced of this. In its 2002 session in Geneva, the UN Commission on Human Rights adopted a resolution which urged all states that still maintained the death penalty to ensure it was not imposed for non-violent acts, such as sexual relations between consenting adults. Following its adoption, Saudi Arabia introduced a statement on behalf of 62 states which wanted to disassociate themselves from the resolution.[5]

It's shocking to think that there is anywhere in the modern world where a person is legally forbidden from choosing their own sexual identity. But it's true. The death penalty is the most extreme example of legally enshrined prejudice against same-sex intercourse. But there are more than 70 countries around the world where the law discriminates against lesbian, gay, bisexual or transgendered people.

Why is sexuality criminalized in this way? The countries that legislate against same-sex intercourse are a diverse group – they don't follow any common religion, and many of them would not be considered by most people to be particularly repressive states. It all seems to come down to the fact that some governments don't like people who go against the perceived norms of society. To an authoritarian and conservative regime, there's something threatening about someone who chooses to reject the "traditional" path of heterosexuality, marriage and family. As Indian gay rights activist Ashok Row Kavi puts it: "Why this sudden hatred of homosexuals? Because it has become a political identity. Governments are trying to suppress it because they see it as a socially disruptive force."[6]

There are many, many stories about how gay, lesbian and

transgendered people have suffered at the hands of the law. One account I found particularly sad, though, was from Romania. In 1992, Ciprian Cucu placed a "lonely hearts" advertisement in a local newspaper. Marian Mutascu answered it, and the two young men fell in love. Cucu's family reported their relationship to the police. The two were arrested and both were tortured in prison. Cucu was raped many times by his fellow inmates. The two received suspended sentences, and their torture was never investigated. Mutascu never recovered from the experience, and committed suicide two years later.[7]

There are also examples of state-wide persecution. In September 1999, Uganda's President Yoweri Museveni issued a public order to police: they must look for homosexuals, lock them up and charge them. Five men and women were arrested the next month – all were held in illegal detention centers, tortured and eventually released without charge. A number of Ugandans fled the country fearing arrest. In November 1999, President Museveni denied any persecution of homosexuals. They could live in Uganda, he said, as long as they kept their sexual orientation hidden.[8]

This need to keep sexual life secret leaves deep scars. Imagine not being able to set up home with your loved one, not being able to tell your friends and family for fear of being reported to the authorities. But this climate of fear and secrecy is all the more disturbing in the face of the HIV/AIDS epidemic. If young people feel afraid to speak openly about sexuality, their chances of getting the kind of information they need to keep safe are slim indeed.

In some societies, homosexuality is treated as an illness, and gay men and lesbians have been forced to submit to psychiatric treatment to "cure" their perceived affliction. Amnesty International reports that in the 1970s and 80s, members of the South African Defense Force were made to undergo "conversion therapy" without their consent. Men would be given electric shocks while they were shown pictures of naked men – the current would be turned off when they were shown pictures of naked women.[9] More recently, a gay rights organization in Ukraine reported that threats of psychiatric treatment had been used as a means of intimidation by police.[10]

Even if a particular country does not criminalize homosexuality per se, there may be other, more subtle ways in which the prejudice continues. There may be an unspoken tolerance for "hate crimes," where reports of attacks on gays and lesbians may be met with hostility and investigated far less rigorously than similar attacks on heterosexuals. Court systems may show a bias against non-heterosexuals by refusing to recognize relationships. There have even been situations where governments have incited hate against lesbians and gay men: Zimbabwe's President Robert Mugabe infamously declared that he didn't believe homosexuals had any rights at all.

Change is on its way in many countries. In June 2003 the US Supreme Court struck down a Texas law that banned most kinds of sexual intimacy for same-sex couples. The decision didn't just affect Texas, either – it effectively struck down similar legislation in thirteen other states. The judges also made it explicitly clear that homosexual couples could enjoy the right to "autonomy" in their relationships, just as heterosexual couples do – the right to raise children, to form bonds within the family, to make decisions about marriage. It's a right enshrined in the American Constitution, and in 1986 a Supreme Court decision said it didn't apply to homosexuals. Now, all that has changed. The American Civil Liberties Union called the Supreme Court decision "the single most significant case that the LGBT [lesbian, gay, bisexual and transgender] community is ever likely to see."[11]

More and more countries are extending offers of asylum to people persecuted in their own countries because of their sexuality. Many activists, though, choose to stay at home, working for change despite the risks involved. The pressure by international human rights organizations to protect people speaking out on these issues brings visibility, and with it, perhaps a measure of protection.

But none of this is enough. Governments need to be pressured to overturn laws that criminalize sexual acts between consenting adults. They also need to ensure that the police and the court system are free from the insidious discrimination that can make gays and lesbians afraid to speak out.

Perhaps most important of all, though, we need to recognize that expression of our sexuality is one of the most fundamental of human rights. And like all other human rights, it should stand apart from the law, as something that needs to be protected above all else.

One in five of the world's people lives on less than $1 a day

Here is the saddest fact about poverty: it really doesn't have to be this way. For less than 1 percent of the income of the wealthiest countries each year, the worst effects of poverty could be greatly diminished.[1] People would have enough to eat, basic services like health and education would be available to all, fewer babies would die, pandemic diseases could be brought under control.

Poverty is not just a matter of a lack of material wealth – the ability to buy bread, say, or basic farming tools. Where there is poverty, people do not get access to medicine or healthcare, so their years of healthy life are diminished. Rather than staying in school or receiving training, children are sent out to work. The cycle of ill health and deprivation is hard to break. People living in poverty are vulnerable, and they are voiceless. Where there is no security of food or income, people cannot make choices. They easily fall prey to crime and violence. A young woman in Jamaica sums up her feelings: she says poverty is "like living in jail, living in bondage, waiting to be free."[2]

In 2000, the United Nations agreed in its Millennium Development Goals to halve the number of people living in poverty by 2015. Seven years later – at the half-way point of the Goals – the UN warned that progress in many areas was too slow. Again and again since 2000, rich and poor countries had promised to work together to alleviate poverty. Richer countries agreed to pledge 0.7 percent of their national incomes, while poorer countries agreed to implement political reforms to ensure aid money was spent wisely and accountably.[3] But agreeing to make a commitment and then actually honouring it are two very different things, and it seems that rich countries are already falling behind in their commitments. Aid contributions from the countries of the OECD's Development Assistance Committee (which account for at least 95 percent of world aid disbursements) rose by 32 percent in 2005 but amounted to just 0.33 percent of gross national income[4] – well below the UN's suggested 0.7 percent. The UN is warning that although some countries are on target to reach the Millennium goal on poverty, many others will not. Overall, the targets should be met – but if we take two large countries out of the equation, India and China, they will not be. Why are some countries succeeding and others failing – and what can we do about it?

In the 1990s, the proportion of the world's population living in extreme poverty – defined as living on an income of below $1 a day, adjusted for relative purchasing power – fell slightly, from 30 per cent to 23 percent.[5] In China, more than 150 million people have moved out of poverty in the past decade.[6]

But in 54 developing countries, income fell during the 1990s. Twenty of these were in sub-Saharan Africa, and seventeen were in Eastern Europe and the Commonwealth of Independent States (CIS). In Eastern Europe, the fallout from the collapse of communism has led to spiralling unemployment and rapid economic decline. In Africa, development has been hit hard by falls in life expectancy caused by the HIV/AIDS pandemic, and small landlocked countries have been hit hardest of all. At current growth rates, it will take until nearly 2150 for sub-Saharan Africa to halve the number of people living in poverty.[7] Some countries are getting richer, yes; but many are getting poorer.

Across the world's population, the divide between rich and poor is growing ever wider. We think of countries like Brazil showing grotesque levels of inequality between wealthy industrialists and the urban poor living in shanty towns, but distribution of wealth across the world's people is even more unequal than that.[8] In 1960, the per-capita gross domestic product (GDP) of the richest twenty countries was eighteen times that of the poorest twenty. In 1995, this gap had yawned to 37 times.[9] Today, the world's richest 1 percent receive as much income as the poorest 57 percent.[10]

Even in countries where poverty levels are declining, there are inequalities which mean not everyone is benefiting from those advances. China's development strategy directs funding towards industry and away from agriculture, so people in the richer coastal regions profit at the expense of the rural poor. In Mexico, the poorest states in the south are far from the US border and so opportunities for trading and employment are few; the richest 10 percent of the population earn 35 times more than the poorest 10 percent.[11] A high degree of inequality in a society leads to a vicious circle: people have less incentive to work hard because advancement in society is very difficult, and this leads to rising crime, social unrest and corruption – which in turn threatens economic stability.[12]

If we cannot succeed in meeting the Millennium Development Goal on poverty, the industrialized world will have failed. We will have failed not only the people that we promised to help, but in some way we will have failed ourselves. Listening to our leaders trumpet the benefits of globalization and worldwide free trade, we believed that we were doing something to help. We must make sure that our governments and our multinational companies prove us right.

First of all, we need to think about reducing poverty as an imperative. When governments look to cut public spending, overseas development aid is often among the first areas to be trimmed – but it shouldn't be. As economist Jeffrey Sachs and director of the UN Human Development Report Sakiko Fukuda-Parr wrote, "the question is not whether the rich countries can afford to do more or have to choose between, say, defense and reducing world poverty. Since less than 1 percent of national income is needed, the question is only whether they will make the elimination of the world's extreme poverty a priority."[13]

Development aid should, for example, be put at a far higher priority than the wasteful and unfair system of agricultural subsidies paid out by the US and Europe. The Organization for Economic Cooperation and Development (OECD) member countries spend around $300 billion a year in supporting their farming sector – more than five times what they spend on development aid.[14] This lavish aid encourages farmers to produce far more crops than they need to, and surpluses are then dumped on the developing world.

If rich countries decided to end agricultural subsidies and remove barriers to imports from the developing world, the results could be dramatic. For every dollar that developing countries receive in aid, they lose two dollars because of unfair trade barriers.[15] Market liberalization needs to go both ways, so that developing countries don't open their doors only to be faced with stiff rich-world trade rules.

But merely dropping trade barriers won't solve the problem. Reducing the crippling debt burdens faced by many developing countries is a crucial part of any poverty-reduction strategy: once they are freed from the need to spend all their resources in servicing enormous loans, governments are able to spend more on vital infrastructure, health and education. G7 leaders committed to cancelling $100 billion worth of debts owed by the 42 poor countries that were identified by the World Bank and the IMF as "highly indebted poor countries" (HIPC); at the time of writing 20 countries had completed the HIPC initiative but aid agencies argue that the structural and economic reforms required to complete the process leave countries more vulnerable, not less. In July 2005, the G8 nations agreed to forgive the debts of all completion-point HIPCs (and potentially many other countries still involved in the process). But aid agencies still called on the G8 to ensure that the debt forgiveness was "new money" – so HIPC countries didn't then miss out on other forms of aid.[16]

It is clear that in order to put in place important development infrastructure – like schools, hospitals, water and sanitation systems – large injections of donor finance will be needed. But this should be in the form of grants, not loans, as the last thing many of these countries need is to take on yet more debt. It also needs to be effective aid, given to the right people at the right time, and with a sense of the distortions that massive injections of money can cause to a society and its people.

The UN Human Development Report summarizes good practices for donors and recipients. On the part of donors, aid should encourage decentralized decision making (by local communities rather than central governments), co-ordination of projects and programs to align with the country's needs, and accountability. Aid should also not be tied to specific conditions. On the recipient's side, there should be institutional reform to promote transparency and good governance, more widespread participation in development issues and an increased level of oversight (by non-governmental organizations, civil society and individuals) to increase accountability.[17] Simply put, donors can do much to make sure the money goes where it's needed, and recipients can make sure it gets spent on the right things by giving people in communities a voice.

Developed nations also need to be prepared to share technology to help poorer countries. This doesn't mean just computer and communications technology, though that is important, but also making patent laws accessible to innovators in developing countries, committing to researching and developing drugs to combat illnesses that are endemic in the developing world, and helping to provide clean energy alternatives to reduce pollution and lower fuel costs. Providing training to help people get the most out of their land may be the most valuable donation of all: for example, the Heifer charity helps families by donating livestock and training to small farmers and communities. Once the farm is back on its feet, the recipients then "pass on the gift" by donating their animal's offspring to another needy family.[18]

Above all, we need to make sure that the forces of globalization do not work merely to make rich countries richer. The benefits need to flow both ways. Developing nations made their voices heard loud and clear at the World Trade Organization talks in Cancún, and put the issue of poverty and trade at the top of the world's agenda. Now it is up to the developed world to rise to the challenge.

On the eve of the Cancun talks, Britain's then chancellor Gordon Brown wrote that afterwards, "globalization will be seen by millions as either a route to social justices on a global scale, or a rich man's camp."[19] The developed world doesn't have much time to change the course of globalization, but then it's not that hard to do what's required. Living up to our promises, giving people a voice, playing fair – none of these things seems unreasonable. In fact, they seem like the very least we should be doing.

More than 12,000 women are killed each year in Russia as a result of domestic violence

"He beat me so hard that I lost my teeth. The beatings happened at least one time each month. He used his fists to beat me. He beat me most severely when I was pregnant ... the first time he beat me, and I lost the baby. I was in the hospital. The second time was only a few days before a baby was born, and my face was covered in bruises. He beat me and I went to my parents. My father refused to take me to a doctor. He said, 'what will I say, her husband beats her.'"[1]

No one should have to live in fear of violence. And no one should have to live in fear of the people who are supposed to love them. Yet every year, around the world, millions of women are victims of assault by their boyfriends or husbands.

In many countries, it's a dirty secret, something that happens between man and wife, an area where the law cannot and should not intervene. Of all the violent crime in society, it's probably the least visible – which makes it the hardest to tackle. But the consequences of inaction are tragic.

One estimate says that 3 million women are physically abused by their husband or boyfriend each year[2] – another that one in three women will be beaten, coerced into sex or otherwise abused during her lifetime.[3] In Russia, it's estimated that between 12,000 and 14,000 women are killed each year by their husbands – that's one every 43 minutes. Contrast this with America, where 1,247 women were killed by an intimate partner in 2000, and the enormity of the problem becomes clear. Russian NGOs say that unless serious injury or death results, abuse is seldom reported, so it's nearly impossible to guess how many women are abused each year.

Russian women's groups have been trying to raise awareness of this silent crisis – trying to get women to speak out about abuse, and pressuring the government to provide facilities for dealing with women who've been victims of violence. But they acknowledge they are dealing with some very deeply entrenched attitudes. One Russian proverb holds that "if a man beats you, that means he loves you." Getting women – and indeed men – to believe otherwise is the first challenge.

One of the few Russian doctors allowed to conduct medical examinations to provide evidence of violence points to Russia's violent history as one reason for these attitudes. According to Yury Pigolkin, "our society is extremely aggressive, going from one war to another. This creates a kind of citizen to whom the principles of conduct generally acknowledged in the US are not applicable. Programs made for Americans are powerless here. This is mainly due to economic factors: when a person is poor, when he's destitute, when he's barely surviving and not able to pay his rent, it's [hardly effective] to impose a fine on him."[4]

It seems that the massive economic and social upheaval in the post-Soviet era has left men demoralized, needing to control. Many insist their wives give up work, leaving the women totally dependent on their husbands. If things turn bad, they are powerless to leave. Housing shortages mean that couples who have divorced are often forced to continue living together. With support from the authorities grudging at best, NGOs aren't optimistic about change. In 2001 there were only six women's shelters in the whole of Russia, with none in Moscow. When one NGO representative asked an Interior Ministry representative to set up a special team to treat and examine victims of domestic and sexual violence, his smiling reply was, "We can't set up something like that just for you!"[5]

Perhaps the greatest challenge – and the first step towards a solution – is overturning entrenched beliefs that violence is acceptable in relationships. Even in Britain, where awareness of domestic abuse is high and there are frequent nationwide campaigns calling for an end to violence in the home, a survey found that one in five young men and one in ten young women think that abuse or violence against women is acceptable.[6]

Certainly, since ancient times women have been treated as living property, passing from the father to the husband on their wedding day. Roman laws of marriage decreed that women should be subject to their husband's rule. In medieval times, disobedient wives were often disciplined in public. And perusal of Blackstone's famous *Commentaries on the Laws of England* suggests that by 1765 little had changed. Blackstone observed:

> The husband also might give his wife moderate correction. For, as he is to answer for her misbehavior, the law thought it reasonable to intrust him with this power of restraining her, by domestic chastisement, in the same moderation that a man is allowed to correct his servants or children ... but this power of correction was confined within reasonable bounds.[7]

Seeing that Blackstone's idea of "reasonable bounds" included beatings with whips and cudgels, it's clear that "misbehavior" carried a heavy, painful price.

While ancient European laws stopped short of sanctioning murder, other countries would excuse a man charged with a so-called "honor killing." A man who had killed his wife or a family member could claim that he had been provoked by her behavior – perceived adultery, for example, or refusing to take part in an arranged marriage. Human Rights Watch reports that some countries, including Jordan, still allow these defenses today.[8]

At the 1995 UN World Conference on Women in Beijing, 189 governments pledged to fight violence against women in all its forms. But in many countries there is little sign that things are getting better. Where the law does provide a measure of protection, it is still often difficult to get authorities to prosecute. Police may often view the matter as something best left within the family – in Pakistan, police may even intervene on behalf of the accused, to try to broker a reconciliation between husband and wife. In other cases, police may drag their feet in collecting evidence about the extent and severity of the injuries – by the time the victim sees a doctor, her bruises have faded and much of the forensic detail has been lost.

Domestic violence is, of course, not just a problem that affects women. Men suffer attacks from intimate partners as well, and hundreds are killed. Men's groups argue that the perception of domestic violence as a female problem makes it difficult for men to report abuse. But the fact remains that women are five to eight times more likely to be assaulted by an intimate partner than men.[9] In 2000, 33.5 percent of the women murdered in the US were killed by their partners – as opposed to less than 4 percent of men.[10]

Violence against women is violence against all people, because it breeds a culture where women fear all men, and men feel wronged by the perception that they are all ticking time bombs, barely able to suppress their urge to strike out. We know this, and yet the problem of domestic violence refuses to go away. Governments need to honor their Beijing commitments – encouraging the police and the legal system to protect victims and punish offenders, and supporting groups that seek to shelter and advise women fleeing violence. But more than that, we all need to challenge the perception that physical discipline and abuse is acceptable. Because it never is.

In 2006, 16 million Americans had some form of plastic surgery

Is cosmetic surgery the ultimate act of vanity – or a courageous step towards self-actualization? Should we be dismayed that millions of otherwise healthy people are choosing to have their bodies cut open and mutilated – or should we be thankful that medical technology has developed to the point where our bodies can be altered to reflect our true selves?

Whatever you think of plastic surgery, it's a booming business. As prices fall and social stigmas disappear, people are flocking to "aesthetic surgeons" in search of perfection – or, at the very least, improvement.

The American Society of Plastic Surgeons recently launched a series of print advertisements featuring real people who were satisfied customers. Andrew, a real estate attorney, waxes lyrical about his liposuction and rhinoplasty: "I sacrificed some of my physical makeup over the years to hard work, long hours and stress, and I wanted to buy some of that back ... when I'm at real estate closings, when we're talking, I like to tell them my actual age and watch their shocked reactions." Laurie, a former competitive body-builder, says her breast augmentation has "helped my motivation, self-esteem and confidence. I did this for me – and nobody else."

In 2006, 16 million plastic surgery procedures were performed in America.[1] This figure includes cosmetic surgery, like nose reshaping, breast augmentation and liposuction; reconstructive surgery, such as scar and tumor removal; and non-surgical procedures, like laser hair removal and cellulite treatment. According to the American Society of Plastic Surgeons, 11 million of these procedures were cosmetic – "a good barometer of the local and national economy" –

and for the first time, breast augmentation was the most popular operation.[2]

The number of procedures has more than doubled since 1997,[3] thanks in part to the growing popularity of the Botox injection, where botulinum toxin is injected into the face to freeze muscles that cause wrinkles. The patient, who might expect to pay $400 for each injection, is left with a smooth, expressionless face.

Botox is now the most commonly performed cosmetic procedure, with 4.1 million Americans going under the needle in 2006. But there are a whole host of new ways to modify your body, if you so choose; bottom implants to make your posterior resemble that of the actress and singer Jennifer Lopez; tiny artificial fillers which are inserted into the skin to plump out wrinkles; and the "body lift," where the skin around your midsection is yanked up to smooth out baggy bottoms and thighs. And this is to say nothing about the alarming variety of adjustments that can be made to one's genitalia – the wonderfully named "designer vaginas," and for the gentlemen, penile enlargements, a concept familiar to anyone who's ever received spam e-mail.

The earliest proponents of cosmetic surgery would have been dazzled at the variety (and severity) of some of these modern innovations. Four thousand years ago, doctors were treating facial injuries so as to minimize damage to a person's looks – and in 800 BC, doctors in India were experimenting with skin grafts.[4] Doctors in medieval England pioneered some rudimentary techniques so as to hide the ravages of syphilis in their more distinguished clients. But plastic surgery reached the mainstream after the First World War, when many eminent surgeons devoted themselves to repairing the ruined faces and bodies returning from the battlefields. The so-called "aesthetic" procedures developed around this time, too, as surgeons realized "how much valuable talent had been ... buried from human eyes, lost to the world and society by reason of embarrassment ... caused by the conscious, or in some cases, unconscious influence of some physical infirmity or deformity or unsightly blemish."[5]

Decades later, the language surrounding plastic surgery has hardly changed. One Canada-based website makes a persuasive case for having one's "defects" rectified. "Most people would agree that what is inside a person is more important than what is outside. But increasingly, we are learning that the outside is important too ... the procedures you are going to read about can help ordinary people improve their appearance and feel better about themselves. They can often lead to improved self-esteem and increased self-confidence. Think of it as a little change on the outside that can lead to a big change on the inside."[6]

This language that centers on the self, that makes us believe that what ails us is not the way we feel about ourselves but the bodies that constrain us – this new way of thinking has helped cosmetic surgery gain a broad acceptance. It's no longer just the province of the rich or the vain. Where once cosmetic surgery was a luxury to which only Hollywood stars and millionaires could aspire, prices are falling. One plastic surgeon quoted in the *Economist* says that ten years ago a breast reconstruction cost around $12,000 – now it can be done for $600.[7] Breast augmentation and nose reshaping both average around $3,000, well within most Americans' reach. More than 70 percent of plastic surgery patients now earn less than $50,000 a year.[8]

Other commentators point to an increasing emphasis on physical perfection in popular culture. Music videos and the so-called "lad mags" – like *Loaded, Maxim, FHM* and countless others – constantly display beautiful, scantily clad women. Their bodies may be altered by digital manipulation, but the message is clear: the perfect female body is large-breasted, long-legged, blemishless. Many actors and models will confess to having surgery, putting an end to the "has she or hasn't she?" rumors. And all of this brings cosmetic surgery even further into the mainstream. Reports that clean-living pop princess Britney Spears had had breast implants led to hosts of young girls contacting their doctors, eager to find out about cosmetic surgery now that their heroine had made it okay.[9]

Perhaps inevitably, the industry now has its own reality TV show. ABC's show *Extreme Makeover* is described as "a real-life fairy tale" where people get to change "not just ... their looks, but their lives and destinies." As well as the usual battalion of hair, make-up and fashion experts, this show's experts include plastic surgeons, eye specialists and cosmetic dentists. In the second season premiere, Seattle radio journalist Dan Restione was transformed from a "plain and pudgy" man whose only exercise was walking across the room to get more doughnuts, into a "hot guy." Facial liposuction, chin implants, porcelain veneer teeth and laser eye surgery have given him "an amazing confidence," according to a colleague.[10] From the pictures, he now has a generic, square-jawed, tanned look. But it's more conventionally attractive than his previous incarnation, and that seems to count more than individuality.

America may lead the world in the race to create perfection, but other countries are catching up fast. Brazil and the UK occupy second and third slots on the plastic surgery league table; according to Britain's first professor of plastic surgery, Professor Angus McGrouther, an estimated 2.5 million cosmetic procedures were carried out in the UK in 2002.[11] Some countries, like South Africa and Costa Rica, are trading on weak currencies by advertising cosmetic surgery holidays – once your initial recovery is over, you can go sightseeing while the bruises fade, and return looking miraculously refreshed.

In an increasingly solipsistic world, perhaps this obsession to stay young and pretty is just an extension of the desire we feel to present the best possible face. Beauty has been prized throughout human civilization, and much as we may feel we are living in a culture obsessed with appearance and materialism, it's a preference that is as old as time. As Western society ages, people feel young and vital well into mid-life – so why shouldn't their exterior reflect that? But there is a danger that by submitting so readily to the scalpel's siren call, we are starting to consider our natural state as ugly, and aging as a disease. Might we one day see a world where we have to fit into an ageless, plasticized definition of attractiveness to be considered successful? Will we lose the ability to choose to grow old gracefully? And what of those who can't afford to keep up? In the name of beauty, we may be forced to face some ugly truths about the human condition.

Landmines kill or maim at least one person every hour

All around the world, more than 100 million remnants of conflicts past and present lie quietly in the ground, waiting for action.

In more than 60 countries around the world, landmines litter the earth. Walking the streets, you see painful evidence all around you. One in every 236 Cambodians is an amputee – and they're the lucky ones. Surgeons from the International Committee of the Red Cross assume that up to half of mine victims die instantly or bleed to death, unable to reach medical care in time.[1]

Margaret Arach was a victim of a mine explosion during Christmas 1998. She was travelling from Kitgum District in Northern Uganda to Kampala to be with her family. Despite reports of rebel attacks, she decided to travel by bus. There were 23 people on the bus when suddenly they heard a loud bang.

"Every able person tried to run. Little did I know that the "bang" had severed off my right foot. I managed to lower myself by the roadside and drag myself further into the tall grass where I remained still lying down. The first rebel who reached me picked my watch … the rebels then set fire to the vehicle, which would have burnt me beyond recognition as I was lying near it. However, with the wind blowing in my direction, I managed to crawl away under the smoke screen to safety."

Sixteen-year-old Taha Ziyadeh was collecting rocks with two friends in Zarqa in Jordan when they found a strange piece. "We thought it would be useful for us. But it was a UXO [unexploded ordinance], and it was the last time I saw my two friends who were killed by the strong explosion … I lost my right leg below the knee."[2]

In this era of computer-targeted missiles and remote-controlled drone bombers, it's remarkable that a weapon as unsophisticated as a landmine is still in use. Landmines were first deployed during the First World War as a means of securing territory. But their cheap price means they are still widely manufactured and used today. The US deployed 90,000 anti-personnel mines to the Persian Gulf for use in the 2003 war in Iraq.[3] They weren't eventually used – but the message was clear. A weapon as crude and undiscriminating as a mine still has a place in modern war.

So what makes landmines so much more of a concern than other conventional weapons? The main problem is their lengthy lifespan. Minefields are seldom cleared when wars come to an end, and the charges remain active for many years. In Poland, mines laid during the Second World War were still killing tens of people each year in the 1970s – and this was despite the clearance of more than 25 million mines from the country.[4]

Mines also can't discriminate between soldiers and civilians – a fundamental requirement of the laws of war. The International Campaign to Ban Landmines (ICBL) calls them an illegal weapon: "The psychological effect of landmines on the enemy is undeniable, but landmines also terrorize and demoralize civil society. Put simply, anything that landmines can do to an enemy's army, they can do to a civilian population. What they cannot do is discriminate between the soldier and the civilian. Their impact cannot be confined to the duration of the battle."[5]

Why do armies still use them, then? In a world where few wars are actually concerned with seizing an enemy's territory, surely their strategic use as a tool of defence is largely obsolete. But one factor is very attractive – their price. Army tacticians believe that, costing as little as $4, mines are cost-effective. And this means they can be used in large numbers, to intimidate, rather than defend. Now, one expert believes, they are used as "a strategic weapon often deliberately aimed at civilians in order to empty territory, destroy food sources or create refugee flows, or simply spread terror and make ordinary people's lives impossible."[6]

These selling points don't just appeal to conventional armies. Landmines are a weapon of choice for what NGOs describe as "non-state actors." In 2005, an annual global report into landmines found that armed opposition groups in ten countries used anti-personnel mines – among them the drought-ravaged African state Somalia.[7] Hundreds of thousands of mines scattered across agricultural lands have terrorized nomadic farmers seeking grazing and brought agricultural production to a standstill.

Progress is being made. On March 1, 1999, the Convention on the Prohibition of the Use, Stockpiling, Production and Transfer of Anti-Personnel Mines and on their Destruction (known somewhat more snappily as the Mine Ban Treaty) came into force, and as of February 21, 2007, 155 countries had become parties. And the treaty is starting to have a significant effect. The ICBL Landmine Monitor found that fewer governments were using anti-personnel mines and that global trade in landmines had dwindled to a very low level of illicit trafficking. Seventy-four countries have destroyed their stockpiles of mines altogether, and in 2005 funding for mine clearance totalled $376 million. Human Rights Watch called the progress "encouraging."[8]

However, there are still 40 countries which have yet to sign the treaty, and between them they hold a stockpile of some 160 million mines. Three permanent members of the UN Security Council – the US, China and Russia – have yet to sign. The ICBL reported that Russia still uses anti-personnel mines on a regular basis. As we have already seen, America has reserved the right to use landmines in conflict. The US is the biggest donor to landmine clearance programs, but the Bush administration seems unwilling to commit to other international efforts to get rid of landmines for good.

The US may have its own reasons for dragging its feet. In 1997, Human Rights Watch approached 47 American companies which were known to have produced components for use in anti-personnel mines. Thirty companies rejected the appeal to forgo any future production. The CEO of Alliant Techsystems paid lip-service to the "terrible problem" of landmines, but went on to say that it was "irresponsible to imply in any way that companies such as Alliant Techsystems have contributed to the world's landmine problems."

The president of Nomura Enterprise Incorporated wrote that "we consider it necessary for the United States to be able to defend itself and its citizens with military force. We truly wish that that were not the case but at this point in world history, it is a hard, cold fact."[9]

The landmine cause has garnered a great deal of publicity in recent years, partly due to celebrities getting involved. Sir Paul McCartney and his former wife Heather Mills are goodwill ambassadors for the Adopt-A-Minefield charity, and the actress Angelina Jolie has publicly supported the International Campaign to Ban Landmines. But few have had the impact of Princess Diana, who angered British government ministers by calling for an international ban on landmines in 1997.

The images of the blonde princess walking through minefields in Angola and talking to amputees resonated around the world, and Conservative government ministers attacked the "loose cannon" princess who had dared to step out of line. Peter Viggers, Conservative member of the Commons Defence Select Committee, fumed: "This is an important, sophisticated argument. It doesn't help simply to point at the amputees and say how terrible it is."[10]

But looking back, highlighting the plight of victims was the most helpful thing the princess could do. The people who are killed and maimed by landmines are largely powerless. The countries that are most heavily mined are among the world's poorest. These countries lack the resources to make a big commitment to de-mining, and their health systems are ill-equipped to help survivors. In terms of international advocacy, their voices are seldom heard. Perhaps, increasingly, the world is starting to listen.

There are 44 million child laborers in India

Every day in India, millions of children who should be at school are sent out to work. For almost all of them, it's a matter of necessity. In a country where two in five people live in abject poverty, getting enough money to feed and clothe a family can be difficult. Where caste and lack of education make well-paid jobs hard to come by, children may be forced to go out and work so they can contribute to the family. The work they get is often hazardous, and the conditions can be close to inhuman.

Ten-year-old Vinod worked for two years in a carpet factory in the Indian state of Uttar Pradesh. "I used to work for 12 to 14 hours in a day on the loom. I was not paid a single penny for a year. A week after joining, I was hung upside down for a minor fault. Whenever I sustained injuries while using a sharp knife to turn the carpet knots, I was denied medical care. Instead my employer used to fill the wound with matchstick powder and burn. My flesh and skin used to burn."[1]

There are children at work weaving saris, cleaning sewers, making glass. There are girls who work as domestic help in other people's homes, and children who take on the major responsibility in their own families for caring for younger children. In fact, it is difficult to say exactly how many Indian children are working. The Indian government claims that 12.6 million children between five and fourteen are in full-time employment. The UN International Labor Organization (ILO) estimates that there are 44 million child workers,[2] and unofficial estimates can be as high as 100 million – this is roughly equivalent to the number of children between five and fourteen who are not in school.[3]

Whichever estimate is closest to the truth, the fact remains that millions upon millions of Indian children are working – and their education, health and future will suffer because of it.

Worldwide, the ILO estimates that there are 246 million child laborers aged between five and seventeen. Of those, 171 million are working in hazardous situations; roughly 8.4 million are involved in what the ILO terms "the unconditional worst forms of child labor," including forced and bonded labor, armed conflict, prostitution and pornography and other illicit activities.

Let's be clear what we are talking about when we use the term "child labor." We're not talking about a child who helps out around the house or a teenager who works for a few hours on a Saturday in a local shop. We're talking about teenagers working as forced labor on cocoa plantations in Côte d'Ivoire. We're talking about six-year-old boys working as camel jockeys in Qatar.[4] We're talking about ten-year-old Sri Lankan girls who are the only servant in a household.[5] These are not kids doing a few hours' work for money to buy luxuries – they're children being forced to undertake adult responsibilities well before their years, working in dangerous environments.

But we'd be wrong to characterize child labor as a problem that only happens in the developing world. A series of high-profile prosecutions in the English county of Surrey exposed school children working sixteen-hour days in conditions described as "fast-food sweatshops."[6] In the US, as many as 800,000 children between the ages of five and eighteen work as migrant or seasonal farm workers, where children may legally be employed at the age of ten.[7] Fourteen-year-old Belinda told UNICEF researchers that she migrates from Texas to Maryland every year, changing schools every six months. At the age of eleven she began working in the fields, being paid 42 cents for picking an 24 pound bucket of squash. "No child belongs in the field and all children deserve an opportunity to enjoy their childhood," she says.[8]

Where child labor is harmful, where it limits a child's access to education or damages their health or welfare, something must be done. But it may not be as simple as calling for trade sanctions and demanding that employers get rid of all their child workers. Children who have been let go by their employers still need money: they may end up working in worse conditions for even lower pay, or being drawn into "street work" like prostitution or crime.[9] Boycotts of particular products are hard to monitor, and where developing economies depend heavily on one or two export sectors, they can lead to devastating consequences for the child employees. Ten-year-old Moyna, who is an orphan, lost her job at a garment factory in Bangladesh as a result of a US Senate boycott. Fifty thousand children lost their jobs, and Moyna now has to rely on family to support her and her grandmother. She told a *New Internationalist* reporter, "They loathe us, don't they? We are poor and not well educated, so they simply despise us. That is why they shut the factories down."[10]

Even when governments try to take action, it can be hard to get it right. In October 2006 the Indian government enacted a law making it illegal for children under fourteen to work as domestic servants or at roadside food stalls. But NGOs were concerned that the government had not done enough to safeguard children who might find themselves without work as a result of the law change. Rita Panicker of the Delhi group Butterflies said there had been little planning for rehabilitation of the young workers, and that it was "ridiculous" to think that a ban alone would solve the problem.[11]

If governments are serious about solving the problems of child labor, why not listen to the children who are involved? The African Movement for Working Children and Youth wants children to be able to work, but to work in accordance with twelve fundamental rights: the right to be taught a trade; to be able to remain in their villages and not be forced to leave for the city; to work in a safe environment; to light and limited work; to healthcare; to rest when sick; to be respected; to be listened to; to learn to read and write; to play; to form organizations and express themselves; and to equitable justice in the case of problems.[12] In other words, working children don't necessarily want an end to work, but they do want an end to exploitation.

It's clear, though, that the children who are most at risk will find it hard to speak out, and in these situations, international law needs to make clear statements that the most hazardous and dangerous forms of child labor need to be eliminated. The United Nations Convention on the Rights of the Child declares that children should be protected from economic exploitation and from performing any work that would be hazardous to their health or development, or interfere with their education. Most recently, the ILO Convention C182 for the Elimination of the Worst Forms of Child Labor called on its signatories to put an end to children's slavery or debt bondage, and the use of children in prostitution, pornography or drug trafficking, or hazardous work. Once children have been taken out of these jobs, the Convention puts an obligation on states who have signed it ("states parties") to help them by providing free education and, where possible, vocational training.

Programs like the Rugmark Foundation can also be very effective in helping children make the transition out of dangerous jobs. Rugmark builds partnerships with carpet producers and importers to make carpets that are free from child labor – factories are independently monitored to make sure they comply. A portion of the carpet price then goes towards the rehabilitation and education of former child workers. The foundation operates in India, Nepal and Pakistan and on average it saves three children a week from the looms.[13]

Vinod, the little boy we met at the start of this chapter, was freed when Rugmark inspectors launched a spot-check on his factory. The owner was told to release the child workers. Now, Vinod attends a rehabilitation group for children. "During Diwali vacation, when I went to my village this time, my mother was happy to see me. She remarked that I had a changed look and was bubbling with energy. Mother tells me to concentrate on my studies and treat it as a mission."[14]

All of the ILO's member states signed up to Convention C182, and it was the fastest-ratified convention in the ILO's history. The political will is there – now the challenge is for governments to translate that into action.

Free and compulsory primary education is thought to be an important step. A child who has a basic education has a far better chance of moving out of poverty – one of the main causes of child labor. If governments are serious about fulfilling their Convention commitments, this must be made a priority. So too must the establishment of a system of independent monitoring. Where there is an effective trade union system, tackling the issue of child labor can greatly increase their standing in a community: if adults are paid a fair wage, children should not have to work. Children's groups should also be allowed a say in how their working lives are regulated.

In the developed world, parents should keep a close eye on the hours their children work – and employers need to take a responsible attitude. Local councils should also make tackling child labor a priority, and do more to run checks on businesses that may be exploiting their young staff. We also need to think about how products we consume every day may have been brought to us through child exploitation. Boycotts might seem like an easy answer, but if we want to exercise our power as wealthy Western consumers, there are better ways. Look for the Fairtrade mark when you're next at the supermarket: you should be able to find fairly traded bananas, cocoa, chocolate, honey and tea, and if you can't, ask for them.

For many children, doing some work about the house is an introduction into adult responsibilities. A paper round or Saturday job may give them a small amount of financial independence and a sense of the importance of managing money – both valuable life lessons. But as soon as work means children can't be children – that they have no time for school, play, friends – the responsibilities have become too great. And that's when we need to do something about them.

People in industrialized countries eat between 14 and 15 pounds of food additives every year

It's the kind of lunch that people across the Western world eat every day: a ham and mustard sandwich on softgrain bread, packaged neatly in a little plastic triangle; a bag of salt and vinegar chips; and a bottle of orange fizzy drink. It sounds tasty, not particularly health-conscious, but certainly a convenient, filling lunch. And it's sitting on my desk.

The ham sandwich contains no fewer than thirteen E-numbers, additives with strange and multisyllabic purposes: emulsifiers, treatment agents, stabilizers, acidity regulators. There are some surprising ingredients too: what are maize grits, and why have I never used them when I've made bread? Why should smoked ham need water? The crisps are suitable for vegetarians and coeliacs, apparently, but still contain flavor enhancers: monosodium gluta-mate and disodium 5 ribonucleotide. And as for the soft drink, well, it does contain orange juice (8 percent) but it also has glucose-fructose syrup, sugar, aspartame and saccharine, preservative, flavoring, coloring and something called "cloud" (stabilizer E1450, if you're interested).

In 2000, the food industry spent around $20 billion on making our food look prettier, taste nicer and last longer. It's big business, and it's driven by the modern need for industrialized countries to feed a lot of people cheaply – and profitably. The food additives industry is adamant that these chemicals make our lives easier. They allow our food to stay fresh longer, and have made the whole concept of "convenience food" possible. Without food additives, they argue, we'd have to spend a lot more time in the kitchen. We'd also have to spend more time shopping, as our food would only last a couple of days before starting to rot. And as for margarine that has no saturated fats, low-calorie dishes and products with added vitamins – forget it. As the Federation of European Food Additives and Food Enzymes Industries has it, "The use of food additives ... has made possible the large-scale preparation of good wholesome food at economical prices ... in fact, many of today's foods would not exist without additives."[1]

It's easy to view the food additives debate as one of chemistry over nature, but it's not quite as simple as that. For centuries, humans used natural substances like salt and smoke as a means of preserving food. In early societies where the success of a hunt could not always be assured and crops could easily fall prey to disease, it was vital to find ways to preserve surplus food.

Nowadays, less than 1 percent of food additives by weight are used to preserve food. Ninety percent are what's known as "cosmetic" additives: flavorings, colorings, emulsifiers to make food feel smoother in your mouth, thickeners, sweeteners. It's these substances that concern campaigners more. By disguising bland and low-quality raw materials, substances like these can convince us we're eating something that's better than its constituent parts. Only those with a very high-level understanding of what each substance does can be sure of what they're eating. And that's worrying.

The worldwide market in flavorings is worth $3.6 billion a year.[2] Synthesizing flavors is a highly complex process, and most manufacturers guard their formulas jealously. Even a taste we might regard as simple – a banana, say, or an apple – is a product of hundreds of chemical reactions. The amount of chemical flavoring that's needed to make my fizzy drink taste more "orangey" is minute. There's also no requirement on manufacturers to go into detail about what's in that flavoring – all they need to say is whether it's natural or artificial.

Even that distinction is tricky. European Union regulations provide that the term "natural flavoring" may only be used for flavoring substances that are extracted from animal or vegetable materials –

but there's no requirement that the natural strawberry flavoring in your yogurt has to come from a strawberry. All it means is that it's been extracted from a natural source.

Reading the websites of flavoring companies is a surreal experience. One website refers to a "natural key lime flavor emulsion ... homogenized, heat-stable, kosher-certified and salt-free." You can buy powdered beer concentrate, liquids that mimic the taste of thick cream or buttery cake. As long as it's derived from a natural source, most consumers won't even know.

Artificial sweeteners are another hugely profitable sector. Britain's Food Additives and Ingredients Association, an industry group, justifies the popularity of sweeteners on health grounds: "Over-consumption is implicated in obesity and diabetes, so sweeteners with no energy content are obviously desirable in many foods."[3] People who worry about their intake can now choose from a wide variety of low-sugar foods without sacrificing the sweet taste they crave.

But there's another potent reason for beefing up sweetness without sugar: cost. While it costs around twelve cents to sweeten a liter of soft drink with sugar, the biggest-selling non-sugar sweetener, aspartame, costs just four cents. Saccharin costs less than half a penny.[4] Around the world, approximately 15,000 tons of synthetic sweeteners are used every year.[5]

Both the food additives industry and regulators such as the UK's Food Standards Agency are satisfied that artificial sweeteners are safe. But campaigners argue that there are considerable doubts about several of the most-used products. Cancer experts have expressed doubts about the testing of one sweetener, acesulfame-K, and have called for more rigorous testing; one retired US Assistant Surgeon General said "there are indications that [acesulfame-K] might be carcinogenic ... a properly designed long-term study in both mice and rats [should] be conducted."[6] Saccharin has been shown to cause cancer in rodents and aspartame has reportedly been linked with neurological effects such as dizziness and migraine.[7]

In Britain, the safety of food additives is determined by the European Commission's food safety body. There are reports of huge pressure behind the scenes, as the food industry seeks to lobby the EU. The US Food and Drug Administration (FDA) isn't immune, either. In 1977 a Canadian study confirmed earlier tests that showed rats developed bladder cancer when fed saccharin in high doses, and the FDA proposed a total ban. After a public outcry, fuelled no doubt by manufacturers, Congress ordered a moratorium – and then enacted legislation requiring products containing saccharin to be labelled as potentially hazardous. Even that labelling requirement has now been relaxed.

It's clear that the British public are worried about food safety – research from the Mintel research company showed that 44 percent of consumers are concerned about this issue, and 36 percent of adults believe there should be clearer labelling for ingredients, additives and "E" numbers. There's no doubt that they're right to be worried. But toughening up labelling requirements won't necessarily solve the problem. While regulatory bodies deem 540 food additive compounds safe for human consumption, there are doubts over the safety of 150 of those. Thirty could cause significant long-term harm to anyone who consumes them.[8]

The EU Food Safety Authority announced in March 2003 that it would change the way it regulated flavorings: from July 2005, only flavorings that were part of a "positive list" would be allowed. The list would only include substances that had been evaluated by an agreed procedure and found to be safe. It's a good start, but still the message seems to be clear: as long as our food is safe, the EU won't concern itself with what it's made of. Real strawberries or strawberry flavoring made from dozens of chemical compounds – it's the same thing, isn't it?

Well, no, actually. What's at issue here is the reality of what we put in our mouths – and the fact that all these food additives are perpetrating a kind of fraud on all of us. If I buy a ham sandwich, I want to taste real ham, not a strange mixture of animal tissue flavored with chemicals. I don't want to have to read the small print of my fruit drink to see if it contains sweeteners. Fresh, well-cooked food has all the flavor and texture it needs.

Some of this is about the choices we make – but much of it is about the choices that are made for us, by retailers and manufacturers. Lobbying for better standards is one thing we can do. But when you're next at the supermarket, take a few moments to read the fine print. If there's anything that you don't like the look of, don't buy it. Manufacturers and retailers won't take long to get the hint.

David Beckham's deal with the LA Galaxy football team will earn him $100 every minute

When football star and former England captain David Beckham announced he would leave Real Madrid and join the American team the LA Galaxy, few of the tabloid headlines had anything to do with his prowess in the midfield. "Dosh and Becks," giggled one British newspaper. "Bank It Like Beckham," punned the US business magazine *Forbes*. The sports network ESPN noted that Beckham "didn't even have to audition to become the next American Idol," while hip-hop star The Game volunteered to "kick Beckham's ass" on any given day. Forget the football, or the soccer, even; it was clear that David Beckham's move from *galáctico* to Galaxy was all about that most modern of sporting abilities, celebrity.

David Beckham's deal with the LA Galaxy was reported to be worth $250 million. Journalists raced to their calculators to work out what this would mean – $984,000 a week, $140,000 a day, $96 every minute – numbers that are absolutely unthinkable to mere mortals. And yet to the modern sports star, it seems, this is just as it should be. These are days, remember, when the average player for Manchester United takes home around $4 million a year – and the BBC can speculate that they're underpaid.[1]

Beckham may look back on his own days at Manchester United as being comparatively lean times. In Los Angeles, as well as an annual salary of $10 million, Beckham will earn 40 to 50 percent of Galaxy jersey sales and an undisclosed share of ticket revenues.[2] There were even suggestions from Tim Leiweke, president and CEO of the company that owns the LA Galaxy, that Beckham might gain financially from the popularity of the entire Major League Soccer

(MLS) competition: Leiweke spoke of "certain aspects of the deal that are ultimately about the upside value of the league as a whole."[3] On top of that, Beckham has personal sponsorship contracts with four companies – Motorola, Pepsi, Gillette and Volkswagen, estimated to be worth some $25 million a year. Do the math, and that comes to about $275 million for the five years of the contract – even more than first estimated. Amazing as this seems, though, David Beckham's estimated new annual earnings of $55 million don't make him the world's highest-paid sportsman. He's surpassed by the Formula One driver Michael Schumacher, whose 2006 earnings were estimated by *Forbes* magazine to be $58 million – and by the very richest of them all, golfer Tiger Woods, who earned an estimated $90 million.[4]

Tiger is so famous that he's become one of those "one name" sportsmen. Ali, Jordan, Pele – all guys who've transcended their sporting prowess to become something bigger, more significant. (In the US, at least, Beckham still needs his first name.) Tiger's become a global phenomenon, something more than a guy who's good at golf.

Like all sports stars, Tiger's millions are not just about what he wins on the PGA Tour – they never have been. In 2006, he earned $9.9 million in prize money.[5] He earns the other $80 million without ever having to pick up a golf club.

Although 2006 was in many ways a challenging year for Woods – his father, Earl Woods, died of cancer – he came back in storming form to win two Major tournaments and become the youngest golfer to win 50 professional tournaments. Off the course, it was a good year too. Woods signed a deal with Electronic Arts giving them the right to use his name for their golf video games for another six years, and he also renewed his highly lucrative multi-year deal with Nike. Neither party would disclose the sum, but the previous five-year contract, signed in 2001, was widely reported to be worth $100 million.

Woods' ongoing relationship with Nike points out very clearly how endorsements from sports stars can affect a brand's performance. Woods signed his first Nike contract in 1996, within weeks of his professional debut. The deal was worth $40 million over five years, and many commentators questioned how could Nike justify such outrageous sums. But over that period Nike saw revenues in its golf division soar from $100 million to $250 million.[6] This led Tiger's late father Earl to speculate that the deal was "chump change ... and this contract will be chump change compared to the next one, because Tiger is only going to get bigger and better."

Nike Golf president Bob Wood made the unlikely assertion that for his company, the deal with Woods wasn't about money. "When the first one came out, everyone said, "what the hell did you do that for?" His representation is enough to reinforce everything we say about ourselves – competitiveness, excellence and a desire to be better."[7]

Others put it differently. Nike is a ubiquitous brand, said *Sports Illustrated*, and so is Tiger Woods – they can't afford not to have him.[8] Nike needs to be stamped into the unconscious of sports fans, so that when they head for their local sports-goods store, they head for the swoosh without even thinking about it. And the MLS will be hoping that in signing a serious football talent – even one who's arguably past his prime – they'll become a serious football competition in the minds of the game's fans.

So sports stars bank the money, sponsors bask in the glory and increase their profits – you could argue that everyone's a winner. But it's worth thinking for a moment about where these massive revenues come from – and who's ultimately paying the price.

In November 2000, a group of sweatshop workers who had been laid off by Nike protested outside the Shangri-La Hotel in Bangkok, where Tiger Woods was receiving an honorary doctorate from a university. They issued an open letter to him, telling him that it would take a Thai garment worker 38 years to earn what he collects from Nike every day. They highlighted the poor working conditions and lack of union representation – and urged Woods to help them pressure Nike to pay Thai workers a living wage. Woods refused to meet the workers and walked past them without speaking. His comment later was suitably non-committal: "They have their own opinions and they have things they want to try and accomplish, and you can't stop them from doing that."[9]

Allegations of sweatshop labor have tainted many of the major sporting brands – and the image of the sports they promote. So too has the rampant commercialism shown by modern-day sports. In the US, fans are starting to use the internet to revolt against the worst excesses of this: from the American football governing body NFL threatening legal action against churches holding Super Bowl parties for their congregations[10] to Major League baseball's plans to display advertising on bases and the pitcher's mound.[11] Fans may love their sport, but they're starting to realize they don't love the business that it's increasingly wrapped in.

In the UK, football attendances are falling as fans become disillusioned. In the English Premiership, travelling fans are often charged in excess of $90 for a match-day ticket. Coupled with expensive transport, glossy programs and high prices charged for drinks and snacks, this puts attending a football match out of the reach of many. While the four biggest clubs – Chelsea, Arsenal, Liverpool and Manchester United – continue to sell out their home games, overall in the Premiership attendances are down by more than 1,000 year-on-year.[12]

Critics also cite the increasing lack of competitiveness in the Premiership – caused in no small part by the huge wealth of the big clubs and the comparative poverty of the rest – as a reason why fans are walking away. Kids who like football are more likely to be attracted to the big clubs with their big stars, rather than following their local team. As one disgruntled fan puts it: "Football has become a vehicle for turning turds ... into millionaires."[13]

At the time of writing, the LA fans' verdict on David Beckham has yet to come. Certainly, the LA Galaxy is already reaping some rewards – 5,000 new season tickets to the club were sold in just two days following the announcement of Beckham's signing.[14] It's not just the fans he'll have to win over; Beckham will need to turn on some sparkling football to justify being paid eleven times more than his next-richest teammate, Landon Donovan, whose MLS contract is just $900,000 a year. So-called "discovery" players receive only $11,700 a year.[15] Becks will have to play many, many times better than those guys.

Ultimately, though, Beckham's employers aren't looking just for goals, as we've already seen. They're looking for something even more elusive, and it's the same something that Tiger Woods brings to golf: celebrity. The LA Galaxy manager Alexei Lalas has already mentioned the attention that will follow Beckham to the US and the exposure it will bring to the MLS league. And Tim Lieweke, president and CEO of the Galaxy's owners, goes further. He believes Beckham will have "a greater impact on soccer in America than any athlete has ever had on a sport globally."[16]

It sounds like hyperbole, but then it seems that's what modern sport is all about. It's no longer enough just to be good at your game: you've got to be good at selling yourself and your sport. But once the big deals start to overwhelm what takes place on the field, that's where the trouble begins. David Beckham's deal with the LA Galaxy isn't the only sign of this trend, of course. But when you consider that in the time it takes you to read this essay, he's earned $1000, it's a sign that something's gone badly wrong.

Seven million American women and 1 million American men suffer from an eating disorder

Everyone knows – or should remember – that the years between ten and twenty are full of upheaval. Bodies change, relationships change and all of a sudden you're not a kid, not an adult, but something in between. No wonder many young people feel like they've lost control of their lives. And around the world, but particularly in the affluent West, young men and women will try to get some of that control back by starving themselves to death.

The prevalence of eating disorders seems sometimes like the bitterest irony of our culture. The typical sufferer is likely to be a high achiever, something of a perfectionist, hard working and eager to please others. They're bright stars. They want to be the best they can be. And for some reason that's not yet fully understood, they decide that losing weight and being thin is the way to do it.

In America, it's estimated that some 7 million women and 1 million men have some form of eating disorder. The most commonly known form is anorexia nervosa, defined by the Anorexia Nervosa and Related Eating Disorders group (ANRED) as "the relentless pursuit of thinness." A sufferer will diet and exercise obsessively, or may stop eating altogether. They will refuse to believe that they are thin; when they look in the mirror, they don't see a skeletal frame, but a bloated and overweight body. Anorexia has the highest mortality rate of any psychiatric disorder – up to 20 percent of sufferers will die.[1]

The other two commonly recognized eating disorders are bulimia nervosa (the "binge and purge" cycle, where a sufferer will eat a large amount of food and then vomit to get rid of it) and binge-eating disorder. Then there are a whole host of other illnesses – officially diagnosed by trying to determine whether a sufferer's relationship with food goes outside what is normal or healthy.

But in our diet- and food-obsessed culture, where ads for junk food crowd around television programs featuring unnaturally skinny women and impossibly buffed men, who's to say what is normal? And if 4 percent of the population has an eating disorder that warrants treatment, what should we be doing about it?

Anorexia and bulimia may have reached the public consciousness only in recent decades, but human beings have been starving themselves for centuries. Ancient Egyptian and Persian manuscripts describe behavior very similar to the starving and bingeing disorders we see today, while the excesses of Ancient Rome are infamous. Saint Catherine of Sienna starved herself to death in the 14th century, while in the 18th and 19th centuries extreme thinness was a symbol of spirituality, a conquering of baser appetites.

The disease was first formally identified in 1689 by Richard Morton, who described a patient of his in London as "a skeleton covered only with skin." But it was not until the early 20th century that physicians began to uncover the psychological nature of the disease.

The death of singer Karen Carpenter in 1983 brought anorexia into the public eye as never before. Ms Carpenter died at the age of 32, having struggled with the disease for most of her life. Her death brought wider awareness of a disorder that appeared to be reaching epidemic proportions. One study found that since the 1950s, the number of anorexia cases had grown by more than a third every five years.[2] Now, it would be hard to find someone who has never known a sufferer.

It would be easy to blame the mass media, and many people do. At first glance, the evidence looks persuasive. Top fashion models now weigh 25 percent less than the average American woman. The growing array of celebrity-based magazines revel in weight-loss stories, tracking stars' "journeys" from miserable normality to successful (and starving) acceptance. The media fuels the message that thin is good, but then it is also extremely quick to judge when a woman is thought to have lost too much weight: witness the furor over the "size zero" craze, in which Hollywood starlets were revealed to have waist measurements equal to the average eight-year-old girl. One study by Harvard Medical School pointed at the impact television had had on Fiji. Like most Pacific Island cultures, Fijians consider a curvy, well-muscled body to be the epitome of beauty. But this started to change after television came to Fiji in 1995. The islands' only channel showed a mixture of programs from America, the UK and New Zealand, with shows like *Seinfeld*, *ER* and *Melrose Place* proving big hits. Some three years later, the images had clearly begun to influence young women. Three-quarters of teenage girls now felt they were "too fat." No one had dieted in Fiji ten years before – now, 15 percent of girls were telling researchers that they had vomited to control their weight. Anthropologist Anne Becker compared the arrival of television to the arrival of British settlers in the islands: "What I hope is that this isn't like the 19th century, when the British came to Fiji and brought the measles with them. It was a tremendous plague. One could speculate that in the 20th century, television is another pathogen."[3]

As clear as that study appears, most research indicates that the picture is more complex than that. One study found that long-term exposure to skinny magazine models did not lead to excessive dieting – unless the girl in question had already expressed doubts about her body and self-image.[4] That view would appear to be borne out by supermodel Karen Elson, who in August 2002 confessed to a lengthy struggle with anorexia. "I used my job to justify my eating disorder … many girls who come into [modelling] already have issues with food, and it gives you an excuse to continue."[5]

That lack of self-esteem may be caused by feelings of inadequacy, the illusions generated by the celebrity stories, the belief that a thin life is a perfect life. But some experts believe that many eating disorder sufferers are seeking control, a way to express their fears. Sometimes a trigger event – a divorce, puberty, stress about exams

– may start the spiral downwards. A young anorexic woman may be trying to fight the transition to adulthood by starving her body into a childlike state. She may be angry, but have no means of expressing it other than to turn her anger on herself.

Pressure from parents and classmates is another important factor. Playground teasing can be cruel, and some anorexics and bulimics can trace the beginning of their eating disorders back to taunts about being fat. The lesson that the fat kid is the dorky, unpopular one takes a long time to forget – particularly since, as we've seen, typical eating disorder sufferers tend to see the world in black and white. As ANRED puts it, "if fat is bad and thin is good, then thinner is better, and thinnest is best – even if thinnest is sixty-eight pounds in a hospital bed on life support."[6]

For young men, the culturally prescribed role of power and strength – both physical and mental – makes diagnosis and treatment of eating disorders all the more difficult. Because most people see problems with food as a female preserve, young men may be ashamed to admit that they need help. Few treatment facilities offer programs specifically targeted at men.

It's clear that the pressure to be thin is spreading across both sexes, all ages, all racial groups. Some 80 percent of women and 45 percent of men say they're unhappy with their bodies. Teachers report girls as young as eight who are dieting to lose weight.

Even if we do the best we can to instill in our sons and daughters that they're beautiful and unique just as they are, young people still have a battle ahead. Kate Dillon, who started her modelling career as an anorexic waif and has now become a successful "plus-size" model, recalls the moment "where you feel one way about yourself … your intuition about who you are is that you're a good person, that you're beautiful, that you're strong, that you're capable. And at some point it's met with an outside force that's telling you, 'no, you're none of those things.'"[7]

It can be hard to override the voices in our heads that tell us we're worthless, that we should be better – let alone the voices that seem to shout from every billboard and every television commercial. But if we want to stop millions of young people starving themselves, we need to do something.

In 2003, the magazine *GQ* was revealed to have digitally manipulated a photograph of the actress Kate Winslet – famous for her beautiful, curvy body – to make her look taller and thinner than she does in real life. The resulting furore did much to demystify the iconic status of the "cover girl." We know the picture of Kate Winslet looked great, but we also know Kate herself doesn't look like that. Nor do most of the models we see in magazine pictorials. Movie stars who flaunt their "perfect" bodies aren't blessed with the "fast metabolisms" we often hear about – they have a battalion of chefs, personal trainers and stylists who can put in weeks of preparation for one red carpet event. The bleary-eyed photos of drunken celebrities staggering out of Soho bars, cellulite and beer bellies on show, are a far better indication of what's real.

The media needs to stop paying lip-service to eating disorders and start tackling the subject honestly. There are signs too that the fashion industry may finally be taking action: after the deaths of two models in 2006 from complications due to anorexia, the Spanish Association of Fashion Designers banned "excessively skinny" models from the catwalks at Madrid's fashion week. The British Fashion Council has also announced that it will set up an enquiry into health issues facing models.

But it's up to us too. Maybe we need to pay a little less attention to what the magazines and TV programs tell us – and start making sure our children grow up able to assess the worth of all the media's conflicting messages. And we need to do everything we can to ensure our children have a sense of their own self-worth and innate beauty, whatever their shape. Some young men and women will still fall into the grip of an eating disorder, of course they will. But by refusing to buy into the cult of skinny, by not equating a normal human body with all its lumps and bumps with ugliness, we may start to change the societal pressures that are feeding this epidemic.

Twenty-eight percent of American teenagers have tried illegal drugs and more than a quarter are regular cigarette smokers

"Drug use among teenagers has become a national nightmare," warns the drugfreeteenagers.com website. "As a parent, you are the first line of defense against your child's drug use." And how is a worried parent best able to arm themselves against assaults on their child's sobriety? With a home hair-testing kit that will allow them to perform a drug test on their teenager.

The website claims that having a drug testing kit at home is like "pre-paid life insurance for your child." But the very existence of such mistrust between parents and children shows that something's gone very wrong.

Since they were identified as a distinct social grouping in the 1950s, teenagers have been marked out by their rebellious behavior. As teens seek to establish a personality and identity that is separate from the family unit, they may reject their parents' values, expressing their individuality through their clothes and music. Teenagers learn the limits of their own abilities by testing them – making mistakes and learning lessons is an important part of forming a personality.

Psychologists refer to a phenomenon they call "adolescent ego-centrism." Young people feel that they are unique in the world and that no one will ever understand them. They may view themselves as special, marked out for greatness, invulnerable. And this may encourage them to take risks, not believing that any harm can come to them. Increasingly, it seems, teens find a source of both rebellion and comfort in drugs and alcohol.

A survey carried out by Britain's National Center for Social

Research and the National Foundation for Educational Research found that 45 percent of fifteen year olds had tried drugs at some point in their lives. Thirty-six percent had taken drugs in the past year. Cannabis was by far the most popular drug – 31 percent of fifteen year olds had used it in the past year.[1]

It's not just illegal drugs that are causing problems. The European Monitoring Center on Drugs and Drug Abuse found that cannabis use among teenagers in Britain had begun to stabilize in 2003, but only because the drug was so widely available that the market may have become saturated. It also found that solvent abuse (sniffing the fumes from gas, aerosols, glue or other volatile substances) was becoming an acute health problem in Europe – about 15 percent of British fifteen to sixteen year olds had used them, and between 1983 and 2000 there had been some 1,700 deaths associated with solvent use.[2]

In America, teenage use of illegal drugs is no less prevalent. The 2003 Pride survey showed that 24 percent of teenagers surveyed admitted to using drugs in the 2002–3 school year – which remained "consistent with the past five-year average." But the author of the survey was ambivalent about the conclusions that should be drawn from that. Dr. Thomas J. Gleaton said the real question was how much teenage drug use was acceptable to the nation. "If one in four teens using drugs is acceptable, we have done well in controlling drugs over the past decade. If a quarter of our youth on drugs is unacceptable, we need stronger action to truly dent teen problems."[3]

Cigarette smoking is another habit teenagers are picking up early in life – nearly a quarter of Britain's fifteen year olds are regular smokers, who consume an average of 50 cigarettes a week.[4] While the proportion of adults who smoke has been steadily declining since the early 1980s, the percentage of young smokers has stayed relatively constant.[5] The same is true in the US, where some 28 percent of teenagers smoke.[6]

And then there is alcohol. Britain's teenagers are drinking twice as much as they did a decade ago. Twenty-five percent of boys between eleven and fifteen reported drinking in the last week, and that 25 percent had drunk an average of 11.7 units of alcohol – about six pints of beer. Forty-nine percent of American twelfth-grade students said they had drunk alcohol in the last 30 days, and about a quarter confessed to "binge-drinking" – consuming five or more drinks in a row – in the last fortnight.[7] It's estimated that underage drinking costs the US $53 billion every year.[8]

National health initiatives seem to be having little effect on these trends. It can be difficult to tackle some of the factors that make drink and drugs attractive to teenagers – but governments are starting to realize that they have to try.

It's often been remarked that today's adolescents are getting older younger. To those of us well past that stage, it could just be the same phenomenon that makes policemen look younger compared with our advancing years – but marketers and branding consultants have been quick to capitalize on teenagers' higher disposable income and desire to look adult. Alcohol and drugs are seen as adult behaviors, and may be a way to seem grown-up in the eyes of classmates.

Teens also use drugs and alcohol for the same purpose that adults do: to relax, to feel more at ease in difficult social situations. Young people will have had their first introductions to alcohol (and perhaps drugs) at home, and will have seen how their parents use these substances to "take the edge off," to "unwind after a hard day."

Some parents decide to take a strict zero-tolerance approach to drugs and alcohol – they're probably the ones who'd be most attracted by the home drug-testing kit. Others are a little more liberal, considering teenage experimentation to be just harmless dabbling. And for most teenagers, that's all it will be. But there are risks associated with drug and alcohol use in teenage years – and this is what most concerns child protection groups.

Firstly, taking drugs or drinking may affect decisions a teenager makes about other risky activities. They may decide to get in a car driven by someone who's drunk or high. They may be pressured into having sex – or, like nearly a quarter of sexually active American teens, into having sex without a condom.[9]

Then, there is the question of what it might lead to. While the so-called "gateway theory" – the idea that experimenting with "soft" drugs like cannabis will inevitably lead to heroin addiction and a squalid death – has been discredited, there is evidence to show that teenagers who start drinking, smoking cigarettes or using cannabis at an earlier age are more likely to take hard drugs than those who start later.[10] Alcohol and tobacco are addictive substances, cannabis less so – but the European survey found that more than half of the young people admitted to drug rehabilitation centers cited cannabis as their main problem drug.[11] And habits picked up in childhood can last a lifetime: approximately 90 percent of cigarette smokers started before they were 21.[12]

Whether you believe in letting teens experiment freely or pre-scribe a strict approach to drugs and alcohol, it's clear that young people are increasingly at risk. Whatever we're doing about the problem, it's not enough.

America's National Academy of Science called for a "deep, shared commitment" to the underage drinking issue, including more vigorous policing of retailers selling liquor to minors and higher taxes on alcohol, especially drinks that are popular with teenagers. It also called for restraint in advertising and controls over the way alcohol and cigarettes are portrayed in film and television. The *British Medical Journal* found "high levels" of self-reported drunkenness in teens linked to consumption of sugary, fruity "alco-pops," and a high awareness of the most-advertised cigarette brands.[13] There have also been reports that one British tobacco company was so scared that it would lose market share to hard drugs that it looked at ways of marketing its products to young people – not exactly a glittering example of corporate responsibility.[14] Governments need to look hard at the way alcohol and cigarettes are marketed, and try not to fear the might of corporate lobbies.

Tackling the underage drug problem may be more complex, but it seems that education may play an important role. A British study found that teenagers who had received effective drug education were less likely to take illegal substances.[15]

But if we are looking at how governments and corporations should act, we must also look at ourselves. The watchful eyes of teenagers are always quick to pick up on adult hypocrisy, and there is plenty for them to seize on. The old argument that marijuana is less harmful than alcohol or cigarettes is one that will be familiar to any parent of teenagers, but we also need to look closely at the way we use drugs – legal or illegal – and the way we talk about them. Do we proclaim our "need" for a morning cup of coffee, say "we're dying" for a cigarette, talk about being a chocolate "addict"? Do we lie about our own illegal drug use in the hope of setting a good example?

Several studies have found that parents are the strongest influence on the decisions children make about whether or not to use drugs or alcohol.[16] If we can have an open, honest and tolerant dialogue with our kids about these issues, then that's probably the best thing we can do. Our young people will feel as though we trust them to act like adults. And though they still may not make the right choices, that trust is a far more effective tool of persuasion than a home drug-testing kit.

One million people become new mobile phone subscribers every day. Some 85 percent of them live in emerging markets

From her tiny office on a busy Kabul street, Sukhriya Hassani rents out cellphone services. For ten cents a minute she helps Afghans do something that most of us take for granted – call a friend, a family member, a business associate. It may mean that she is hassled by thugs who don't like the fact that a woman does business with men, but for Hassani (a widow at 25) it means she can send her son to school and take classes herself.[1]

Hassani is one of 50 Afghan women employed by the mobile phone network Roshan, which boasts 1.2 million customers in Afghanistan. Compared to the international giants, that's a tiny user base – but when you consider that Afghanistan had little infrastructure of any kind after two decades of war and occupation, it's a remarkable achievement. No longer do people have to walk to a neighboring country if they need to make a phone call – the outside world can come to them.

Every single day, 1 million people become new mobile phone subscribers. Of those, 850,000 live in the developing world.[2] In India alone, 6.6 million new customers sign up every month, and by 2010 the government predicts that there will be more than 500 million mobile phone users in the country.[3]

It's easy to see why mobile phones have captured India's heart. Once upon a time, getting a land-line telephone in India was a long and tortuous process; waiting lists of 5–10 years were common and many opted not even to bother. Now, cheap call costs mean that mobile phones are available to everyone. Rickshaw drivers, fishermen, farmers – one top executive told the *Economist* that even "an unemployed person with a phone suddenly feels part of the nation."[4]

What this could mean for development is exciting indeed. A study conducted by the Centre for Economic Policy Research and Vodafone calculated that a developing country with an extra ten phones per 100 people would have seen a 0.6 percent rise in its GDP.[5] Small business owners confirm this: in South Africa, 62 percent said they'd increased their profits after getting a mobile phone.[6]

As well as helping businesses grow, mobile phones strengthen communities. Most mobile owners in South Africa allow their family members to use their phone for free, and in Tanzania 85 percent of phone users said they had more contact with their families after getting a mobile phone.[7] One young woman in Kenya told the BBC that, in her opinion, the cellphone boom in Africa has had "about the same effect as a democratic change of leadership."[8]

But while mobile phones may be changing the developing world, there is a long way to go. The "digital divide" – the gap between those who can benefit from technology and those who cannot – is still a real concern. It's not just a question of access any more; the statistic quoted in the first edition of *50 Facts That Should Change The World*, that 70 percent of the world's population had never heard a dial tone, is no longer true. The real challenge is to make sure that people all over the world can get the real benefits of that access.

Every year, the wired-in world generates a huge amount of information. In 2006 it's estimated that the world generated 161 exabytes of information. That's 161 followed by 18 zeros – or enough information to fill 161 billion iPod shuffle music players.[9] The information ranges from e-mails and web searches to digital photographs to videos shared on YouTube and internet-based phone calls – and by 2010 it's estimated that nearly three-quarters of the digital information in the world will be generated by ordinary consumers.

It seems as if the rose-tinted predictions of tech-evangelists have come true: technology really has enabled everyone it touches to get their voices heard. And every day, there are more and more of those voices. With much fanfare, the number of internet users in the world reached 1 billion in 2005. But at the time of writing, only 16.7 percent of the world's population had internet access, and not surprisingly, they are almost overwhelmingly in the developed world.

In North America, nearly 70 percent of people can access the internet; in Asia and the Middle East it's around 10 percent, and in Africa less than 4 percent.[10] Given the geographic and economic difficulties in getting land-line telephones into remote rural areas in developing countries – let alone telephone lines capable of delivering consistent, fast internet connections – that divide might look almost impossible to bridge.

Here's where the mobile phone comes in. As anyone who's listened politely through a sales pitch in a mobile phone store knows, you can access the internet – a cut-down version, at least – on a phone. Now although you need a fairly modern phone to access images and video, there are many crucial services that can be offered without these frills.

For an example, look at TradeNet in Ghana. The company's aim is to create a platform for farmers and traders to share information – and they can do this via text message. Where once farmers might have had to wait for a passing trader to buy their goods and had no idea of what was a fair price, TradeNet's subscribers can check market prices in real time and send out an offer to buy or sell goods to thousands of others. Once buyer and seller get in touch, they do the deal direct. And all this using a mobile phone's Short Message Service (SMS) function – something that's found on even the most basic handsets.[11]

And then there's Wizzit, a cellphone-based banking service that's launched in South Africa. Some 16 million South Africans don't have bank accounts, and using this service they don't need one – they can send money to relatives or pay bills using their phones, and they're also issued with debit cards which work just like those of other banks.

In February 2007 a pilot scheme for allowing international phone-to-phone money transfers was announced – hoping to cater to the needs of migrants sending money back home to their families. The World Bank estimates that some $232 billion was remitted by migrants around the world in 2005;[12] a cellphone-to-cellphone system would cut down on losses due to fraud or charges, and would mean smoother, cheaper money transfers.

Soon, even more will be possible. Third-generation (3G) mobile phone technology is poised to bring the mobile internet within reach of the developing world. The World Wide Web Consortium, directed by Tim Berners-Lee, has turned its attention to streamlining the mobile internet so it can be accessed easily around the world. The GSM Association industry group challenged manufacturers to produce a low-cost 3G mobile phone: the winner, Korea's LG Electronics, designed a phone that should be 30–40 percent cheaper than the current average price for a 3G phone. There may even be advantages to coming to this kind of technology late. Boffins talk of the "leapfrogging" phenomenon, in which countries that are later to adopt technology may end up with better standards and faster penetration, because the rich world has already done a lot of the experimentation.[13]

Governments can clearly reap many benefits of having a technologically engaged population. We've already seen that it will have a big impact on a country's economy – and it will open up the possibilities of a more transparent relationship between a government and its citizens. But it also allows others to communicate with a government's citizens too, and this may be a somewhat more unwelcome prospect for regimes which don't relish opposition parties summoning supporters to rallies via mass text message.

So there are clearly dangers that governments may seek to regulate what their citizens can and cannot do with their phones – in the way that many already seek to regulate the internet. Many governments, including China, Iran, Vietnam, Myanmar and North Korea, practice heavy internet censorship: for example, banning opposition party websites, arresting bloggers who criticize the government, and blocking websites of international human rights groups. Others, like Saudi Arabia and the UAE, filter all internet traffic.[14] For some countries, the barriers to freedom of speech aren't just caused by a lack of technology. But many believe that mobile technology is evolving faster than governments' efforts to censor it.[15]

The digital divide has threatened in the past to worsen the gaps between world's haves and have-nots. The rich world, with access to more information than it could ever need, would get richer; the poor world, lacking the power and the resources to change their situation, would suffer further. Fortunately, there seems to be some real progress. In the modern, globalized world, information really is power. With governments and big business starting to see the potential in universal access to technology – and citizens seeing the very real difference it will make to their everyday lives – there's every chance that the digital divides will disappear altogether.

Cars kill two people every minute

On August 17, 1896, 44-year-old Bridget Driscoll became the first person to be killed by a motor car. Mrs. Driscoll and her teenage daughter were visiting London to watch a dancing display. On a terrace in the grounds of Crystal Palace, she was hit by a car which was offering demonstration rides to the public. The car was travelling at four miles per hour when it hit Mrs. Driscoll, and the impact proved fatal. As he delivered his verdict of accidental death, the coroner said "this must never happen again."[1]

But it has. Since then, some 25 million people have been killed in road traffic accidents. If current rates continue, an estimated 1.17 million more will die each year – two people every minute of every day – and a further 10 million people will be injured or crippled. It's a problem of such magnitude that it's led many to speculate whether the inventors of the motor car had any idea what they were unleashing on the world.

In the 20th century, death by road accident had become an epidemic in the Western world. In 1930, there were just over a million cars in Britain, and 7,300 people died on the roads – more than twice the number of deaths in 1999, when there were 27 million cars.[2] By 1960, President John F. Kennedy identified traffic accidents as "one of the greatest, perhaps the greatest of the nation's public health problems."[3] By then, nearly 40,000 people were dying on the roads each year in the US; today, that figure is pretty well unchanged, despite there being three and a half times as many vehicles.[4] Now, the people most affected by road accidents are the world's poor.

The statistics paint a sombre picture. Seventy percent of road deaths every year occur in developing countries. Sixty-five percent of those killed are pedestrians. The majority of people hurt or killed in road accidents in the developing world are not the vehicle occupants; they're walking, they're on motorcycles, they're on bicycles or other non-motorized vehicles.

The problem is getting worse, too. A study by Harvard University and the World Health Organization (WHO) projected that by 2020 road traffic accidents would be the third biggest cause of death or permanent injury in the world. They're already the second biggest cause of premature death for men aged between 15 and 44 – beaten only by HIV/AIDS.

As well as the tragic loss of life, that last statistic hides a whole host of other problems. Men in the prime of life tend to be the bread-winners in a family. Even if their injuries are not fatal, they may greatly reduce their ability to earn. When the family loses its main income, especially in poorer countries, there are few safety nets to catch them. The effect on the family's standard of living can be disastrous.

In some low- and middle-income countries, road crash victims occupy up to 10 percent of hospital beds.[5] The WHO estimates that road accidents cost countries between 1 and 2 percent of their gross domestic product (GDP). The developing world loses some $100 billion each year – twice the amount of development assistance it receives.[6] Once you factor vehicle ownership rates into the accident statistics, the five countries reporting the most deaths are all in sub-Saharan Africa: Ethiopia, Rwanda, Guinea, Nigeria and Lesotho.[7]

In countries where there is a high level of car ownership, the number of deaths seems to be declining. In developed countries, the number of road accidents has fallen by about 25 percent since the early 1970s – despite massive increases in the number of cars on the roads.[8] In Britain, there are now 24 million cars, ten times as many as there were in 1950 – and yet the number of road deaths has fallen from just over 5,000 to 3,508 in 2003.[9] The so-called "highly motorized countries" account for 60 percent of the global vehicles, but only about 14 percent of the global deaths.[10]

So what's the difference? Why, once again, are developing nations over-represented in a public health crisis? And what can be done?

If you drive a car in a richer country, it's more likely to be a newer vehicle, and subject to safety checks required by law. Your car is likely to have a number of safety components installed: airbags, for example, or anti-lock braking. You'll be driving on well-maintained roads. And there are likely to be strict laws preventing you from doing things that will impair your driving skills: drinking, for example, taking drugs, or talking on a mobile telephone.

In some developing countries, many people drive without ever having passed a test. The number of vehicles on the road is dramatically increasing in many countries, and the roads often haven't kept pace with this sudden surge in drivers. They may be narrow, badly surfaced, potholed. Due to corruption or stretched resources, the roads are poorly policed. If an accident does happen, it may take a long time for emergency services to attend, thus increasing the chance that people will die at the scene or be left with permanent disabilities. And if the ambulances do come in time, the medical treatment may be prohibitively expensive. In Ghana, one study showed that only 27 percent of people injured in road crashes used hospital services. The most common reason cited for not seeking healthcare: the victims couldn't afford it.[11]

Most governments are aware that the high rate of road deaths is a problem, but it can be difficult to generate the impetus to do something about them. They will never attract the whirlwind of publicity surrounding the SARS outbreak in 2002–3 – which claimed 774 lives in nine months. Vehicle accidents claim that many lives in just eight hours.

Some are starting to realize that road deaths are not just a string of isolated tragedies; when taken together as a whole, they are hindering development. And there are some success stories. In Fiji, vehicle insurers agreed to pay 10 percent of their premiums to fund a National Road Safety Council – whose programs led to a 44 percent fall in road deaths over the four years to 2002.[12]

The key seems to be convincing governments that road safety is a tremendously cost-effective investment. In 1999 the World Bank initiated the Global Road Safety Partnership (GRSP), which aims to convince governments that road safety is not just a moral responsibility, but can also help to smooth the path out of poverty. The GRSP quotes a study which found that road crashes cost a particular country $30 million each year. A comprehensive road safety plan, incorporating improvements in highway design, education and so on, cost just $150,000 a year and led to savings of $1.5 million as road accidents decreased.[13] Around the world, GRSP initiatives range from providing school children in South Africa with high-visibility jackets and backpacks, to encouraging Vietnam's 10 million motorcycle riders to wear helmets. In Hungary, GRSP partners helped to introduce reflective road signs, speed limits and road markings at dangerous sites.[14]

In the developed world, meanwhile, governments are seeking to continue the downward trends in vehicle deaths. Britain's "Think!" campaign aims to make drivers see the consequences of their actions – how drinking, taking drugs or driving too fast will affect their ability to cope with certain situations. A number of European countries have launched campaigns promoting "designated drivers" in an attempt to curb alcohol-related accidents. In the US, the American Automobile Association Foundation for Traffic Safety has recently completed projects about unlicensed drivers, "distracted driving" (for example, where drivers eat and drink behind the wheel, or use mobile telephones) and child seat safety.

Perhaps the saddest aspect of a road death is the sense of waste. Road traffic accidents are, for the most part, completely avoidable. They take the lives of young, fit people. Nelson Mandela wrote of the loss he felt on hearing his eldest son had been killed in a car accident: "I do not have words to express the sorrow or loss I felt. It left a hole in my heart that can never be filled."[15]

If they could hear Mr. Mandela's words, the inventors of the motor car might wonder what they had unleashed. Now it is up to governments – and all of us – to make sure the car's impact is as benign as possible.

Since 1977, there have been more than 120,000 acts of violence and disruption at abortion clinics in North America

In September 2003, a former Presbyterian minister became the first person to be executed for killing a doctor who performed abortions. In 1994, Paul Hill murdered Dr. John Britton and his driver James Barrett outside the Ladies' Center in Pensacola, Florida. Hill gave himself up to police, saying he had killed Dr. Britton to prevent "innocent babies" from dying.

Before his execution, Hill said he was looking forward to dying for his cause: "I believe the state, by executing me, will be making me a martyr," he told reporters, and he said that, given the chance, he would kill again to save unborn children. Many protesters waiting outside Starke Prison on the day of the execution hailed Hill as a hero. In a last statement before his execution, Hill called for more violence. "If you believe abortion is a lethal force, you should oppose the force and do what you have to to stop it."[1]

The battle over America's unborn children has raged since the landmark Supreme Court judgement in *Roe v. Wade* legalized abortion in 1973. By a seven to two majority, the court ruled that the state did not have the power to prohibit abortions, as a woman's decision to terminate a pregnancy was included in the freedom of personal choice in family matters enshrined in the Fourteenth Amendment of the US Constitution.

Since then, several Supreme Court decisions have limited the freedoms protected by *Roe v. Wade*, and some states have adopted legislation that aims to discourage abortion – by providing that a woman must be given information that could discourage her from the operation, for example, or requiring a compulsory waiting time between the first consultation and the abortion procedure. A January 2003 survey by the Alan Guttmacher Institute found that 30 years after *Roe v. Wade*, abortion rates in the US were at their lowest level since 1974, and that emergency contraception had played a big part in the decline.[2]

For some, though, these downward trends are not enough. They are not satisfied that the current administration is seeking to restrict abortion as much as possible. Some people feel so strongly about what they see as the killing of unborn children that they take their feelings to the clinics. The National Abortion Federation (NAF) keeps statistics on incidents of violence and disruption at abortion clinics, and since records began in 1977 there have been more than 120,000 incidents at clinics in the US and Canada.[3]

These incidents cover a whole range of disruptive and violent behavior – from picketing abortion clinics and harassing patients and staff, to photographing women who are attending clinics and posting their pictures and medical records on the Internet; from sending envelopes filled with substances resembling anthrax, to bombings, arsons and murder.

Seven people have been murdered by anti-abortion activists. On October 23, 1999, Dr. Barnett Slepian was standing in his kitchen in Buffalo, New York, when a sniper shot and killed him. Dr. Slepian's wife and four sons were nearby. He was the fifth doctor to be shot by a sniper, but the first to die. After a two-year manhunt, James Kopp was arrested in France and extradited to the US. In March 2003 he was found guilty of second-degree murder. He was also charged with trying to kill a Canadian doctor, and was wanted for questioning in relation to two other attacks in Canada. Kopp was sentenced to 25 years to life imprisonment. He refused to apologize for what he had done.

Kopp did not act alone. He is reportedly a member of the underground network "Army of God," a terrorist network that has been linked to the bombing of an abortion clinic and a gay bar in

Georgia, the kidnapping of an Illinois abortion provider, hundreds of anthrax threats to abortion clinics and a host of other violent incidents. The group's website is a bizarre mixture of scriptures, photos of aborted babies, anti-homosexual and anti-Islamic propaganda. But it makes it clear that those who resort to violence are heroes.

The group considers itself to be fighting a war against the US government – in the words of anti-abortion activist Neal Horsley, "the war that had gone undeclared in this nation ever since 1973 when the government of the USA in *Roe v. Wade* effectively declared war against the children of God." He goes on: "Like the bombs planted by the IRA in Ireland, the bombs might be terrorist but they are not cowardly when war has been declared and responsibility for the military actions are accurately assigned."[4]

Horsley is the man behind the infamous Nuremberg Files, a website which features a list of names of doctors and other staff that work at abortion clinics. Horsley claims to be collecting evidence with a view to seeing all abortionists on trial. As the website says, "Our goal is to record the name of every person working in the baby slaughter business across the United States of America so, as in the Nuremberg Trials in Nazi Germany, we can punish these people for slaughtering God's children."

Many felt that the Files amounted to a hit list. The site is decorated with lurid images of what appear to be body parts, dripping with blood. The list of "baby butchers and butchered" includes names and states – where a person has been wounded, their name is greyed out, and where there has been a fatality, it is struck through.

Among recent additions to the Nuremberg List is President George W. Bush. The Files' authors objected to his approval in August 2001 of federal funding for existing lines of stem cell research – which involves taking cells from aborted embryos. Horsley described President Bush's decision as "a covenant with the devil." It's a strange irony that Bush is condemned by the Nuremberg crew, as many pro-choice activists consider that his administration poses a serious threat to *Roe v. Wade*. The National Organization for Women (NOW) highlights his August 2003 ruling that federal family planning funds should not be paid to any international organization that performs abortions or refers women to abortion services, and the June 2003 bill which banned a number of abortion procedures used in the second or third trimesters of pregnancy, regardless of the threat to a woman's health. He has even, NOW believes, likened abortion to terrorism.[5] But despite all of this, President Bush is still on the Nuremberg List – in the eyes of anti-abortionists, he's guilty of crimes against humanity.

In 2002 a Federal Appeals Court held that the Nuremberg Files site contained "true threats" of violence against abortion providers, and that these were not political speech covered by the First Amendment right to freedom of expression. The case, brought by two abortion-provider organizations and four doctors, had been struck down earlier in 2001, but the events of September 11 made the Appeals Court think again. However, the new ruling only applied to a poster campaign where doctors had been identified as "the deadly dozen." Neal Horsley's response: the six judges who supported the ruling were added to the Nuremberg List.[6]

If we believe in free speech – and we should – we must realize that it's a right that applies to people whose views we may find unpalatable or offensive. But when does forceful expression of one's views cross the line, and become intimidation?

With such an emotionally and ethically complex subject, it's unlikely that the decision whether or not to have an abortion would ever become completely free from some kind of pro-life pressure. There's no law to stop campaigners setting up outside clinics, distributing leaflets, chanting and praying for those inside. But when people start linking arms to keep women out of the clinic, there's a problem. When people start publishing names and addresses of doctors who provide abortions, there's a problem. And when the rhetoric spills over into violence, there's a very serious problem.

We must make sure that we respect the rights of people to express their anti-abortion views, however repellently, and however much we may agree or disagree with them. We also need to make sure that our law enforcement agencies don't single anti-abortionists out for particularly tough treatment – such attention feeds these groups' mythology of persecution, and only serves to reinforce their belief in the rightness of their cause.

There are many people who strongly disagree with abortion – but the vast majority of those do not feel compelled to launch a violent campaign against people and clinics that provide abortions. Both sides of the abortion debate need to see the violent few for what they are: terrorists subverting a legitimate debate for their own ends.

Global warming already kills 150,000 people every year

There's no kinder way to put it: climate change is already happening, and it's already claiming lives.

In 2003, Europe experienced one of its hottest summers ever. Across the continent, temperatures soared; in France, the thermometer hovered around 40 degrees Celsius for a fortnight, while Belgium had the hottest summer since records began in 1833. In cities, where temperatures tend not to fall at night, there was little respite from the choking heat.

It was only once the heat had subsided that the human cost of the extreme weather began to be counted. In France, undertakers were forced to store bodies in a refrigerated warehouse. At first it was estimated that the heatwave had claimed some 35,000 lives across Europe. But three years on, the Earth Policy Institute issued its revised death toll: it now believes that more than 52,000 Europeans died from heat in the summer of 2003.[1]

The Institute pointed out that heatwaves are silent killers – coroners' reports rarely list heat as a cause of death, and it's only when death counts can be compared with a "normal" year that the true toll can be determined. And the Institute warns that, because of this, policy-makers and the public haven't yet grasped the full extent of what happened that summer – and what risks we may face in the future.[2]

The heatwave had other serious consequences, too. Crop yields slumped as fields turned from green to brown, and Europe's agricultural output fell to its lowest level in a century.[3] Wheat harvests were down 20 percent in France and nearly 650,000 hectares of forest were destroyed in fires.[4] As Europe's vegetation withered and died, its ability to absorb carbon dioxide from the air was hugely reduced – thus, cruelly, leading to far higher emissions across the continent.

Even in terms of death toll alone, this was the worst natural disaster Europe had faced in 50 years.[5] And the World Health Organization warns that worse is to come. Every year, the WHO estimates that climate change leads to more than 150,000 deaths and 5 million illnesses – and that this toll could double by 2030. Warmer temperatures mean that diseases spread more quickly. Bacteria that cause diarrheal diseases flourish in hot weather, contaminating water supplies. Mosquitoes and rats thrive too, migrating into areas which were previously too cool for them to venture – leading to the spread of potentially fatal diseases like malaria and dengue fever. Meanwhile, there are reports that malaria is making a modest reappearance in Italy, a country that was declared malaria-free in 1970.[6]

Many of these diseases can be prevented by providing clean water and by preventative medicine, but this comes at a cost – and with many poorer nations already struggling to provide healthcare services to their people, it could be tough for them to cope with the increased demands on their resources. It's thought that global warming could cause as many as a million additional deaths from malaria each year.[7]

And then, of course, there is malnutrition. We've already seen how a heatwave affected the growth of cereal crops in Europe; changes in temperature may make some crops simply impossible to cultivate, and those that can still be grown will require far greater amounts of water. Of course some countries may experience an increase in agricultural production – Siberia, say, may suddenly become a more hospitable place to grow crops – but the *British Medical Journal* anticipates a "net negative impact" on agricultural production.[8] Unable to produce staple foodstuffs and without the funds to change to other kinds of farming, it is the poorest communities in the world who will suffer the most.[9]

Scientists are now clear in their assessment of the problem: global warming is happening, and it's almost certainly caused by human action. In February 2007 scientists across the world compiled a report for the Intergovernmental Panel on Climate Change (IPCC) which spelled it out plainly. If we do nothing, average temperatures could increase as much as 6.4 degrees Celsius by the end of the century. Even a rise of 4 degrees would have catastrophic consequences. Hundreds of species would become extinct, there would be food and water shortages in many countries, and rising sea levels would leave hundreds of millions of people without homes. And the scientists said it is "very likely" – in scientist-speak, that means 90 percent sure – that this is all caused by human action. As Achim Steiner, executive director of the UN Environment Programme, said: "February 2007 may be remembered as the day the question mark was removed from whether people are to blame for climate change."[10]

The IPCC report made it very clear: it's worse than we've thought, and we've done it to ourselves. And unless we, as a species, take drastic action, things are going to get very bad. But in a way, this may give us cause for hope. In 2007, there's no excuse for not doing something about global warming. Our governments can no longer couch their discussions in paternalistic language, urging us to do our bit while being reluctant to take strong action that might cost them votes. Slowly, we might be starting to realize that there's something bigger at stake here. And maybe, just maybe, a change is coming.

In 2006, a former chief economist of the World Bank, Sir Nicholas Stern, authored a report into the business impact of climate change.[11] His conclusion was stark: global warming could shrink the world's economy by 20 percent. He concluded that "our actions over the coming few decades could create risks of major disruption to economic and social activity, later in this century and in the next, on a scale similar to those associated with the great wars and the economic depression of the first half of the 20th century." But he suggests that taking action now would cost just 1 percent of the world's gross domestic product. Sir Nicholas set out a tough prescription: emissions from power generation will need to be cut by 60–70 percent, and there will have to be an end to deforestation and huge cuts to emissions from transport. And he argues that the bulk of these emission cuts should be borne by the rich world.

Sir Nicholas claimed that he was "optimistic ... that we have the time and knowledge to act. But only if we act internationally, strongly and urgently."[12] There's nothing that scares businesspeople quite as much as a threat to their bottom line. The prescription was set out: now it was up to governments to take up the challenge.

In April 2007, the UN climate panel met in Brussels to hammer out a final version of a second IPCC report on the likely effects of climate change. Governments and scientists argued for four days about the precise wording of some of the conclusions, but there was little doubt about the importance of the report; one of the co-chairs of the working group told the BBC that "the real secret is that governments buy in."[13] In other words, government involvement was key to any success this report will have.

So what comes next? At the time of writing, the IPCC was to release two more reports, one of which would focus on ways to put the brakes on climate change. Taken together, the IPCC reports should end the argument between those who believe we should do everything possible to reverse climate change and those who believe we should adapt to its effects. Both of these approaches need to be taken together, and quickly.

Politicians are starting to respond – maybe not quickly enough, but something's definitely happening. In the UK, the Labor government and the Conservative opposition are battling to outdo each other for the "green" vote, with Tory leader David Cameron proposing a target of 80 percent emission cuts by 2050. The EU has agreed a tough new goal of 20 percent cuts by 2020, although the McKinsey consulting firm warned that it could cost member states up to 80 billion euros a year to meet them.

The US is traditionally seen as the big bad enemy in the movement to stop climate change, but there are some very encouraging signs that here too, things may be changing. The Supreme Court ruled in April 2007 that the government does indeed have the authority to curb emissions, opening the door for Congress to pass legislation to address global warming. Twelve states and thirteen environmental groups, frustrated with the lack of action on the part of the Bush administration, brought the action – which now leaves the way clear for the next president of the USA to curb emissions. All the Democratic and Republican candidates have made climate change a major part of their policy platforms.

So how can we play our part? Fortunately, this is one area where each action you take – no matter how small – plays some part. Greenpeace suggests a twelve-step plan for saving energy (and the planet): these include turning heating or cooling equipment down (or off altogether), choosing energy-efficient lightbulbs and appliances, and turning off electrical equipment when it's not in use.[14] And while you're at it, talk to your electricity provider about switching to a "green" tariff. The more people do it, the more pressure on these companies to invest in renewable energy sources.

Think about other ways in which you can cut down your emissions. Make fewer car journeys – it's an obvious one, but it's important. Also, when it comes to planning your next holiday or business trip, think about the options. Aviation is the fastest-growing contributor to climate change – and it's fuelled by our love of travel and the artificially low cost of flying. Pledge to take fewer flights, don't fly if you can take a train or a boat – and if you must travel, consider donating to a carbon-offsetting scheme. The British government is formulating a code of best practice for these schemes which should be in operation by autumn 2007.[15]

On top of all this, get active. Sign up to one of the on-line petitions on climate change. Research the issues, find out what you can do – talk to your MP, talk to your community and keep on talking! The impetus to make a change will only come if we, as individuals, keep piling pressure on our governments to put the future of our planet at the very top of the political agenda.

The scientists and the economists have started the ball rolling – working out what could happen, having the guts to spell it all out and scaring our governments into doing something. If we all act together, then maybe we can prove the scenarios wrong. Because let's face it – there really isn't any alternative.

In Kenya, bribery payments make up a third of the average household budget

For most Kenyans, a request for "kitu kidogo" ("something small" in Swahili) is an almost daily occurrence. It's hard to get anything done without paying bribes, they say. Getting your child into public school means greasing a few palms. If you're sick and you need medicine or a hospital bed, you're out of luck unless you pay a few key people. Birth or death certificates, jobs, business licences – all these involve a bribe. In the words of one Nairobi resident, "you can get documents to prove that your father died ten years ago, wake up the following day, and get your father a passport."[1]

Given that background, it's no wonder that Eric Wainaina's song "Nchi ya Kitu Kidogo" ("Country of Bribes") proved such a huge hit. Its infectious melody is in sharp contrast to the lyrics, which chronicle the daily bribery that has become a part of Kenyan life. In August 2001 Wainaina sang it in front of an audience including the country's vice president and a host of government officials. His microphone went dead as he started to sing the second verse – but the message had got through. Kenyans were starting to realize that the corruption at every level was something they didn't have to accept.

The Kenyan Urban Bribery Index details just how much average people pay out in bribes. The January 2001 report found that people paid an average of sixteen bribes a month – which accounted for about a third of their income.

Transparency International defines corruption simply as "the mis-use of entrusted power for private gain." This covers a broad range of activities – from multinational companies that pay bribes to get preferential access to government contracts, to police officers who stop drivers at road blocks asking for money to supplement their meager wages. When corruption becomes endemic in a society – as it is in Kenya – something subtle happens to the way people feel about it. People may not like having to pay the bribes, but they come to accept them as part of daily life. Transparency International's Kenya director, Gladwell Otieno, puts it like this: "People start to feel it's inevitable and normal, so when they have an opportunity they do it themselves."[2]

Mrs. Otieno believes that Kenya's new government may be able to do something about this – but they need to act quickly. At the end of 2002, Kenyans elected a new president, Mwai Kibaki, who entered office on an anti-corruption platform. On taking office, President Kibaki told his parliament that "corruption had undermined our economy, our politics and our national psyche." It was time for change, he said, and that change was going to start at the top.

Weeding out corruption is an imperative for any society, but for the developing world it's all the more vital. Kenya was once considered an African success story, but the corruption problem has taken its toll. The country is now the tenth most corrupt in the world.[3] The World Bank calculates that Kenya's poverty rates grew over the 1990s, at a time when global rates were declining. Growth rates had slowed from 4 percent in 1990 to 1 percent in 2001. Infant mortality rates rose, primary education enrolment fell.[4] It was clear that Kenya's development was going into reverse, and corruption was partly to blame.

Why does corruption hurt the poor so badly? When more than half the population live in poverty, they're denied access to things they sorely need: education, healthcare services, jobs. Meanwhile, bribes and kickbacks add an estimated 20–25 percent to the cost of government procurement. Resources, already scarce, may not be allocated where they are needed. The market becomes distorted and inefficient, and people's basic needs are ignored – thus worsening the cycle of poverty. A bad record on corruption will deter foreign investment in key projects, which itself slows development. The possibility of state interference and requests for kickbacks introduces an element of uncertainty that, in today's climate, few businesses are willing to risk.

What's almost worse is that multinational corporations are often implicated in the cycle of corruption. Courts in Lesotho have convicted two Western companies – Canada's Acres International and Germany's Lahmeyer International – of bribing their way into contracts for a massive dam construction project.[5] Two American businessmen were indicted for their roles in a huge scam where payments on Kazakh oil and gas projects were routed into bank accounts belonging to senior government officials.[6]

Until 1999, there were no international conventions to prevent companies based in one country from using bribery and inducements in another. It was widely acknowledged that this went on – in fact, some European countries even allowed bribery payments to be tax-deductible. The OECD Convention on Combating Bribery of Foreign Public Officials in International Business Transactions entered into force in February 1999 , but in 2006 Transparency International noted that there had been "little or no enforcement" of the Convention in almost two-thirds of the signatory countries.[7] This is despite studies that have shown "very high" levels of bribery in developing countries by corporations from Russia, China, Taiwan and South Korea. Corporations from the US, Italy and Japan – all signatories to the Convention – were also seen to have a high propensity to bribe.[8] The Convention may have been a good start, but it seems to have had little impact on how corporations view bribery.

In Kenya, the Kibaki government embarked on a radical clean-up of the most corruption-prone sectors of society. But it's clear there are still big problems. Two years after President Kibaki was elected, his anti-corruption tsar John Githongo resigned. Githongo claimed that $500 million had been sucked out of Kenya's economy by corruption since the Kibaki government came to power – enough for 10,000 primary school classrooms.[9]

But if the government is struggling, it seems that ordinary Kenyans are starting to rebel against the culture of bribery. There are stories of people not only refusing to pay their "something small," but frog-marching the errant official to the police station seeking punishment. In this respect, Gladwell Otieno believes, Kenya is typical of the African problem. Along with Nigeria, Kenya has become a byword for corruption. But she notes that countries that try to clean up their act don't get an easy ride. There is a need for early successes, she says; the window of opportunity for tackling the bribe-takers is very short, perhaps only 18 to 24 months. After that, public confidence will start to wane. "Those who benefit from corruption are reforming themselves, judging the situation, adopting new networks. Those who have been corrupt have enormous resources, they can keep cases going in court for dozens of years and they can buy the best lawyers. I think the reformers are on the weaker side in terms of numbers and resources. It's an out-and-out battle."[10]

If development goals are to be met, it's a battle that must be won. And the West needs to play its part. Ignore the arguments that this is another example of the developed world pushing its values on the rest of the world. The tradition of giving gifts may be an important part of building business relationships, but there is a clear difference between public gifts and private graft.

Shareholders need to push multinationals to reject the culture of bribery, and governments need to make sure they punish people who transgress the law. The framework is there, but administrations are reluctant to act first and put their corporations at risk. All the signatories to the OECD Convention need to take their responsibilities seriously. The World Bank and the International Monetary Fund (IMF), which had been criticized for being too lax in setting standards for transparency and accountability, have realized that aid must go hand in hand with good governance.

As for the situation in Kenya – well, Gladwell Otieno feels hopeful, "depending on the day." It's hard to estimate what corruption has cost the country, or indeed what it will cost to eradicate it. If the average Kenyan could keep for himself what he has been paying in bribes, the change could be remarkable.

As he appeared before the parliament to register his list of financial interests, President Kibaki told the public: "For the few months I have been head of government, I have known that we have more than enough resources to do all we intend if only we can stop corruption."[11] Seen individually, cases of corruption may only be "something small" – but when they're standing in the way of development, they are large indeed.

The world's trade in illegal drugs is estimated to be worth around $400 billion – about the same as the world's legal pharmaceutical industry

Civilizations come and go, systems of government prosper or fail, but throughout human history the drive to escape reality has remained a constant. Seven thousand years ago, the Sumerians were using opium – proved, scholars say, by the fact it had its own pictogram in their written language. In 3000 BC, the Chinese started drinking tea, while Egyptian documents describe places used to make alcohol. Opium use was once widespread in Asia, and it has been traded in the region for centuries; in the 19th century, Britain fought two wars with China over it. While we may argue about the legality or morality of a certain drug, one thing is for sure: human beings have always found a way to get high, and perhaps they always will.

The first law to prohibit the use of a drug came in 1875, when San Francisco banned the smoking of opium. The drug had been introduced to the US by thousands of Chinese men who had come to America in the middle of the 19th century to help build railway lines. When white people started visiting the opium dens, though, there was outrage. The San Francisco authorities learned that "many women and young girls, as well as young men of respectable family, were being induced to visit the opium-smoking dens, where they were ruined morally and otherwise."[1] But it seemed that the law merely drove the dens underground – in fact, the illegality merely added to the decadent thrill of the drug.

Thus the first prohibitive drug law failed to have any effect – and there is no evidence that any laws banning drugs in any jurisdiction have ever worked. Nevertheless, the widespread use of drugs has become a political issue of huge importance. In 1971, US President Richard Nixon declared drugs to be "public enemy number one" and declared war on their use and supply. Since then, many governments have issued their own campaigns against users, dealers and traffickers, and the phrase "war on drugs" has entered the lexicon of our times. In 2007, the US federal government will spend $12.9 billion dollars on its National Drug Control Strategy,[2] and state and local governments will spend at least another $20 billion.[3]

On the face of it, there are some persuasive arguments in favor of a prohibitive approach to drugs. Traditional economic theory would dictate that cutting the supply of a particular commodity will eventually decrease demand – so if the drug supply lines are cut, users will eventually be forced to give up their habits. As well as being considered immoral by much of the population, drugs are dangerous. They create massive loads on healthcare and policing systems, and greatly contribute to crime. Addictive drugs rob the user of any ability to make up his or her own mind whether to take them. Accordingly, it is right for a state to step in to prevent its citizens from harming themselves.

So far, so apparently sensible. But there's one big problem with this analysis: the War on Drugs just isn't working.

There is little to suggest that any of the global efforts to crack down on the drugs trade have had any effect at all. The UN estimates that 200 million people around the world abuse drugs, and that the global trade in illicit drugs is worth $400 billion a year.[4] In other words, the illegal drugs market is worth about the same as the worldwide trade in pharmaceuticals[5] – and it makes up about 8 percent of all international trade.

In the US, drug use levels have remained more or less constant for the past decade, even though federal spending on drug control has risen by 50 percent. While the Drug Enforcement Administration trumpets its supposed successes, police chiefs and community workers told ABC News that prohibition has been useless in preventing people from turning to drugs. By cracking down on dealers, the government has done nothing but drive up the prices. And where there's money to be made, people will flock to any business.[6]

That's backed up by research produced by the Cleveland police force in the north-east of England. The study concluded that not only were attempts to restrict supply not working, there was little evidence that they ever could.

The report set out the case against current policy in strong terms. "If there is indeed a "war on drugs" it is not being won; drugs are demonstrably cheaper and more readily available than ever before... If a sufficiently large (and apparently growing) part of the population chooses to ignore the law for whatever reason, then that law becomes unenforceable."[7]

This powerlessness could have real consequences for the global attempt to clamp down on terrorist activity and organized crime. The US State Department, through its Bureau for International Narcotics and Law Enforcement Affairs, has done its best to promote a connection between drug trafficking and terrorism. The State Department claims that there is "often" a link between terrorism and organized crime; drug traffickers benefit from terrorists' organised networks and military skills, while terrorists get the benefit of a stream of income.

This much is probably accurate. But again, it is prohibition that has created this lucrative underground trade, and prohibition that fuels the struggles between groups to control trafficking routes. An intensification of the war on drugs in South America – largely funded by the US – only served to increase prices of cocaine, and the levels of violence surrounding the trade.[8]

And then, of course, there is the human cost of prohibition. It's estimated that 36 percent of HIV/AIDS cases in the US are linked to use of injected drugs: a direct result of laws restricting access to clean needles.[9] Drug users are forced to become criminals; sourcing drugs is illegal, and many addicts are forced into crime to support the cost of their addiction. In some countries up to 50 percent of thefts are committed by addicts,[10] and some 30 percent of people arrested by Britain's police are dependent on one or more illegal drug.[11]

More than 30 years after President Nixon's initial declaration of war on drugs, it's becoming increasingly clear that the war can't be won – at least, not with the weapons we are currently employing.

Some drug policy groups are suggesting a change of tactics. Instead of seeking to prohibit drug use, they argue, we need to move to a strategy of harm reduction. This means acknowledging that a drug-free society probably could never exist, because there will always be some people who choose to use drugs. So we must seek to reduce the negative consequences – for them, and for the rest of society – as much as we can.

Proponents of the harm reduction strategy argue that marijuana should be legalized. Hard drugs, like heroin, cocaine and crack cocaine, would be available only on prescription from doctors, so that usage levels could be monitored. The government would over-see manufacture of drugs so that purity levels could be guaranteed, thus reducing overdoses and health problems caused by other substances used to "cut" drugs.

To the anti-drug campaigners, though, this is complete anathema. They argue that even though governments might become involved in the licensing and import of drugs, there would be no control on supply; one in five cigarettes smoked in Britain has been smuggled into the country, so it's easy to see how state control can be confounded. Others argue that it would place young people in even greater danger. Without the moral force of the law to prevent them from turning to hard drugs, how would we prevent our children from experimenting with them, and possibly becoming addicts?

A few jurisdictions have shown that harm reduction strategies can work. In the Netherlands, marijuana is sold through "coffee shops" and the amount sold to each customer is regulated by police. The result: while 37 percent of Americans have admitted to using marijuana at some point,[12] only 16 percent of Dutch people had done so.[13] The Dutch minister of health has said that the Netherlands has succeeded in making pot boring for young people. And it's believed that the coffee shops have done much to separate the markets for soft and hard drugs, so that curious teens in search of marijuana are not also being exposed to more dangerous drugs.[14]

However, critics point to Switzerland's attempt to decriminalize heroin use in the early 1990s, by allowing drug dealers and heroin users to congregate in a park in central Zurich. Drug deaths spiralled, crime levels shot up and the park was closed in 1995. Now, heroin addicts may obtain the drug on prescription, and the state funds needle exchange programs and places where addicts can inject drugs safely. While interior minister Ruth Dreifuss says Switzerland is merely facing up to "social reality," the UN International Narcotics Control Board regularly criticizes the Swiss policies. Marijuana is sold in some hemp shops because of a legal loophole, but in September 2003 the Swiss parliament voted against decriminalizing marijuana completely.

With cocaine and ecstasy use now at epidemic levels, Britain has made the first tentative steps towards a harm reduction approach. In January 2004, cannabis was downgraded to a class C controlled drug. Police no longer automatically arrest people caught in possession of the drug, and the maximum penalty for possession fell from five years' imprisonment to just two. The then Home Secretary David Blunkett said he wanted British police to concentrate on reducing the supply of heroin, cocaine and crack. With these drugs, it seems, prohibition is still thought to be key.

Perhaps it is too much to expect governments to wholeheartedly accept harm reduction strategies – not yet, in any case. But they need to stop thinking of the war on drugs a simple matter of cutting off supply lines. Every year, millions of people around the world use illegal drugs. That's probably never going to change. So rather than punish addicts by turning them into criminals, we need to look at how we can keep them safe. For any kind society, that has to be a first step.

A third of Americans believe aliens have landed on Earth

The renowned cosmologist Carl Sagan puts the case for life in other galaxies simply. A character in his fictional work *Contact* observes that, given the vastness of the Universe, "if it is just us, it seems like an awful waste of space."

It seems as if a sizeable minority of the population would agree with that. In 2001, 30 percent of people surveyed by the US National Science Foundation agreed that "some of the unidentified flying objects that have been reported are really space vehicles from other civilizations," and a 2000 survey by *Popular Science* magazine found that 45 percent of Americans believed intelligent aliens have visited Earth.[1]

It's not just the US that is entranced by the idea of life on other planets. In Britain, a 1999 poll revealed that 61 percent of British teenagers believed in aliens and UFOs – while a mere 39 percent had any belief in Christianity.[2] In China, a belief in aliens is one of the few fringe opinions that has been allowed to grow into an organized movement. A Chinese magazine about UFOs boasts a circulation of 200,000 and the director of the Beijing UFO Research Association says he receives so many "visitation reports" that he won't even bother investigating them unless people have pictures of their experiences.[3]

The phenomenon of UFOs – unidentified flying objects, thought by some to be piloted by aliens who pop past Earth every so often just to keep an eye on what we're doing – is comparatively recent. It wasn't until the 1940s that the appearance of "flying saucers" began to be taken seriously. The modern cult of alien-watching centers largely on the most famous of all alien sightings – the events of July 1947 near the small New Mexico town of Roswell. In 1997, some 80,000 people attended the 50th anniversary of the incident that's made the town famous – and, in the minds of many believers, has never been adequately explained.

On that day, something crash-landed in the desert near Roswell. Whatever it was, the US Air Force quickly retrieved it, and covered it up. The *Albuquerque Journal* for Wednesday July 9, 1947 describes how a rancher found a "strange object" in a field. An army press officer at first described it as a flying saucer, but further press statements sought to calm the growing commotion: it was only an army weather balloon, move along, nothing to see here. UFO enthusiasts see this as proof positive that a massive cover-up was already under way.

Behind the official statements, though, were contradictory accounts from military personnel and eyewitnesses. Several people claimed to have seen the bodies of dead aliens being taken to the now famous "Area 51" at Roswell Air Force base. A video of an "alien autopsy" surfaced mysteriously in 1994, claiming to show military personnel examining a body recovered from the UFO crash.

In July 1994 the US Air Force conducted an exhaustive review of all the documentation surrounding the Roswell incident. The enquiry was adamant that their story stood; debris of a balloon was picked up near Roswell at that time, the remains of a failed research project. The alien bodies were just test dummies which were being carried by the balloons. And the reports that military units quickly arrived at the scene to dispose of the "evidence" – they were just clearing up after the experiments. The title of the report makes the Air Force's position clear: "Roswell: Case Closed."

But the conspiracy theorists are not convinced, and nor, it seems, is the American public. A CNN/*Time* poll held in June 1997 found that 80 percent of Americans think the government is hiding knowledge of the existence of alien life forms.[4] And who knows, maybe they're right. One adviser to the US government's Project Blue Book study claimed that the Air Force was placed under huge pressure to keep UFO investigations "manageable." Sightings reported by anyone under eighteen were automatically disregarded, for example, and towards the end of the project military staff were allowed to dismiss cases if they believed they were filed by crackpots.[5]

To believers, all of this proves that our governments want to cover up evidence of alien visits. Their theories are a rebellion against official explanations, and certainly it is easy to see why, if aliens had landed at Roswell, the US government might not want people to know. Conspiracy theories presume that human beings behave as they always do: cooperating, cheating, deceiving.[6] Sometimes, when scientists and politicians are called on to explain a phenomenon, their answers don't seem to fit with the facts – and from that, conspiracy theories are born.

For some reason, humans want to believe that there is intelligent life out there, and that it wants to seek us out – just as we want to believe in other phenomena for which there is no scientific proof. The US National Science Foundation noted that belief in "pseudo-science" like astrology and extra-sensory perception, and in aliens, ghosts and the like was "widespread."

There's no proof that any of these UFOs have been piloted by curious extra-terrestrials. At best, all we have are phenomena which can't easily be explained away. After all, UFO visits have been widely reported only in the past 50 years – a mere blip in a planetary history that spans 4 billion years. A senior astronomer working on the SETI Institute's Project Phoenix noted that beings in other galaxies would be able to "see" Earth only because we emit high-frequency radio signals – and we have been doing this only for the past 70 years. Even if the aliens immediately jumped in their spacecraft in search of this mysterious planet, and even if they could travel at light-speed, there would only be four star systems close enough to have been able to reach Earth by 1947 – the date of the Roswell incident.[7]

Few doubt the theoretical possibility that there is life out there, though. And maybe it's closer than we think. Dr. Frank Drake conceived a mathematical formula which can be used to calculate the number of planets that might harbor life-forms with sufficient technology to communicate through space. It takes into account the rate of formation of stars (like our Sun) and the fraction which have planets, the fraction of those where life could develop, and so on. Using this formula, Drake estimates some 10,000 communicative civilizations in the Milky Way alone.[8]

It's this optimism that fuels the search for life in the stars. When Congress slashed NASA's funding for the Search for Extra Terrestrial Intelligence (SETI) it spurred on a large non-profit movement. The SETI Institute is conducting the world's most comprehensive research in the field, while the SETI League has co-ordinated thousands of radio telescopes operated by amateur and professional astronomers, each one surveying Sun-like stars and looking for signals of life.[9] And by 2015, NASA's Terrestrial Planet Finder should have begun its quest to find small Earth-like planets orbiting stars.

But what if these programs find something? How would we contact these distant beings – but perhaps more importantly, what on earth would we say? Will these aliens be kind – or will they be hostile? It may take a long time to tell. Assuming Drake's estimate is right, the nearest aliens might be 500 light years away. A conversation would take a very, very long time. That doesn't mean we shouldn't give it a go, of course – but what should we say about ourselves, and how should we say it?

At first it was thought that mathematics and physics could provide a common language which would be understood by any society advanced enough to build space-exploration structures. But that would paint a very dour picture of life on Earth. What could we tell aliens about our lives, our cultures, our planet?

Maybe the answer is still to be found in the golden records carried by the Voyager 1 and 2 probes. Launched in 1977, the Voyager space probes carry recordings of life on Earth: images of plants, countryside, mountains and people, greetings in 55 languages, the song of a whale. Selected by a committee chaired by Carl Sagan, the recordings include symbols which indicate how the record should be played. There's something marvelous about this kind of optimism. If aliens exist, and if they ever find the probes, and if they work out how to play the records, it might still be 40,000 years before the probes make an approach to another planetary system. The SETI Institute is trying to determine how some of these more aesthetic messages might be transmitted in radio broadcasts.

The belief that there are other beings out there – beings that might want to talk to us, and be our friends – speaks of a fundamental human need. We are by our very nature social beings, and the thought that we might be alone in the whole of existence is a lonely one indeed. The knowledge that there are other Earths out there allows us to hold a mirror up to ourselves, to find out fundamental truths about how we got here and what we're here for.

Sagan sums it up: "The nature of life on Earth and the quest for life elsewhere are two sides of the same question: the search for who we are."

More than 150 countries use torture

"He had a pair of pliers in his hand. He kept asking where the mobile was. I told him I had not seen it. He then told me to bring my thumb forward. He got hold of my thumb and placed it between the pliers. He pressed it hard and crushed my thumb. I do not remember what happened next."[1]

This account describes the treatment of a Bengali torture survivor at the hands of the police. By any standards, it's a barbaric act. What makes it more shocking is the fact that the victim was just nine years old at the time. All over the world, governments are endorsing torture – either by enshrining its practice into law or by turning a blind eye to the behavior of police and security services – cruelty that flies in the face of international human rights legislation.

Torture is defined as the intentional infliction of severe mental or physical pain or suffering for a specific purpose. It speaks of the darkest side of human nature: the will to dominate, to harm another who refuses to do our bidding. Elaborate woodcuts from the Middle Ages depict torture techniques used to extract confessions from people suspected of crimes. Physical coercion was thought, in those days, to be a legitimate means of obtaining testimonies. Painful and disfiguring techniques like the rack, the iron maiden (a box large enough to fit a man's body, which was filled with spikes) and the choke pear (a metal object which would be inserted into a victim's mouth, whereupon spikes would emerge and pierce them) may have given way to more modern techniques such as electrocution and administration of drugs. But the principles remain the same.

Amnesty International estimates that between 1998 and 2000, more than 150 governments allowed torture to be carried out in their countries. That's two-thirds of the countries in the world. Why do these governments use torture? And why do they think it's acceptable?

Countries that use torture can be divided into several broad groupings. There are those which are considered to have a low regard for human rights as defined by international organiztions – this includes a number of countries which observe Sharia or Islamic law, which includes amputation of limbs and stoning among its list of possible penalties. Then there are those where control over police or security forces is lax – allowing officers to act with impunity, and providing few mechanisms to call them to account. And then there are countries where torture happens infrequently, perhaps as a result of conflict. Added together, that's a significant list.

Some countries stop short of institutionalizing torture, settling instead for a variety of techniques that have been dubbed "torture lite." This can include rough treatment, forcing prisoners to assume "stress positions" for long periods, or psychological techniques to induce fear and confusion. The Geneva Convention prohibits these, and anti-torture NGOs say they consider all ill-treatment to be worthy of investigation. Yet many nations, particularly in the light of the so-called "war on terror," consider these to be justifiable practices. If it encourages prisoners to divulge information that might save lives, this school of thought dictates that a little force, some slight coercion, is perfectly legitimate.

In December 2002, an article in the *Washington Post* quoted CIA agents who confirmed that agents routinely use "stress and duress" interrogation techniques. Prisoners at the US airbase at Bagram in Afghanistan were reported to be kept standing or kneeling for hours, wearing black hoods. The suspects would be bombarded with bright light, keeping them awake for hours on end.

For those who played the game, there would be rewards – a few creature comforts, some feigned respect. For those who didn't, there was the prospect of being turned over to foreign intelligence services whose torture practices were well documented by the US government and human rights groups. In the words of one official, "if you don't violate someone's human rights some of the time, you aren't doing your job."[2]

The tragic events of September 11, 2001 have given US intelligence services a new impetus to get as much information as possible about further attacks. It was rumored that the CIA had upped its game, employing what was known (in classic military phrasing) as "operational flexibility" in its handling of suspects. The then head of CIA counter-terrorism, Cofer Black, told a joint meeting of the House and Senate intelligence committees that 9/11 had seen a change of policy. "This is a very highly classified area, but I have to say that all you need to know [is]: there was a before 9/11, and there was an after 9/11. After 9/11, the gloves came off."[3]

Each year the US State Department issues a Human Rights Report which details the situation in countries which receive US foreign aid and all those which are members of the UN. A number of countries were criticized for using "stress and duress" techniques similar to those reportedly used at Bagram airbase. There were also strong criticisms of torture techniques used in countries to which detainees had been rendered (transferred). Egypt was reported to suspend prisoners from ceilings or door frames, beat them with fists, whips and metal rods and administer electric shocks; Jordan was criticized for beating prisoners on the soles of the feet and allowing prolonged suspensions in contorted positions.[4] These accusations come from the State Department's own reports. There can be no way the US government is unaware of them.

In July 2003 the Bush administration unequivocally rejected the use of "cruel" treatment in interrogation of suspects. President Bush reiterated his position in October, in response to claims that detainees at the US military facility in Guantanamo Bay, Cuba, had been tortured. But the taint of hypocrisy remains. In October 2003 more than 600 prisoners were being held there without trial, with children as young as thirteen among them. Twenty-one detainees were reported to have attempted suicide and many more were suffering from depression.[5] Human rights groups maintained that the totality of the conditions in which the detainees were being held constituted cruel, inhuman and degrading treatment. Taken along with the shocking images of prisoner abuse at the Abu Ghraib jail in Iraq, Amnesty International argued that the US prohibitions against torture and ill-treatment no longer appeared to be "non-negotiable."[6]

In the face of accusations of hypocrisy, Harvard law professor Alan Dershowitz has argued for the use of a "torture warrant." Professor Dershowitz argues that in extreme cases, where there is immediate peril of an attack and a suspect is considered to hold information that might avert a tragedy, the President or Supreme Court could issue a directive that torture should be allowed. "I would talk about non-lethal torture, say, a sterilized needle underneath the nail, which would violate the Geneva Accords, but you know, countries all over the world violate the Geneva Accords. They do it secretly ... if we ever came close to doing it, I think we would want to do it with accountability and openly and not adopt the way of the hypocrite."[7]

Professor Dershowitz's argument raises an issue much debated by ethicists. If you know someone holds vital information that would prevent the deaths of many people, then are you justified in using violent or brutal means in extracting that information? The subtle shifts that have come about since the September 11 attacks have this at their very heart.

These shifts may have greater implications. Firstly, a tacit acceptance of torture by Western nations will greatly inhibit their ability to put pressure on countries where torture is a daily routine for law enforcement and security bodies. By using torture themselves, these governments in effect institutionalize torture as a legitimate practice. One member of the World Organization Against Torture explained how this would in effect feed terrorism rather than proscribe it: "When torture is no longer absolutely prohibited, law enforcement attitudes change. Over time, the mentality that torture is acceptable comes to infect the entire system, and even persons accused of normal crimes get the same treatment as suspected terrorists ... Terrorists do not suffer in such an environment: rather, they thrive in it."[8]

Regimes that have been criticized in the past would no doubt welcome an opportunity to point to Western hypocrisy. "Stress and duress" would join a continuum of barbaric practices used by governments around the world. It would be considered alongside reports of floggings and amputations in Yemen, allegations of rape and sexual violence by Russian forces in Chechnya, tooth extractions and suspension from chains in Saudi Arabia.

Secondly, there is a concern that the quality of evidence obtained by these means is unreliable at best. As early as 1764, the Italian philosopher Cesare Beccaria warned that a man being tortured would be compelled to find the quickest way to free himself, telling his captors what they wanted to hear: "His answer, therefore, will be an effect as necessary as that of fire or boiling water, and he will accuse himself of crimes of which he is innocent: so that the very means employed to distinguish the innocent from the guilty will most effectively destroy all difference between them."[9] Some may tell the truth under duress, but many others will lie. The torture has achieved nothing.

The long-term effects on torture victims can be devastating. Amnesty International's medical co-ordinator Jim Welsh notes that torture "strikes at the whole root of being human. Someone has you in their power and they're going to hurt you to the greatest extent possible."[10] As well as the physical impact of what has happened to them, torture survivors may suffer flashbacks and anxiety for years.

The international community has worked hard to build a consensus against torture. The Universal Declaration of Human Rights prohibited torture and ill-treatment in 1948, and this applies to all states. The UN Convention against Torture and Other Cruel, Inhuman or Degrading Treatment or Punishment is binding on those states that have signed it, of which there were 144 at March 2007. There are a number of other instruments which prohibit torture. The combined effect is to prohibit torture in all circumstances. So why are states still trying to seek exceptions – and why is torture reported in countries that have signed the UN Convention?

Under international law and under any humane legal system, torture must be prevented. Governments must take all steps to ensure that allegations of torture are investigated and the perpetrators are punished. And we must keep the pressure on governments to make sure they do this. There should be no more discussion of exceptions to international law, even in the context of a war on terror. Torture merely feeds the fire of terrorism, and restricts the freedom we all deserve.

Every day, one in five of the world's population – some 800 million people – go hungry

At the beginning of the 21st century, when the rich world is enjoying the benefits of scientific and medical research and looking forward to long, prosperous lives, it is difficult to comprehend why so much of the world's population should still go hungry.

The statistics tell of a problem of immense proportions. Eight hundred million go hungry every day. Two billion people suffer from chronic malnutrition. Eighteen million die each year from hunger-related diseases. Two billion people suffer from micro-nutrient deficiencies, which lead to chronic health problems. Around half of the deaths of children under five (10 million each year) are associated with malnutrition. Famines occur where there is an acute and extreme shortage of food for a large number of people, but hunger can persist over many years and its long-term effects can be just as devastating. The World Health Organization (WHO) says that hunger and malnutrition are among the most serious problems facing the world's poor.[1]

And yet, incredibly, this is not caused by food shortages. The world produces enough food each year to feed all of its inhabitants: if it were shared out evenly, everyone would have enough to eat. Nutritionists consider that a healthy diet provides 2,500 calories of energy a day. In the USA, the average person consumes 3,600 calories a day. In Somalia, they get 1,500.[2]

Food production has kept pace with global demand, and prices for staple foods like rice and other cereals have fallen. So why are so many still suffering?

The Nobel Prize-winning economist Amartya Sen is one of the world's foremost authorities on the causes of hunger. He notes that hunger is caused not by a country's inability to produce food but by a lack of income. Poor people have no money to secure a constant food supply, and no resources to grow their own food. Professor Sen argues that political circumstances are often to blame. Famines may threaten the existence of a democratic government, but where democracy is absent or compromised, the government will often lack the motivation to tackle the problem. "Indeed, as a country like Zimbabwe ceases to be a functioning democracy," Professor Sen writes, "its earlier ability to avoid famines in very adverse food situations (for which Zimbabwe had an excellent record in the 1970s and 1980s) becomes weakened. A more authoritarian Zimbabwe is now facing considerable danger of famine."[3]

Armed conflict also places a major strain on food security. The UN Food and Agriculture Organization (FAO) found that of eighteen African countries facing food emergencies in 2001, eight were involved in conflict and a further three were suffering its after-effects.[4] In times of war, a government will divert resources away from food production in favor of the military effort. Food distribution and transport networks are disrupted, and where an area is under dispute it may be too dangerous for subsistence farmers to tend their land. In Rwanda in 1995, war displaced three out of four farmers and cut the harvest in half.[5]

Hunger is also, callously, used as a tool of war. One side may try to starve the other into submission, seizing or destroying food stocks and diverting food aid from the needy to the armed forces. Lands may be mined or water sources polluted. In the aftermath of conflict, it is difficult or impossible for communities to rebuild their food sources. Armed violence in Southern and Western Africa and Central America has left generations of young people without any farming skills at all – the only reality they knew was conflict, so the only training they have is in the art of fighting.[6]

This disappearance of traditional farming techniques is also happening in areas hit hard by the HIV/AIDS crisis. Malnutrition has been linked to an earlier onset of AIDS symptoms after HIV infection, and it increases the likelihood of opportunistic infection – thus further shortening the lifespan of the sufferer. In a family where one or both parents is sick, the family will lose valuable income and may be forced to sell assets like livestock in order to pay for healthcare and burials. Some societies do not allow widows to inherit land, so it may be lost to the family. Young children may be forced to leave school in order to work or care for sick relatives. The specialized knowledge that parents might have hoped to pass on to their children may be lost.[7]

Where a country is already weakened by epidemics or war, natural phenomena like droughts or floods become far more difficult to overcome. Corruption, mismanagement and bad government mean that the country may lack funds to import food when it's needed – so a food shortage can very quickly turn into a famine.

Having enough to eat is a basic human right, and hunger is a huge impediment to development. People who have enough to eat can work better and generate more income. One study in Sierra Leone showed that, on average, a 50 percent increase in calories per farm worker would increase agricultural output by 16.5 percent.[8]

So how to achieve this? There are huge surpluses of food in the rich West – so much so, in fact, that food is sometimes destroyed in order to keep prices buoyant. A lot of surplus food is sent to poorer countries as aid, but agencies are well aware that this does not constitute a long-term solution. The key is to change the factors that led to the poverty in the first place: by raising the average income in a region so that hungry people, and in turn their governments, can buy what they need.

In Afghanistan, for example, aid agencies are helping to feed a population ravaged by two decades of war and a severe drought. Some of it has involved distributing food donated by the West, but other initiatives have provided seeds, tools and fertilizer for farmers to grow their own crops. These efforts, coupled with better weather and pest control, meant that the 2003 harvest was forecast to be

50 percent bigger than the year before. But Christian Aid expressed strong concerns that the UN was still sending massive wheat shipments to the region, causing prices for locally grown wheat to plummet and farmers to turn to more lucrative crops – like opium.[9] The key is not to make countries dependent on handouts, if at all possible; instead, the international community should help guide hunger-stricken societies towards a degree of self-sufficiency. As hunger decreases, the country's income will rise, and it will be better able to cope with food shortages in the future.

But even that path is complicated. African nations are currently debating the role that genetically modified food should play in the fight against hunger. The US has suggested that high-yield GM crops could help the fight against hunger by raising farmers' incomes. There are even suggestions that genetic modification could invent crops that might target micro-nutrient deficiencies. Some countries have enthusiastically welcomed the prospect of GM food aid, while others have declared it "poison." There are certainly long-term issues to consider here, not just about the possible effects of GM food on consumers and the environment, but about the culture of dependence that it could create. Poorer countries would become more reliant on developed countries and large multinational companies to supply the GM technology that they cannot afford themselves.

One of the most important factors in reducing hunger is thought to be education. The FAO estimates that some 300 million poor children in the world either do not attend school or do not receive a meal during the school day.[10] Basic education is the most effective development tool there is. In countries with an adult literacy rate of 40 percent, per capita gross domestic product (GDP) averaged $210; where the rate was at least 80 percent, per capita GDP was $1,000 and more.[11] Girls who go to school marry later and have fewer children. Farmers who have a minimum of four years' education are up to 10 percent more productive.[12]

The World Food Summit in 1996 set a target of cutting the world's hunger problem in half by 2015. To do that, the number of hungry people needs to fall by 33 million every year – currently, it is only falling by 6 million a year. Progress needs to be accelerated. In October 2003, the World Food Program noted that contributions to its fund were not keeping pace with the demand for food aid. In 2003, it needed $4.3 billion to feed 110 million people around the world, and contributions fell short by $600 million (or nearly 15 percent).[13]

Global bodies like the WHO are urging the world to recognize that proper nutrition and health are fundamental human rights. Combating hunger will allow poorer nations to carve a path towards development. Director-General Emeritus of the WHO, Gro Harlem Brundtland, urged that "a strong human rights approach is needed to bring on board the millions of people left behind by the 20th century's health revolution."[14]

Article 25(1) of the Universal Declaration of Human Rights (1948) asserted that "everyone has the right to a standard of living adequate for the health and well-being of himself and his family, including food." The human rights approach puts the primary responsibility on governments to do everything possible to ensure people have access to food. But we all have a responsibility to remember the scale of this problem. We can support charities working to promote food security, and we can urge our own governments to do what they can to help – and that includes pressuring them to honor aid commitments.

The victims of famine may occasionally make it onto the front pages or news bulletins, but most victims of hunger go unnoticed. Hunger affects the poor, the powerless. It's a complex problem that requires a huge international effort. We are all responsible, but we can all do something about it.

Black men born in the US today stand a one in three chance of going to jail

America may be the land of the free, but an increasing number of its residents have, at some time or another, had their freedom taken away. In June 2002, the number of people behind bars hit 2 million, and the US became home to the world's largest prison population – overtaking Russia. In 2005, 7 million Americans were on probation, in prison or on parole: more than 3 percent of the adult population.[1] One in every 37 Americans has spent time in jail – up from one in 53 in 1974. If current trends continue, one in every fifteen American children born in 2001 will go to jail in their lifetime.[2]

But look closer at the statistics, and some even more worrying trends emerge. Of those children born in 2001, a white male has a one in seventeen chance of going to prison. For Hispanic males, there's a one in six chance, and for black men, it's one in three. When you consider that black people make up 12.9 percent of the American population, you can start to see the scope of the problem. A sixth of all African-American men are current or former prisoners, compared with one in 38 white men.[3]

Clearly, something is going wrong. America's prison population has skyrocketed in the past 30 years: in 1970, there were just 200,000 inmates in state and federal prisons.[4] Since then, policies like the "three strikes and you're out" legislation adopted in 1994 – which provides for a 25-years-to-life sentence for anyone convicted of a third felony – have led to a massive increase in the numbers in jail. Black men make up a large percentage of those charged for violent crimes (42.5 percent in 2001), so they are disproportionately affected by the longer sentences.[5]

The so-called "war on drugs," too, has done a terrific job of filling up jails. The Sentencing Project group reports that 70 percent of those sentenced to state prisons in 1998 were convicted of non-violent crimes; drug offenders made up 57 percent of federal prison inmates in 1999.[5]

It's in these areas that we start to see how the law is racially biased. Official US government statistics show that 13 percent of people who admit to using drugs at least once a month are black. But black people make up 35 percent of those arrested for drug possession, and 74 percent of those imprisoned for it.

In a hugely influential speech to the American Civil Liberties Union in 1999, Ira Glasser called American drug policy "the new Jim Crow."[6] He was referring to a particularly shameful part of American history, the period when segregation of blacks and whites was enshrined in law in southern states of the US. In the mid-19th century, Jim Crow was the nickname given to characters in "minstrel" shows, in which white performers would blacken their faces and perform racist songs and dances. The term became a symbol of black inferiority in the popular culture of the day – and by the end of the century, laws that discriminated against blacks became known as Jim Crow laws.[7] Glasser argued that America's drug laws now have that same quality: they have created an "epidemic [of] incarceration" and drug prohibition has become an effective replacement for segregation.

One way and another, America's drug laws work against minorities. There is a huge disparity in sentencing between crack cocaine (used more by black and Hispanic people) and powder cocaine (used more by white people). Although there have been attempts to reduce it, the current law states that possession of 500 grams of cocaine nets the same mandatory five-year sentence as possession of 5 grams of crack.

Or consider this: drunk driving is the most frequent category of arrests in America, with 1.8 million each year. Drunk drivers kill 22,000 people annually, while deaths from overdoses, disease or violence associated with drugs come in at around 21,000 each year. Yet almost all US drunk-driving cases are dealt with as misdemeanors, punished by fines, loss of driving licence or community service. Typical penalties for possession of drugs – even soft drugs like marijuana – are up to five years' jail for a first offense. Drunk drivers are predominantly white males.[8]

Minorities in America are frequently subjected to forms of racial profiling. In one section of the I-95 highway running through Maryland, 17 percent of drivers are black, but 73 percent of those who are pulled over and searched are black. In the majority of cars searched in this manner, no drugs are found – and where they are, they are just as likely to be found in cars driven by white people.[9] In New York City, less than a quarter of the 45,000 recorded "frisks" in 1997 and 1998 resulted in arrests, and two-thirds of those frisked were minorities.[10] In September 2003, the City of New York agreed to settle a class action lawsuit that charged the New York Police Department with engaging in illegal racial profiling in stop-and-search situations. As part of the settlement, the NYPD agreed to prevent all its officers from targeting minority groups for unwarranted searches.[11]

Black women, too, are far more likely to end up in prison than their white counterparts. In 1980 there were 12,300 women in state and federal prisons in the US; in 2002, there were 96,000. Forty-three percent were black. Only 31 percent were in prison because of violent offences.[12]

This mass incarceration of women has serious repercussions for their children. Around 65 percent of women in prison have families, and the children are frequently denied visits on the grounds that their mother is "unfit." Many states have laws which entitle them to begin action to terminate a woman's parental rights on the grounds of incarceration.[13] Three-quarters of women in prison were regular drug users, nearly 40 percent had monthly incomes of less than $600, and more than half had been physically or sexually abused.[14] It's hard to see how any of these problems will be helped by a spell in prison.

Indeed, being imprisoned for a felony in America can lead to consequences that continue long after you've served your time. Forty-six American states have disenfranchisement laws which take away the voting rights of anyone serving time for a felony. Ten states take them away permanently.

Being barred from voting means that rehabilitated felons who have served their time are denied the right to participate in civil society. Felony disenfranchisement laws effectively remove the freedoms guaranteed by the Fifteenth Amendment to the US Constitution, which gave black people the right to vote. This was further secured by legislation in 1965, which eliminated arbitrary requirements placed on voters – like the requirement of literacy – designed to prevent black people from voting. Today, 1.4 million black men – 13 percent of the black male population – cannot vote because of felony convictions. In Alabama and Florida, 31 percent of black men are permanently barred from voting.[15] As Ira Glasser puts it, "what the Voting Rights Act of 1965 provided, drug prohibition has to a significant degree taken away."[16]

This racial disparity in prison populations is most clearly illustrated in the US, but it is starting to occur elsewhere. In Britain, 1 percent of the black adult population is now in prison. African and Caribbean people make up 2 percent of Britain's population, but 16 percent of the prison population.[17] In 1998–9, black people were six times more likely to be stopped and searched than white people. Britain already has higher incarceration rates than any other country in Europe, and there are concerns that the UK could be heading for a US-style love affair with prisons.

Tackling the problem of these racial inequalities is all the more crucial when you consider that spending time in prison leads to cultural and social exclusion, which in turn breeds the kind of environment in which children are likely to turn to crime and enter the prison system. It's estimated that half of former prisoners struggle to get jobs. Those who do find work earn around half as much as people from similar backgrounds who have not spent time in jail.[18] The failure of the prison system to provide comprehensive job training or rehabilitation does not help this. With no other way to support themselves, former offenders may find themselves enmeshed in the same environments that caused them to fall foul of the law.

Politicians and policy-makers often argue that prison works. But it's hard to see how locking up millions of people can be seen as any kind of victory over crime. Where the demand for drugs is pretty constant, locking up large numbers of people for drug crimes merely leads to the recruitment of more willing workers. With so many people in jail, being locked up is hardly a deterrent – in fact, some see it as a chance to catch up with their friends inside. Some criminologists believe that the US could be reaching a "tipping point": when more than 1 percent of a population is in prison each year, social networks are paralyzed, and crime becomes impossible to keep under control.[19]

It costs the US something like $30,000 to keep a prisoner in jail for a year. Imagine what might happen if that kind of money were diverted elsewhere: into street-level crime reduction programs, into development in inner cities, into drug and alcohol treatment programs. As well as saving taxpayers' money, we might start to see a real drop in crime rates. We might see poverty levels fall, too, and children from minorities staying in school, choosing another path.

The issue of policing – particularly policing of drug crime – is already far too tied up with race and class. If we don't address this, the way we administer justice will continue to create further disadvantage, further exclusion, further hatred.

A third of the world's population is at war

As the US and its allies ponder the wisdom of keeping their troops in Iraq, more than a third of the world's population continues to be involved in conflict. In 2005, 27 countries around the world were fighting in 32 armed conflicts – a combined population of 2.33 billion people.

Some, like the Israeli–Palestine conflict, are long-term disputes that still show no real signs of resolution. Others, like the confrontations between Hindus and Muslims in the Indian state of Gujarat, were ongoing disagreements that spilled over into serious violence. But they all take a toll on all concerned – not just the governments, not just the combatants, but all the people who live in the theatre of war.

Project Ploughshares,[1] which compiles an annual list of the world's wars, defines "armed conflict" as a political conflict involving armed combat between armed forces of at least one state, or one or more armed factions seeking to gain control of all or part of a state. A conflict makes the Ploughshares list when more than 1,000 people have been killed by the fighting. In introducing the 2002 report, former Canadian senator Lois Wilson summed up the ugliness of war – and the complex nature of peace. "Peace is not just the opposite of war," she wrote. "The eloquently visual Mandarin language uses three symbols/words for peace. The first word for peace literally means rice in the mouth, or economic security. The second means a woman with a roof over her head, or social security. The third means two hearts beating together in understanding and friendship, or human security."[2]

For the people living in war, those basic securities are lacking. For them, armed conflict goes beyond the television pictures or column inches. It is a daily reality which drives them off their land, deprives them of food and water, kills their family and hinders any chance of development. Not all of the residents of our warring countries experience this, of course. But for many, conflict has become a way of life.

For the past twenty years, Sudan has been fighting a bitter civil war. The government in Khartoum has been fighting rebels based in the south of the country, and the military strategies of both sides have often put civilians directly in the line of fire. UN Secretary-General Kofi Annan referred to "shameful attacks on civilians at or near food distribution sites."[3] Sudan now hosts the world's largest number of internally displaced people: some 4 million Sudanese have fled their homes because of the conflict and drought, more than 10 percent of the population. Only a minority can be housed in official refugee facilities, and most of the others live in squatter camps.[4]

In the Democratic Republic of Congo, a conflict often referred to as "Africa's world war" claimed more than 3 million lives between 1998 and 2002 – either as a direct result of the fighting or through disease and malnutrition.[5] At least six other countries became involved in the battle between the government of President Joseph Kabila and numerous rebel groups. Although a power-sharing government was sworn in in 2003 after a national peace agreement was signed, fighting continued in the east and the ability of the government to cope with the needs of its population was very limited.

Aid workers from the International Rescue Committee (IRC) described the situation in Congo as the biggest humanitarian crisis on the planet. The director of IRC operations in the DRC, Werner Vansant, detailed what he had seen: "This is not a war of troops fighting against troops, it's a war against civil society, where infrastructures are destroyed and looted, all medicines stolen from health posts, key people like nurses are killed in villages, agricultural fields are destroyed."[6] Hunger and disease spread quickly and, without medical care, they take a heavy toll.

In the aftermath of war, rebuilding communities takes time;

undoing the damage done to the land takes even longer. During the Vietnam War, American troops sprayed the defoliant Agent Orange over jungle areas and agricultural lands. Twenty-five years later, those areas are still contaminated, unable to grow food. Two-thirds of Kuwait's underground aquifers, a major source of drinking water, are still polluted by oil spilled during the First Gulf War. NATO bombing campaigns in Kosovo targeted chemical plants and oil refineries; the result of one bombing raid in the city of Pancevo was that black rain fell on the city, releasing carcinogenic chemicals like dioxin in concentrations many thousands of times higher than recognized safety levels. The rains polluted the soil and poisoned crops – and those who ate them.[7]

This is the truth about modern war. Forget about all the high-tech equipment, the computer-and-satellite-targeted bombing raids, the preposterous claims to "shock and awe." This is the so-called "fourth generation" of war – a type of conflict that is poorly defined, with few obvious battlefields.

The first generation of war was all about order. Battlefields were precisely executed operations. The concepts of uniform, strictly hierarchical promotion systems and rank and file all stem from this time. In the mid-19th century, though, another style of fighting began to emerge. Machine guns and artillery saw the order of battlefield break down somewhat. Attacks were still linear, though, and battle lines and impenetrable defences were key. Victory would come through attrition and superior firepower. The third generation, devised by Germany during the First World War, relied on tactical changes and unsettling the opposition.

Now, the fourth generation is upon us, and the state no longer has a monopoly on war. Increasingly, combatants may be rebels, militias, loosely grouped with few distinguishing characteristics. These enemies are hard to pin down, even harder to fight – there is no capital to invade, no seat of power to bomb, and when one is killed there are dozens of recruits to take their place. And they seek new ways of getting their point across: their emphasis is not on traditional targets, but on striking at cultural or social icons as a means of drawing attention to their cause. Winning battles isn't important. Winning the propaganda war is what counts.

These non-state actors (NSAs) may be rebel groups, dissident armed forces personnel, guerrillas or armies appointed by the de facto governing bodies of disputed land. Since many NSAs fight on the ground without access to high-tech equipment, and most combatants are not highly trained in fighting techniques, collateral damage is frequent. Booby traps and mines are frequently used to secure land and scare the local population. The International Campaign to Ban Landmines says that NSAs in every armed conflict have anti-personnel mines in their arsenal.

Whether the NSAs want to overthrow a government, annex territory or effect some wholesale change to society, for those concerned about protecting civilians their form of warfare is a troubling development. NSA fighters often don't wear uniforms, making it much easier for bystanders to get caught up in the conflict. It is also harder and harder for the superpowers to tell when a battle has been won or lost. They may gain control of an area, but the NSAs may carry on the fight, leading to long periods of sometimes heavy-handed occupation, attacks against the occupying forces, and continued insecurity for civilians.

The big military powers have little idea of how to deal with these new adversaries. To traditional military thinking, the NSAs don't fight "fair." Most military analysts agree that the superpowers don't know how to handle fourth-generation war. That may be true. But what's urgent is that they figure out how to protect civilians as much as possible.

International humanitarian law lays down the minimum protection that should be given to civilians in armed conflict, and NSAs are bound by these laws just as states are. One of the key requirements is to allow humanitarian assistance teams access to needy people. This can be difficult at the best of times, when the security situation is precarious. The usual means of getting states to comply – through diplomatic or economic pressures – don't apply to NSAs.

But as long as the humanitarian agencies are "independent and impartial" actors on behalf of civilians, they have the right to safe and unimpeded access. It's also vital to ensure that both states and NSAs are aware of their responsibilities. Here, though, it can be difficult for humanitarian workers. James Darcy of the Humanitarian Policy Group of the Overseas Development Institute says it's often difficult to know who he's dealing with, "where to point the finger of responsibility, not to become complicit in strategies that are actually abusive of civilian populations."[8] Some rebel groups will try to infiltrate civilian groups, making it all the more crucial that fighters and bystanders are kept clearly separated.

As well as helping those in need, the access can do much to improve the situation generally. According to Kofi Annan, "negotiations for unimpeded humanitarian access may also become the basis for a future transition to peace and recovery, in no small measure by simply being one of the few, if not the only, forums where the parties to the conflict are talking to one another." National immunization days and "days of tranquillity" to provide targeted services had had some success in Liberia and Sierra Leone, he said.[9]

There is also a need to reinforce to all combatants that they will be made accountable for their actions. The establishment of specialised criminal courts for the former Yugoslavia, Rwanda and Sierra Leone has gone a long way to removing the perception that combatants can carry out crimes against civilians with impunity. After the conflicts have ended, the UN recommends disarmament as soon as is practically possible, coupled with a thorough reconciliation process. This way, the battered civilian population can see that justice is being done.

It is impossible to prevent conflict having an effect on the ordinary people in a country that is at war. Aid agencies and international institutions are adamant that all sides must live up to their responsibilities under international law. War is an enemy of development, a huge drain on a population. The psychological effects of displacement can take years to heal. Where a conflict has robbed a society of entire generations, the scars run deep indeed.

US President Dwight Eisenhower once remarked, "every gun that is made, every warship launched, every rocket fired, signifies in the final sense a theft from those who hunger and are not fed, those who are cold and are not clothed."[10] Fifty years later, the face of warfare may have changed, but President Eisenhower's words ring as true as they ever have.

The world's oil reserves could be exhausted by 2040

The greatest addiction of the modern world is oil. Since the first modern oil fields were discovered in Pennsylvania in the early 1860s, we have become totally dependent on it. We need petrol to fuel cars, airplanes and ships; we need crude oil to provide energy for electricity generation and as a raw material in plastics, solvents, fabrics and detergents. It's no exaggeration to say that without it, society and industry would shudder to a halt.

Some time in the future, though, we may have to learn to live without oil. While estimates vary as to how far away that is, almost all of them agree that the world's oil reserves are finite – and that there will come a time when we will have to learn to live without it.

The Organization of the Petroleum Exporting Countries (OPEC) tries to put a positive spin on the problem. OPEC is a cartel which represents eleven of the major oil producers, and it calculates that the world has just over a trillion barrels of oil in proven crude oil reserves. OPEC's World Energy Model puts the world's oil demands at 76 million barrels a day, which could rise to 90 million barrels by 2010. At the current rate of production, OPEC believes that its members' oil reserves will last another 80 years.[1]

But given that OPEC's main role is regulating the supply of oil and maximizing gains for their members, that's exactly what you might expect them to say. Some scientists believe that the world's reserves of oil could be exhausted in four decades, and that a crisis will come far sooner than that. According to Colin Campbell, a geologist who has worked for Texaco and Amoco, the key is not to ask when oil will run out, but when production will start to become uneconomic. He estimates that by 2010 prices will start to rise as the world's oil reserves start to decline.

Why so soon? Dr. Campbell argues that 80 percent of the oil produced today comes from fields that were found before 1973.[2]

There may be new discoveries to come, of course, but they're likely to be smaller fields where the oil is harder to extract. Exploration has been so thorough that only very deep waters and arctic regions have not been tested, and the prospects there are not good.

A geologist named M. King Hubbert (who worked for Shell) first suggested a theory of decline in the 1950s. The first oil fields to be discovered are the big ones that can be exploited cheaply. When they're exhausted, the industry is forced to turn to smaller fields where extraction costs are higher. Dr. Hubbert believed that there would always be oil in the ground, but as more and more of it was extracted it would become uneconomic to exploit the remaining reserves. He predicted that world petroleum output would peak at a certain point, and after that, production would fall into a long-term decline.

Dr. Campbell believes that that peak will come in about 2005 – and after that, the period of decline in production will begin. "I think it will fall by roughly 3 percent a year. Demand, on the other hand, is growing at 2 percent a year. That means there's a shortfall, and by about 2020 there will be a shortfall of something like 40 percent."[3]

The world will start to run out of the cheap and abundant sources of oil on which industrialized countries are so completely dependent. The oil industry points to what it calls "unconventional oil," in other words, oil that is present in other forms like tar sands or bitumen fields, or in areas that are not currently able to be exploited. But it will take a massive technological advance to make these sources economically viable, and that could take many years.

In 2000, the CIA issued a report which looked ahead to 2015, trying to anticipate global movements and their impact. The report said that while the global economy would become more energy-efficient, sustained economic growth (particularly in China and India) would drive a nearly 50 percent increase in the demand for energy.[4] It's clear, then, that the developed world will have to start considering alternative sources. But what are they – and how quickly can they be brought on-stream?

One of oil's essential roles is that of power generation. Most electricity in the developed world is generated using coal, natural gas or petroleum, but that needs to change. The British government issued a White Paper on energy in March 2003 which set clear targets: by 2010, 10 percent of Britain's electricity should come from renewable sources, and by 2020 that should double to 20 percent. The US Department of Energy is reluctant to overstate the problem, saying that "renewables will never provide 'the' answer to all energy problems," but admits that under some conditions they are proving to be of "great value, especially overseas."[5]

Water, wind and sun can all provide sources of power. Hydro-electric generation is becoming increasingly unpopular; due to the dams they require, the environmental impact of these plants can be severe. But water power can be harnessed in other ways. Various sites around the UK are experimenting with tidal power generation: acting like underwater windmills, turbines capture the energy of the moving tide. Wind technology is well advanced, although energy companies wishing to erect wind turbines frequently face challenges from local residents who complain that the turbines are unsightly.

Biomass is another potential renewable energy source. Electricity can be generated by burning waste products from agriculture, forestry and food preparation. The incineration process emits green-house gases, but it's possible to install equipment that will reprocess gas and waste products.

Bio-fuels may also be useful in tackling another huge area of energy use – that of road transport. Automotive fuels account for nearly half of US oil consumption, and in 1999 Americans drove a whopping 2.6 trillion miles – enough for 14,000 round trips to the Sun.[6]

Brazil's scheme of fuelling cars with ethanol (distilled from fermented sugar cane, which is in plentiful supply) has been a huge success, replacing some 40 percent of the country's gasoline usage. During his visit to Latin America in early 2007, President George Bush expressed a great deal of interest in Brazilian "flex-fuel" technology, and the White House has pledged to substitute 20 percent of its oil demands with ethanol by 2017.[7] But both this technology and the "bio-diesel" fuel made from vegetable oils create other problems. The harvesting and refining process causes air and water pollution, and the ethanol industry in Brazil has been linked with wholesale deforestation to make room for cane crops. Bio-fuels also place enormous pressure on farmers to cultivate crops for energy rather than food. The US economist Lester R. Brown of the Earth Policy Institute points out that this will create an "epic" competition between the 800 million motorists who want to keep using their cars and the 2 billion people who don't have enough to eat.[8] In the US, the Bush administration has put considerable weight behind the development of hydrogen as a primary vehicle fuel. In his 2003 State of the Union address, the President announced a $1.2 billion grant to develop a commercially viable hydrogen fuel cell. It's easy to see why the US is excited: hydrogen is a highly efficient fuel which produces minimal emissions. Once hydrogen production becomes economical, the US could fill all its own energy needs, rather than having to rely on oil imports.

But the commercial viability of hydrogen could be a stalling point. In its natural form, hydrogen is a difficult gas to contain, and it's still very expensive to produce. Leakage of hydrogen into the atmosphere could be more dangerous than the greenhouse gas emissions from fossil fuels. Then there are transport and storage issues: at the moment, it's difficult to get hydrogen to filling stations, and unless it is widely available motorists won't choose a hydrogen-powered car over a gas one.

Despite these concerns, the moves towards a hydrogen economy rather than a fossil fuel one have begun. Electronics giants Sanyo and Samsung are working on producing fuel cells for small electronic devices like phones and laptops. The first public hydrogen filling station opened in Iceland in March 2003. There was only one prototype van on hand for a refill at the opening, but demand looks set to grow. BMW, Honda and Mercedes Benz have produced small numbers of concept cars, while nine European cities have held trials of hydrogen-powered buses. General Motors says it is confident that the first hydrogen-powered vehicles will be ready for commercial production by 2010,[9] and it has entered into a partnership with Shell to test-drive a fleet of mini-vans in and around Washington. The collaboration with the oil industry is seen to be pivotal to the success of the new fuel.

It may be too early to tell whether hydrogen will be a real solution to the world's long-term energy problems. It may enable us to continue our love affair with the car, but there are still questions about how this technology could adapt to industrial use and large-scale power generation. Governments should approach the question of alternative fuels in tandem with initiatives to encourage people to cut down on car use – encourage employers to offer flexible and home-working, invest in public transport networks and create pedestrian-friendly cities. Now, though, it seems as if thinking about energy sources has acquired some sense of urgency. And it's just as well – we may only have four more decades to get it right.

Eighty-two percent of the world's smokers live in developing countries

It is hard to overstate the public health disaster wreaked by tobacco. Every year, nearly 5 million people die as a result of smoking.[1] It is the number one preventable cause of death in the world. Five hundred million people alive today will die prematurely from tobacco-related diseases. As Gro Harlem Brundtland, Director-General Emeritus of the World Health Organization (WHO) put it, "It is rare – if not impossible – to find examples in history that match tobacco's programmed trail of death and destruction. I use the word programmed carefully. A cigarette is the only consumer product which when used as directed, kills its consumer."[2]

Over the coming years, more and more of those deaths will come in the developing world. There are more than 1.1 billion smokers worldwide, and 82 percent of them live in low- or middle-income countries.[3]

In the industrialized West, the number of smokers has been steadily declining. In 1955, 56 percent of American men smoked; by 2001, this was down to 25.2 percent.[4] British figures show a similar decline: from 51 percent in 1974 to 28 percent in 2001.[5] Fifty percent of men in low- and middle-income countries are smokers. In China alone, more than 300 million men smoke, leading one tobacco industry giant to conclude: "Thinking about Chinese smoking statistics is like trying to think about the limits of space."[6]

The increasing liberalization of global trade has fuelled the developing world's taste for tobacco. The US threatened a number of Asian countries with trade sanctions if they did not open up their markets to American tobacco manufacturers. Japan, South Korea, Thailand and Taiwan eventually dropped import restrictions, and the market share of Big Tobacco in the region soared. In order to keep up with their new rivals' sophisticated promotion strategies, national tobacco companies intensified their own marketing efforts. Before the Taiwan market was opened up, 26 percent of boys and 15 percent of girls in Taipei had tried smoking. By 1990, four years after the US companies gained access, the figures were 48 percent for boys and 20 percent for girls.[7] Business was booming.

The WHO reports that tobacco advertising in Cambodia rose by 400 percent in just four years during the 1990s. In Malaysia, tobacco companies account for 20–25 percent of all advertising, despite the fact that they are not allowed to advertise cigarettes directly. Companies have responded by marketing a range of spurious products "such as the Benson and Hedges bistro, Dunhill accessories, Marlboro clothing, Kent Horizon tours, Peter Stuyvesant Travel and Salem Cool Planet concerts."[8]

Women and young people in developing countries offer a particularly tempting prize to tobacco companies. Compared with their counterparts in the industrialized world (where about 22 percent of women smoke), women in lower-income countries smoke far less – just 9 percent are regular smokers.[9] The tactics employed to appeal to women in the US in the 1920s – one brand encouraged women to "reach for a Lucky instead of a sweet," another hired young women to stride down New York's Fifth Avenue smoking their "torches of equality"[10] – are hardly more subtle now. In Japan, cigarette advertisements depict "real-life" European women proclaiming their independence, while in India they show women in Western clothing and affluent settings, enjoying the material trappings of financial autonomy.[11]

The tactics used to snare young people are even more insidious. Nearly one in ten Chilean children surveyed by the Center for Disease Control said they had been offered free cigarettes by tobacco company representatives.[12] The brands themselves have been pushed as yet another desirable Western consumer commodity – half of school students in Cambodia own a product that has a cigarette brand logo on it.[13] In Sri Lanka, a tobacco company hired glamorous young women to drive around in branded jeeps and cars, handing out free cigarettes.[14] In Ukraine, the world's second-biggest cigarette market after China, one brand sponsored gala parties and made videotapes showing affluent young men and women enjoying themselves, surrounded by cigarette company logos. The state TV channel, too poor to make its own programs, showed numerous repeats of the thinly veiled advertisements.[15]

As smoking rates rise in the developing world, so, eventually, will the death toll. In the words of one tobacco control expert, "if the Chinese smoke like Americans, they'll die like Americans."[16] The WHO estimates that by 2020, there will be some 8.4 million deaths a year from smoking-related diseases, reaching 10 million in about 2030. By then, smoking will be the leading cause of death worldwide.

The health risks associated with smoking are well publicized in most industrialized countries: we all know (or should know) that smoking heightens the risk of heart disease and various forms of cancer. But many smokers in developing countries have little conception of the risks. One survey found that 61 percent of Chinese smokers thought their habit did them little or no harm.[17] Forget the scary warning labels you see on cigarette packets in the West – many countries have little or no requirement that warning labels be put on packs, and in October 2003 a Japanese court ruled that the warning "be careful of smoking too much" was perfectly adequate.[18]

As well as all the dangers normally associated with tobacco smoking in the developed world, smokers in developing countries may face even greater risks. A study in India found that half of the men who died from tuberculosis – some 400,000 a year – would not have done so if they had not been smokers. The researchers explained that smoking lowers the immune system and damages the lung's defences against infection.[19] For HIV/AIDS sufferers, smoking can increase the risk of opportunistic infections such as pneumonia or emphysema.[20]

The burden on health systems – which, in developing countries, may already be underfunded and sorely stretched by other public health problems – is significant. The World Bank estimates that smoking-related health problems take up as much as 15 percent of developed countries' health budgets.[21]

If there is no legal imperative for tobacco companies to adopt a responsible attitude towards their customers, and if individual countries are reluctant to take on the might of Big Tobacco, then perhaps it's up to the international community to take a tougher stance. The WHO, noting wryly that the tobacco industry and corporate responsibility were an inherent contradiction, decided to formulate its first treaty. It has introduced its Framework Convention on Tobacco Control (FCTC), which aims to address all aspects of the problem – from advertising to taxation. The FCTC was adopted by the World Health Assembly in May 2003 and it entered into force in February 2005.

Each state party will have to adopt a national mechanism for tobacco control and incorporate a whole host of legislation to discourage demand for tobacco – suggestions include taxing cigarettes at a higher rate, printing large and clear warning messages on packaging, and launching public education campaigns about the dangers of smoking. Parties also agree to a comprehensive ban on all tobacco advertising, promotion and sponsorship.

The tobacco industry was not included in the treaty consultation process, and the WHO conducted its own inquiry into the industry's efforts to undermine tobacco control activities.[22] Some companies (such as Philip Morris International) publicly applauded the signing of the FCTC, but others had a more mixed view. British American Tobacco's chairman Martin Broughton had already made his feelings clear: "[The WTO's] priorities are different from those of Health Ministers in the developing world, for whom issues like malnutrition, lack of sanitation, infant mortality and AIDS loom much larger."[23] However, many developing countries have already reaffirmed their commitment to ratifying the framework.

The moves suggested by the FCTC could be very effective. Taxation, according to the World Bank, "albeit a blunt instrument, is the most effective and practical method of deterring children and adolescents from smoking." Counter-advertising is also an effective strategy: in Canada, 90 percent of smokers noticed the disturbing labels on packets of cigarettes, and 44 percent were more motivated to quit.[24] In Turkey the introduction of warning labels saw consumption drop by 8 percent over six years. Partial restrictions on advertising are largely ineffective, but comprehensive marketing bans make sure that tobacco companies do not just switch their marketing efforts towards other strategies.

Tobacco is an addictive substance, and it is hard for adults to give up habits that they learned at a very young age. Governments can help with this by providing information to help aspiring non-smokers and subsidizing tools to help them in their quest, such as nicotine patches and gum.

If we encourage adults to quit smoking and kids not to start, we can save millions of lives. The world now has a clear agenda to reduce tobacco supply and consumption. The 5 million deaths each year from smoking are preventable deaths. It's up to governments, tobacco companies and healthcare providers to take action to prevent them.

Britons buy 3 billion items of clothing every year – an average of 50 pieces each. Most of it ends up being thrown away

In April 2007, the opening of a new cut-price fashion store in London's Oxford Circus caused a near riot. The doors of the new Primark store were torn off their hinges and two staff were hospitalised as shoppers rushed to pick up jeans costing £8 and cotton T-shirts at £3 each. By noon, there was a queue down the street, with waiting time estimated at a couple of hours.

There's little doubt about it – British people love to shop, and there's nothing they love quite as much as a good bargain. Between 2001 and 2005, spending on women's clothing soared by 21 percent and men's by 14 percent as Britons took advantage of a buoyant economy and comparatively cheap credit. During the same time, prices for clothing actually fell by 14 percent in real terms – so over four years, the number of garments bought per person increased by over a third.[1] Shopping has become one of the nation's favorite leisure activities. In fact it's reached the point where one department store in London advertises its sale with huge posters reading: "I shop therefore I am," and "You want it, you buy it, you forget it." Irony, of course, sold separately.

The falling cost of clothing, combined with the end of import quotas as mandated by the World Trade Organization Agreement on Textile and Clothing, have led to a boom in the "value" clothing sector. It's now worth some £7.8 billion in the UK alone, about a quarter of the fashion market, and retailers like Primark and Matalan and the supermarkets Asda and Tesco (which have lucrative clothing businesses) have prospered. These retailers have become famed for turning out lightning-fast imitations of catwalk trends – their clothes are now often featured alongside thousand-dollar items in high fashion magazines. Celebrities would once have considered it career suicide to be associated with such mass-market brands, but they're now signing lucrative deals to be the public face of supermarket clothing ranges. But, as many NGOs point out, this boom comes at a cost. It's a human cost, it's an environmental cost. And even given the ridiculously cheap price of those jeans, it's one that you may not feel happy to pay.

The pressure group War on Want took the opening of the new Primark store as a chance to highlight its concerns about the ethics of clothing production. Simon McRae, a senior campaigner at War on Want, says it is "naive" to think you can buy a $24 copy of a $6,000 Gucci leather jacket (popularized by none other than Victoria Beckham) and think that no one has been exploited in the process.[2]

In December 2006 War on Want released its "Fashion Victims" report, detailing how its researchers had found workers in Bangladesh working 80-hour weeks and being paid just 10 cents an hour to make clothes for Primark, Tesco and Asda's "George" fashion range. All three retailers had made public commitments to paying their suppliers a living wage – calculated to be just $44 a month in Bangladesh – and yet some factories were found to offer a starting wage of just $16 a month. Many workers told of hundreds of hours of unpaid overtime and being kept locked in unsafe buildings while they worked.[3]

Eighty percent of the people employed in the clothing industry in Bangladesh are women, a trend that is echoed across the developing world. Many are young – between 15 and 20 years old, around the same age as the young women who flock to the British high streets on Saturdays, determined to get their fashion fix.

Primark, Asda and Tesco have all signed up to the Ethical Trading Initiative (ETI) – an alliance of companies, NGOs and trade unions which aims to ensure that working conditions in companies that supply the UK market meet international labor standards. But it's not enough just to sign up to the ETI – you have to practice what you preach as well. The Labor Behind the Label group surveyed all high-street signatories to the ETI in September 2006 and found that only two retailers seemed to be engaging with the issues raised: Gap and Next. The survey found that none were making a serious commitment to tackling ethical issues.[4]

If we really want to clean up the textile and garment industry, though, we need to go right back to basics. Even the most basic of raw materials, cotton, places the environment and the people who farm it under stress.

Cotton prices are at their lowest point ever, and they're expected to keep falling – due in no small part to the subsidies that America's government pays to its cotton farmers, leading to oversupply on the world markets. Farmers are struggling to make their land more and more productive, and they're using more and more chemicals in an attempt to increase their yields. Due to this intensive farming, the cotton plant has become fragile and susceptible to pests – so its production now uses more insecticides than any other crop on earth. Cotton now uses 10 percent of the world's pesticides and, of that, 25 percent of the world's insecticides.[5] Farmers are often lacking in education and often don't know how to apply the chemicals properly – even when they do, the pesticides can contaminate water supplies and kill beneficial insects along with pests.

Agriculture takes up about 69 percent of the world's fresh water supplies, and rice, wheat and cotton are the biggest consumers of water. As demand for water increases and supplies dwindle, ineffective use of irrigation could lead to even greater strains on water supplies, with potentially catastrophic consequences. One report highlights the case of the Aral Sea, once the fourth-largest lake on earth. In the 1940s the Russian government wanted the country to become self-sufficient in cotton, so it diverted water for irrigation from two huge rivers in Central Asia. Since 1961 the Aral Sea, which received most of its water from these two rivers, has shrunk by three-quarters. In the five countries that share the Aral Sea basin, more than 20 million people depend directly or indirectly on irrigated agriculture. The Sea has now split in two, dust storms have contaminated agricultural land with salt, and the water that eventually drains back to the Sea is becoming more saline and polluted by agricultural chemicals. Local residents have lost their jobs, their environment is wrecked and recent surveys predict a complete drought in as little as fifteen years. Restoration plans are under way, but it's hard to disagree with the conclusion that this is one of the largest ecological disasters that man has created.[6]

Man-made fibers are not much better. While a very few new textiles are able to use recycled plastic materials, many use highly toxic chemicals in their production: to make fibers suitable for spinning and weaving, to prevent shrinkage, and to make clothing softer and wrinkle-free. Petrochemical dyes pollute waterways and the production of nylon is a major source of the UK's emissions of nitrous oxide, a greenhouse gas.[7] And the chemicals which are added to clothes to make them "flame retardant" and "non-iron" are considered to be probable human carcinogens.[8]

Then there are the emissions involved in transporting the clothes from the countries where they're made to our retailers. In total, 4.2 billion ton-kilometres of freight were required to meet the UK's demand just for T-shirts – the equivalent to sending one kilogram of goods approximately 105 million times around the world.[9]

Then, once we've tired of our fashionable clothes – or once they've fallen apart – there's the question of how they're disposed of. Although most of us are used to the idea of taking used clothes to charity shops, only about 30 percent of the UK's clothing is disposed of in this way. The rest is sent either to landfill or to be incinerated. A report by the Institute of Manufacturing at Cambridge University estimates that buying one cotton T-shirt, washing and drying it and then throwing it away, results in nearly twice the T-shirt's weight going to landfill and 4 kilograms of carbon dioxide being released into the atmosphere.[10]

So what can we do? Well, first of all, we need to take action as consumers. If you're concerned about the labor that's gone into your clothes, let retailers know you're not happy. This is a competitive market, and consumers hold real power. Simon McRae from War on Want says: "Boycotting will simply close factories, taking jobs away from local people. What we need [people] to do is speak out about the fact they dislike these practices and put pressure on companies to change them."[11] Some activists suggest you should cut the labels out of your clothes and send them to the manufacturer, together with a letter explaining that you like their clothes but don't like how they're made. It would certainly be an attention-grabbing tactic. In the UK, head for the Clean Up Fashion website and monitor the latest developments at your high-street retailers – there are also suggestions about what you can do to take action.[12]

While you're at it, write to your favorite retailers and ask them when they're going to start designing fair trade and organic ranges. In 2006 Marks and Spencer announced it would launch a fair trade range because it said that's what its customers wanted; the company surveyed shoppers and found that a third had put clothes back on rails amid concerns about where they'd come from and how they were made.[13]

The fashion industry clearly needs to take action here, too. There's a clear perception that "eco-clothing" has to be either hippie-style or prohibitively expensive – nowadays, with the market for ethical products growing hugely, that's no longer true. There also needs to be a change of emphasis away from disposable fashion, designed for maximum impact and minimum lifespan, and back towards durable, well-made items.

And while we're thinking fashion, don't forget that second-hand clothing – or vintage, as it's now termed – is a very good ethical choice. Clothes from the past are well made, usually cheaper than their new equivalents, and at least you'll never run the risk of going to a party and seeing someone in the same $24 frock.

It doesn't have to be a question of not shopping; in fact, the NGOs make it clear that that's the last thing we should do. We just need to be a bit more conscious when we get out the plastic, and think of the true cost of what we're buying.

A quarter of the world's armed conflicts of recent years have involved a struggle for natural resources

A country's natural resources may provide opportunities to build wealth, create employment and foster development. Or they can breed jealousy, trigger violent confrontation and leave a society in ruins. Abundant natural wealth can prove to be a country's biggest curse.

This wealth can be within the land itself (like oil, minerals, metals or gems) or can cover its surface (water, timber, drug crops). In about a quarter of the roughly 50 wars and armed conflicts of recent years, natural resources helped to trigger or exacerbate violent conduct, or helped to finance its continuation. More than 5 million people died as a result of these conflicts in the 1990s.[1]

The war in the Democratic Republic of Congo (DRC) has claimed an estimated 3 million lives since 1998.[2] The country's resources were not just a prize to be fought over; they provided a means of paying for the military campaigns, and a rich source of revenue for unscrupulous governments. DRC has substantial deposits of gold, diamonds and a mineral ore called coltan (short for columbite-tantalum) which is an important component of mobile phones and computers. In their raw state, these minerals have little value to the people of the DRC. But the massive demand for them in the West has led to death and deprivation for millions.

A United Nations report in October 2002 accused the armies of Rwanda, Zimbabwe and Uganda of illegally plundering the DRC's mineral wealth.[3] It found that state armies had fuelled inter-ethnic battles within the DRC as a means of justifying their own presence in mineral-rich areas. If the troops maintained control of these areas, "arrangements" with companies could be made. Rwanda protested, but the evidence didn't look good. Rwanda's president, Paul Kagame, had famously said the war in DRC was "self-financing." This was echoed by Adolphe Onusumba, president of the Rally for Congolese Democracy, the rebel group sponsored by Rwanda. "We need to maintain the soldiers. We need to pay for services ... we raise more or less $200,000 per month from diamonds. Coltan gives us more: a million dollars a month."[4]

The fighting officially ended in late 2002, after a series of peace agreements between the DRC and its adversaries: Rwanda, Uganda and a brace of rebel groups. A new constitution setting up a power-sharing government was signed in April 2003. However, Rwanda and Uganda are still accused of funding militia groups fighting in the east of the country. In its fourth report, released in November 2003, the UN panel of experts concluded that "illegal exploitation remains one of the main sources of funding for groups involved in perpetuating conflict."[5]

In Colombia, the natural resource fuelling the battle between the government and the Revolutionary Armed Forces of Colombia (FARC) rebel group is cocaine. The civil war has lasted some 40 years and escalated substantially in the 1990s, fuelled by funds from the drug trade. FARC styles itself as a peasant revolutionary group, but to American officials, they are narco-terrorists. It's estimated that FARC nets as much as $400 million each year from the cocaine trade.[6] Because Colombia's government has little real control outside the major cities, FARC and other rebel groups have been able to set up sophisticated trading networks – they sell drugs, gems and gold, and buy arms to fuel the war.

DRC and Colombia are two examples of wars being fought over an abundance of resources. But experts believe that in the coming years we may see more and more conflicts being fought as a result of scarcity of resources. Wars have been fought over oil – we need only look at the 1991 Iraqi invasion of Kuwait, and the Western world's swift response, to see that. But there is one commodity that may prove even more contentious: water.

In 1985, when he was Egypt's minister of state for foreign affairs, Boutros Boutros-Ghali warned that "the next war in the Middle East will be fought over water, not politics."[7] Boutros-Ghali envisaged a future where population growth would mean greater and greater demands on water resources. People obviously need drinking water, but they also need to grow enough food to minimize the need for costly imports. While the average person should consume two liters of water a day, it may take more than 1,000 liters to produce their daily food.[8] Accordingly, agriculture consumes about 70 percent of the world's fresh water – but in developing countries the figure is closer to 90 percent. Where you have a number of states reliant on the same water source, it's easy to see how tensions begin.

The Consultative Group on International Agricultural Research (CGIAR) suggests that if present trends continue, one in three of the world's people will be affected by a water shortage by 2025.[9] Africa could be badly affected, with as many as 500 million people without access to clean water. The shortage will also affect food production, with a 23 percent shortfall of crop yields expected. Countries will be unable to finance the food imports they need, resulting in widespread hunger and malnutrition.

This is where conflict could start. The Nile river complex flows through ten countries, where half the population lives below the poverty line. The population in the Nile basin is expected to double in the next 25 years, raising tensions even higher. Thanks to two colonial treaties – the 1929 Nile Water Agreement and the 1959 Agreement for the Full Utilization of the Nile – Egypt and Sudan have extensive rights over the river's waters. The other countries along the banks of the river have called for a more equitable system of rights, but Egypt and Sudan have been reluctant to re-negotiate the treaties.[10] The Nile Basin Initiative has brought the river states together to try to form a partnership for its management. But for the initiative to be a success, it will have to reassure Egypt that its only water source will not be threatened.

Another potential flash-point could be the River Ganges. India plans to tackle its water worries by interlinking more than 30 rivers in the country and diverting water towards drought-prone states. But experts fear that this could lead to water shortages in Bangladesh, whose government has called India's plans a "weapon of mass destruction in the offing."[11] India has agreed to involve Bangladesh in future discussions on the project, but the Bangladeshi government says that the livelihoods of more than 100 million people are at risk.

But, as Dr. Boutros-Ghali predicted, the most likely area of conflict is the Middle East, where 5 percent of the world's population lives on just 1 percent of its water. In the mid-20th century Israel sent tanks and aircraft to destroy Syrian bulldozers trying to divert tributaries of the River Jordan, and in 2002 it threatened action when Lebanon started pumping water from a river feeding the Jordan. Palestinians complain that Israel's control over water allocation leads to an erratic and expensive supply, and that the underground aquifer they share has become damaged through overuse. Israelis in the West Bank use four times as much water as their Palestinian neighbors.[12]

Water is a source of security, and of prosperity. It's easy to see how it has become nearly as important an issue as land. And with a world water shortage looking very likely, some of these tensions could spill over into armed conflict. Former Russian president Mikhail Gorbachev, who now heads the International Green Cross, warned that the world could be facing a "grave situation ... a great majority of countries have not reaffirmed their commitment to cooperate on water resources. We are facing some real conflicts."[13]

And in February 2006 Britain's Defense Secretary John Reid pointed out that climate change would only hasten violence and political conflict over water. He warned that Britain's armed forces would have to ready themselves for tackling conflicts over water.[14]

War is no longer a matter of annexing territory – it's about generating wealth and securing resources. Where the conflict relates to precious mineral deposits, much can be done by increasing accountability for the parties involved in plunder and raising awareness about the bloody origins of some of our well-loved Western luxuries. In the past, we've been unconcerned with what's gone into our laptop computers and where the gems in our jewellery are sourced. Recent campaigns relating to "blood diamonds" have done much to change this.

Where resources are at issue due to their scarcity, the problem may be more complex. In the coming decades, our basic rights to food, fuel and clean drinking water will sorely test our planet's ability to provide for us. International institutions are calling for strict observance of water laws and a multi-party approach to drawing up water management agreements. But as the Earth's population continues to grow, there will be few easy answers.

Some 30 million people in Africa are HIV-positive

It is the biggest epidemic ever to face humankind, and we are not fighting it well. Every fourteen seconds, a young person becomes infected by the HIV virus. At the time of writing, 36 million people are living with HIV or AIDS, and by 2050 the disease may have claimed as many as 280 million lives.[1]

Sub-Saharan Africa has been hit the hardest. More than 20 million people there have died from AIDS, and 12 million children have been orphaned by the disease. Life expectancy is tumbling – by as much as 30 years in some countries.[2] As the breadwinners sicken and die, communities are left starving, and the impact on regional economies has been fierce. And this is to say nothing of the personal cost, the heartbreak, the families destroyed. Even if a huge global response swung into action tomorrow and instigated effective prevention, treatment and care, these countries will feel the effects of HIV and AIDS for many generations to come.

It seems bitterly unfair that countries which have struggled under the effects of famine, repressive colonial regimes and civil war should now be hit by such a crisis. Certainly, epidemiologists and international institutions have looked hard at the epidemic in sub-Saharan Africa and tried to figure out just why the virus has taken such a huge toll there.

Predictably, the answers are complex. It is thought that the HIV virus originated in primates in Africa, and made the leap to humans some time in the early 20th century. The HIV virus may have "crossed over" several times, on different continents. But the spread in Africa would have begun long before any preventive action could be taken.

When AIDS was first recognized in the USA in the early 1980s, the vast majority of infections occurred among gay men and intravenous drug users. In Africa, though, the main spread of AIDS came from heterosexual sex. Widespread poverty has worsened the situation: malnutrition affects the body's ability to fight off infection, meaning that people may be more susceptible to infection, and once they are infected, they will become ill more quickly. Where men are forced to move away from their families to look for work, the risks increase; they're more likely to visit sex workers or have multiple partners. They then go back home and infect their wives, who may then give birth to HIV-positive babies.

Conflict is also placing people at great risk of HIV infection. Where large groups of people are forced to flee their land due to fighting, it is hard to ensure they are educated about the risks and how to protect themselves. A UN worker in Sierra Leone reported that during the brutal civil war, tens of thousands of girls and women had been abducted and raped by soldiers from the warring factions. Many of them ended up working as prostitutes in the bigger towns, and with the country's infrastructure struggling to rebuild itself, there is little that can be done to protect them: "Nothing is left standing in Sierra Leone except hope."[3]

Governments in Africa were slow to react to the growing AIDS epidemic. For some administrations, the AIDS issue became intensely politicized. President Thabo Mbeki of South Africa publicly questioned the link between the HIV virus and AIDS, and courted a number of well-known "AIDS sceptic" scientists to back up his views. In a 2001 lecture, President Mbeki implied that the West blamed Africa for the disease: "Because we are germ carriers and human beings of a lower order that cannot subject its passions to reason, we must perforce adopt strange opinions [that HIV causes AIDS] to save a depraved and diseased people from perishing."[4]

In August 2003, the South African government announced that it would introduce anti-retroviral drug treatment for half a million people. Activists hailed this as an end to the denials and the beginning of real hope for South Africa's AIDS sufferers. Yet in September 2003, President Mbeki sparked more controversy when he told the *New York Times* that he did not know anyone who had died of AIDS –

although one of his own staff, and several senior ANC members, had died of the disease. His remark was seen by AIDS activists as adding insult to injury.

Denial didn't come just at government level. It's also alleged that the international community chose to overlook projections of the massive death toll from AIDS. In 1990, the CIA published a report forecasting 45 million HIV infections by 2000, the vast majority of which would be in Africa. Seven years earlier, a small team of foreign scientists saw hospital wards in Kinshasa full of young women suffering from AIDS. It was clear to Belgian scientist Peter Piot that the virus could be transmitted through heterosexual sex, and as such, it could lay waste to entire communities. But Piot and his team were rubbished by other scientists, and it was not until the late 1990s that international institutions started to give priority to the emerging crisis in Africa.[5]

Piot is now the Executive Director of UNAIDS, and he says that "denial has been a characteristic of this epidemic at all levels."[6] Certainly, denial is helping to fuel transmission in other regions, and just as in Africa, the devastation is only now starting to be known. Up to a million people in China's Henan province are infected with HIV because of a large blood-selling operation. Once the blood-collectors had extracted the valuable plasma, they would pool the remaining blood and re-inject donors with it. This way, they could give more blood without risking anaemia. It also assured a rapid spread of HIV across the province. Human Rights Watch notes that not one Chinese official has been prosecuted for their role in what it calls one of the world's worst blood scandals, and a health official was thrown in jail for sending an official government report on HIV/ AIDS to a group of activists.[7] China refused to acknowledge the country's AIDS problem until 2002, when in a single day it revised its HIV infection statistics. One day there were 30,000 people living with HIV, the next there were 1 million.[8]

In India, the government insists that HIV infection is limited to high-risk groups like sex workers, drug users and men who have sex with men. There have been reports of AIDS activists being harassed and intimidated, while sex workers have been subjected to violent attacks. Government programs provide no information or care for married women in states where HIV has spread to the general population, despite the fact that they may be at the highest risk of infection.[9]

In many countries, HIV/AIDS is not just slowing development, it is forcing it into reverse. Life expectancy is spiralling downwards, child mortality rates are rising, and the number of people living in extreme poverty is expected to increase.[10] In Burkina Faso, in West Africa, it's estimated that 20 percent of rural families have reduced or abandoned their agricultural work because of AIDS.[11] With incomes falling, paying for funerals and healthcare becomes far more difficult, and families are forced to sell land or livestock. If these precious assets are sold, they are usually lost for good, and the family's livelihood will be further diminished.

This is why providing a source of cheap anti-retroviral drugs has become so critically important for sub-Saharan Africa. In 2001, when a group of international pharmaceutical companies challenged the South African government's plans to import cheap generic AIDS drugs, the outcry shamed the whole industry. The drug companies' arguments about protecting their patents were shouted down by activists, and the companies eventually dropped the case.

Thanks to this pressure, a number of pharmaceutical firms have announced they will cut the prices of anti-retrovirals to poorer countries. But some critics say this still isn't enough. Of the $70 billion spent each year in researching new drugs, less than 10 percent is spent on finding solutions for 90 percent of the world's health problems.[12]

There are some success stories starting to emerge from Africa. In the east, prevalence of HIV infection is falling in some countries: most notably Uganda, where infection rates in pregnant women have fallen for eight successive years.[13] Large-scale information campaigns seem to be working, and condom distribution schemes have led to an increasing number of young people practicing safe sex.

But all HIV/AIDS prevention and treatment programs need funding, and securing financial commitments from richer countries seems to be a problem. UN Secretary-General Kofi Annan told a major international conference that the world was not on track to begin reducing the scale and impact of the epidemic by 2005, thus missing key UN targets set in 2000. The special envoy on HIV/AIDS, Stephen Lewis, was scathing in his criticism. He said the lack of cheap AIDS drugs in Africa was a "grotesque obscenity ... we can find over $200 billion to fight a war on terrorism, but we can't find the money to provide the anti-retroviral treatment for all those who need such treatment in Africa!"[14]

Secretary-General Annan estimates that $7–10 billion is needed each year to address the epidemic in low- to middle-income countries. Yet the world spends about $2 billion every day on funding its military efforts.[15] One could argue that it's a question of priorities. And if the rich world doesn't do everything it can to help developing countries fight HIV and AIDS, those priorities are disgracefully skewed.

Ten languages die out every year

Imagine, just for a moment, that you are the last native speaker of English. No one else you know speaks your language. You don't see any point in teaching it to your kids, because no one will ever speak it to them, either. Imagine the loss you would feel. All those untranslatable English-language ideas – a stiff upper lip, a stitch in time, a New York minute – would disappear. No one would ever sing "baa baa black sheep" or "ring-a-ring o' roses" again. All those minute clues about history, culture, collective memory – all gone.

There are around 6,000 living languages in the world – and at least half of those are under serious threat. In every part of the world, languages are disappearing. In fact, one scientist has said that languages are facing a bigger risk of extinction than birds and mammals. Professor Steve Sutherland of the University of East Anglia calculated that the past 500 years have seen 4.5 percent of languages die out – compared with 1.3 percent of birds, and 1.9 percent of mammals.[1]

Some 300 languages have more than a million speakers. They're the healthy ones – Mandarin Chinese, English and Spanish are the most widely spoken. Ten major languages are the mother tongues of almost half the world's population. But the median size for languages in the world is just 6,000 – so half the languages in the world are spoken by that number or fewer.[2]

Languages, like so many other forms of human expression, come and go, and thousands have done exactly that without leaving any trace of ever having existed. Only a very few – Basque, Greek, Hebrew, Latin among them – have lasted more than 2,000 years. But it seems that the pace of their disappearance is becoming ever quicker. UNESCO claims that the rate of language extinction has now reached ten every year.

The Ethnologue, a database of all the languages spoken in the world,[3] claims that 417 languages are spoken by so few people that they are in the final stages of becoming extinct. Spare a thought for the one living speaker of Luo in Cameroon, the single remaining exponent of Klamath in Oregon, the handful of people that speak the Saami Pite language in Sweden and Norway.

Where once languages flourished in small isolated areas, there are now very few that are not in regular contact with the rest of the world. Speaking an internationally recognized language is a clear advantage for people who want to make the most of the opportunities contact brings. Eventually, people may not realize their children are not learning their native tongue.

Languages may also be lost through migration, as people move from small rural communities to urban centres, or when environments are destroyed by the search for oil or timber. Natural disasters can also devastate populations, and along with them, their language – like the speakers of the Paulohi language in Maluku, Indonesia, of whom all but 50 were killed by an earthquake and tidal wave.[4]

Governments also have a case to answer in the extinction of languages. The perceived need to establish "official languages," in which a country would educate its children, conduct its political affairs and carry out its business, had a disastrous effect on many small languages. Up until the 1970s, Aborigines in Australia were forbidden to speak in their own tongues – which once numbered more than 400. Now, according to the *Atlas of the World's Languages in Danger of Disappearing*, only about 25 Aboriginal languages are still commonly spoken.

What is lost if a language is lost? There are some who argue that the extinction of languages is merely a symptom of the gradual evolution of our species, where universal communication is prized, and increasing homogeneity is just an evolutionary side-effect. Obviously there could be great benefits if everyone in the world spoke the same language – some industries already reflect this, with English a must for pilots and air traffic controllers. But it's clear that there is far more at stake than mere convenience. As languages are lost, whole ways of life and sets of knowledge may be lost along with them. Complex religious and social rituals disappear, oral histories die through lack of telling. Information about plants, animals and environments gathered through generations may never be passed on. And the richness of human invention, our unique gift of talking about what we see around us, would be much the poorer.

Put simply, language expresses something about identity, about our place in the world. Ani Rauhihi, a Maori teacher in New Zealand's North Island, sums it up: "If you grow up not speaking your language, you won't know who you are."[5]

That need for a feeling of identity and connection to one's past is a big factor in the resurgence of the Maori language. Maori is the language of New Zealand's native population and was the predominant language spoken there before the arrival of the European settlers. But by the early 20th century children were punished for speaking Maori at school and very few schools taught the language. By the 1980s less than 20 percent of Maori knew enough of the language to be regarded as native speakers, and many urbanized Maori people had no contact at all with their language and culture.[6] Now one in four Maori people in New Zealand speaks the Maori language and around 40 percent of Maori pre-schoolers are enrolled in total-immersion schools.[7] Maori is also an official language.

It is even possible for a language considered dead to be revived into a flourishing and dynamic tongue. Hebrew ceased to be used as a spoken language in about AD 200, but continued to be used by Jews as a "sacred tongue." In the late 19th century, a revival movement headed by Eliezer Ben-Yehuda aimed to reestablish Hebrew as a spoken language to provide a common tongue for Jews. The new language came to be a key factor in the Zionist movement, so that when Jews moved back to their homeland they would have a common language. Ben-Yehuda coined thousands of new words and pioneered Hebrew usage in home and school. Now Hebrew is spoken by more than 5 million people, 81 percent of Israel's population.

It seems the world may be starting to realize what it is about to lose. UNESCO is actively promoting multilingualism and the need to preserve intangible aspects of culture as well as the more traditional monuments and national parks. Joseph Poth, head of its languages division, has spoken of the need for "trilingualism"[8] – we should all speak our mother tongue, a "neighbor" language and an international language. Even teaching an endangered language in schools creates a rescue system, he says.

It may be too late for the languages where only a few speakers remain. Chances are they're elderly, they speak their mother tongue very little and have forgotten many of the words they once knew. But it seems that at last the value of these languages is being recognized, and that is the first step to stemming the tide of loss.

More people die each year from suicide than in all the world's armed conflicts

There can be few people who have not, in times of stress, wished fervently to be somewhere else. The idea of escaping from one's problems is a human instinct: the "fight or flight" reaction is deep within us all, and in some situations, fighting on seems like a far tougher option. But there is a huge difference between wanting to run away from one's problems – wanting to escape into another life, someone else's shoes – and wanting to die. And there is just as big a difference between wanting to die and actually doing something about it.

In the US, more people die by their own hand than are killed by others – in 2000, there were 1.7 times more suicides than homicides.[1] A study carried out in Britain in 2002 showed that nearly one in six adults had considered attempting suicide at some point in their lives. The Office of National Statistics found that just over 4 percent of people between 16 and 74 had attempted suicide.[2]

In the past 45 years, suicide rates have grown by 60 percent worldwide. The World Health Organization (WHO) estimates that a million people died from suicide in 2000, and ten to twenty times more attempted suicide. It is now the third biggest cause of death among people aged 15 to 34 worldwide, and kills more people than all the world's armed conflicts.[3] It is not just an affliction of the developed world: the former Soviet states of Belarus, Kazakhstan, Latvia and Lithuania all show alarmingly high rates of suicide.

So why are so many human beings choosing to take their own lives? What makes a person decide that their own existence has grown too much to bear?

While suicide is a complex issue which involves many social and cultural factors, many studies have shown a link with major depression. About two-thirds of people who kill themselves are depressed at the time of their deaths,[4] and although most studies are reluctant to say that depression actually causes suicide, the two are strongly associated.

Depression is more than just feeling a bit down or overwhelmed; at its worst, it is a debilitating illness, leaving its sufferers unable to sleep or eat and filled with feelings of immense sadness and guilt. It is sometimes thought of as a modern affliction, a result of the rich world's leisurely preoccupation with the self. But that couldn't be further from the truth. Depression was once referred to as "melancholia," a diagnosis recorded around the 5th century BC by philosophers like Hippocrates. Arateus described symptoms that sound all too familiar to modern clinicians: "The patients become dull or stern, dejected or unreasonably torpid ... they also become peevish, dispirited and start up from a disturbed sleep."[5] Depression is a reality for people in the developing world, too: one survey of AIDS-stricken regions in Uganda showed that 21 percent of residents were clinically depressed,[6] while studies in a Pakistani village showed that 44 percent of the population were suffering from some kind of depressive disorder.[7]

Research suggests that depression may be triggered by stressful events in a person's life: a medical emergency like a stroke, a heart attack or cancer may cause a period of depression.[8] The same goes for personal tragedy or upheaval: a bereavement, perhaps, the end of a relationship or financial problems. Whether depression is present or not, suicide is more likely to occur during periods of crisis.

One group struggling with the pressures of modern life appears to be young men. Since 1950, suicide rates for English and Welsh men under 45 have doubled. A report by Bristol University researchers suggested that "the society in which young people live has changed in such a way that a number of things that may have protected young men against suicide are now less present: for instance, a stable job or secure marriage."[9] The research suggested that the rise in drug and alcohol use, soaring divorce rates and widespread unemployment had all taken their toll on young men. People living in deprived industrial areas in England and Wales were the most likely to be treated for depression – the least likely were those living in comfortable, middle-class suburbia.[10]

Women are more likely to attempt suicide, but men are more than four times more likely to die.[11] Men are thought to be less likely to admit to depression and stress, and it can be difficult to diagnose. The US National Institute for Mental Health suggests that men are less likely than women to seek help, and may mask their depression with drugs or alcohol, or working long hours.[12]

Another group that are prone to misdiagnosis are the elderly – and here again, men are at a particular risk. In the US, white men over the age of 85 are at the highest risk of all, with a suicide risk more than six times that of the general population.[13] The elderly are more likely to "complete," with one suicide for every four attempts (compared with one in twenty overall). Contrary to popular belief, only a tiny percentage (2–4 percent) have been diagnosed with a terminal illness.[14] The problem is that depression in older people can often be dismissed as just a normal part of aging, and as many as three-quarters of depressed older Americans do not receive the treatment they need.[15]

By 2020, WHO predicts that depression will be the second-largest contributor to the global burden of disease. By then, there are expected to be 1.5 million deaths by suicide every year.[16] It is described as a serious public health problem which entails tremendous costs to society – through the lost years to the victim, and the grief and suffering on the part of their friends and family.

Fortunately, depression can be treated. Some 60–80 percent of sufferers can be helped if they are diagnosed and given access to anti-depressant drugs and appropriate therapy.[17] But tackling suicide is more complex than that. Many countries still consider it to be a taboo subject: for example, the former USSR kept its records on suicide strictly secret and did not release them until after the *perestroika* era.[18] The more scant the information, the harder it is to look at risk factors for that particular society.

There is also the question of how much public health bodies should seek to involve themselves in matters of individual choice. Albert Camus famously declared that "there is but one truly serious philosophical problem, and that is suicide."[19] If a person decides to end his or her life after a long period of rational thought, then it's hard to see how society can justify intervening. In the case of someone who is terminally ill, it's at least arguable that the person has a right to decide when and how they should die. But most people who attempt suicide are not in that situation, and their circumstances make rational thought impossible. What society needs to do is provide more help and support to people struggling with suicidal thoughts – to make them aware that there are alternatives, that people can help them.

One of the first steps is to identify groups of people who are at risk: people who abuse drugs and alcohol, depression sufferers, people who have attempted suicide before. The British government's national suicide prevention strategy also suggests attempting to remove some of the methods used in attempts: improving security at "hot spots" like bridges and cliffs and limiting the prescription of certain kinds of drugs. When Britain changed its household gas supply from lethal coke gas to a less toxic form, the suicide rate dropped by a third, and new regulations making it harder to obtain large quantities of pills led to a 34 percent drop in death by acetaminophen poisoning. As a consequence, Britain's suicide rate in 2003 was the lowest since the Second World War,and among the lowest in Europe.[20] Meanwhile, the US, with some 200 million firearms in private hands, is the only country in the world where self-inflicted shooting is the most common method of suicide.[21] By taking away the means to make impulsive decisions, suicide levels can be reduced.

Risk factors will also vary between countries: in Eastern Europe, for example, the economic slumps that hit many countries in the post-Communist era have led to widespread unemployment and soaring alcoholism rates. Each country needs to research the underlying causes of depression and suicide and do what it can to reduce their effects.

Then, there is the crucial question of reducing the stigma of mental illness. In societies which prize coping, the ability to perform under pressure, mental toughness and the need to triumph in the face of adversity, it's little wonder that so many find it so difficult to ask for help. Five thousand people in England kill themselves each year, but only 1,200 have had some prior contact with mental health services.[22]

Advertising campaigns can do much to raise public awareness about mental health issues – assuring people that it's okay to ask for help before problems become insurmountable. WHO also strongly promotes training for health professionals in recognizing danger signs and making some kind of treatment available for all who need it.

The poet and philosopher George Santayana once wrote: "That life is worth living is the most necessary of assumptions, and were it not assumed, the most impossible of conclusions."[23] If we are serious about suicide prevention, then reaffirming that "assumption" – and not judging those who, through whatever circumstances, have come to doubt it – is what we must do.

Every week, an average of 54 children are expelled from American schools for bringing a gun to class

On April 24, 2003, fourteen-year-old James Sheets walked into the school cafeteria at the Red Lion Area Junior High School in Pennsylvania. It was a Thursday morning and nothing seemed out of the ordinary. James took a seat near the front of the cafeteria, opened his backpack and pulled out a large revolver. He aimed it at the school principal Gene Segro and pulled the trigger. He then turned the gun on himself.[1]

Four months later, in Cold Spring, Minnesota, John Jason McLaughlin, fifteen, allegedly shot and killed two schoolmates. McLaughlin, who had been teased by other kids for his short stature and severe acne, shot Aaron Rollins and Seth Bartell outside the school weights room. Rollins died immediately, while Bartell died two weeks later. At the time of writing, McLaughlin faces murder charges.[2]

It's shocking to think of the waste of young life, the huge impact on the kids who witnessed the shooting, the terrible loss felt by small communities. The shootings at Columbine High School in April 1999 – where two former pupils killed twelve students and a teacher before killing themselves – provoked an outcry around the world, and a period of intense soul-searching for America. The call for tougher gun control seemed near-universal. And yet, it seems, not much is changing.

A survey by the US National Institute of Child Health and Human Development suggested that nearly a quarter of boys had carried a weapon (a gun, knife or club) in the past month, and some 15 percent – nearly 2 million students – had taken one to school.[3] Another study by the non-profit Josephson Institute of Ethics reported that almost half of high school students said they could get a gun if they wanted to.[4] And many of those kids need only take a look around their own homes. Nearly one in three American households with children have a gun in them.[5] In a 1994 survey, the National Institute of Justice found that more than half of all privately owned firearms were stored unlocked, and 30 percent of all handgun-owning households had an unlocked, loaded gun in the home.[6]

The consequences of leaving guns within reach of children can be devastating. In a study of 37 school shooting incidents between 1974 and 2000, two-thirds of the students involved had taken their guns from their own home or that of a relative.[7] When homicide, suicide and accidental death are all taken into account, the death rate from guns in the US is by far the highest in the developed world; one study found that, for children under fifteen, the firearm-related death rate in the US was nearly twelve times higher than the average of 25 other industrialized countries.[8]

We can blame the images in movies and television, ultra-violent video games or teenagers' obsession with particular musical artists. We can point to the association between guns and power, wealth, status. We can shake our heads at lax gun laws and gasp at parents who keep guns in their houses without taking proper safety measures. The gun lobby claims that it is educating children that guns are not to be touched; the anti-gun protesters claim that gun owners' groups deliberately seek to stifle laws that would protect children. All agree that we must encourage kids to resolve their problems in a non-violent way; but will encouraging responsibility be enough to keep guns out of the hands of children?

Worldwide, the violence wreaked by handguns and other small arms is reaching alarming proportions. Aid agencies point to the huge increase of arms sales as a result of the so-called "war on terror," with many countries (including the US and Britain) relaxing controls on arms sales to governments known to have poor human rights records. They claim that the world's 639 million small arms are the real weapons of mass destruction.[9] Slightly less than a third of these – nearly 200 million – are in America, in private hands.[10]

This widespread sale and use of guns is encouraging us to think of guns as a normal, necessary part of life. Developing countries spend an average of $22 billion a year on arms – a sum which would enable those countries to meet the Millennium Development Goals of universal primary education and reducing infant and maternal mortality.[11] They're not just a weapon in the hands of the few – we are starting to see them as a priority, an integral part of our lives.

In America, the issue of gun ownership strikes at the very heart of the nation's values. The Second Amendment to the US Constitution guarantees that every citizen shall have the right to keep and bear arms. For gun owners, this is as close to a fundamental human right as you can get. For those who argue for a tighter approach to gun control, however, the Second Amendment is not so clear-cut, as it specifically refers to state militias, a part-time fighting force which operated in the days of the founding fathers, but which has no equivalent in today's world. In 1991, former Supreme Court Justice Warren called the Second Amendment "the subject of one of the greatest pieces of fraud, I repeat the word "fraud," on the American public by special interest groups that I have ever seen in my lifetime … [The National Rifle Association (NRA) have] misled the American people and they, I regret to say, they have had far too much influence on the Congress of the United States than as a citizen I would like to see – and I am a gun man."[12]

The NRA is an immensely powerful group: with around 3 million members it is the largest of the pro-gun bodies, and in 2001 *Fortune* magazine voted it the most influential lobby group in the US.[13] And its influence goes all the way to the top: in April 2003, Florida's Governor, Jeb Bush, told the NRA's annual meeting that "were it not for your active involvement, it is safe to say that my brother would not have been elected president of the United States."[14]

The power of the pro-gun lobby was shown yet again when the US Senate considered a bill which would give legal immunity to gun dealers and manufacturers in civil lawsuits. The NRA had lobbied hard for the bill, and it was passed by the House of Representatives in April 2003.

Things were not so easy in the Senate, however. In March 2004, anticipating that the bill would be passed, Democrat senators tacked on two amendments – renewing a ten-year ban on the sale and manufacture of assault weapons, and requiring background checks on customers at gun shows. So the NRA urged senators to vote against the amended bill. And they did; it was defeated 90 votes to eight. Democrat Senator Dianne Feinstein marvelled that the NRA "had the power to turn around at least 60 votes in the Senate. That's amazing to me."[15]

In September 2004, the assault weapon ban legislation lapsed – after Republican legislators failed to make time to vote on another proposed bill which would have extended the ban. This happened despite statements made by President George Bush during his 2004 campaign – in the third presidential debate he told millions of viewers that he believed the ban should have been extended.[16] Campaigners are now pressing for the ban to be reinstated, but for the moment, powerful assault weapons like AK-47s and Uzis will be legally sold and manufactured in the US.

The crazy thing is this: most Americans are in favor of tighter controls. Almost 80 percent of people think it is important to reduce children's access to guns, and 70 percent feel that more needs to be done to educate parents about keeping children safe from guns.[17] There is widespread support for several policies which would reduce the illegal sale of guns: 81 percent of people favored limiting sales to one handgun per person per month, 82 percent approved of mandatory registration of handguns, 77 percent agreed with background checks for private handgun sales.[18]

There is evidence, too, that tighter gun laws work. A 1976 law in Washington DC which virtually banned new handgun sales or ownership was associated in a 25 percent decline in gun homicides and suicides in the following decade. Litigation, especially on behalf of victims of gun crime, is also thought to be an effective tool.[19] The Brady Campaign to Prevent Gun Violence points to the keenness of schools to create "peanut-free zones" for children who are allergic, and the motor industry's willingness to install latches inside car trunks to prevent children getting trapped in them. Why should the gun industry be immune?

Both sides of the gun argument agree that children must not be allowed to have access to guns. The NRA points to its "Eddie Eagle" gun safety program for kids, and says that parents need to take responsibility to make sure their children are safe. Tighter regulation, it seems, is not the answer. In the wake of the Columbine shootings, the then president of the NRA Charlton Heston wrote to members, asking for "patience, prayers and presence...our spirits must endure this terrible suffering together, and so must the freedoms that bring us together."[20]

The other side argues that guns need to be kept out of kids' hands, and in order to do that, the law needs to be made watertight: under-21s should not be allowed to buy guns from any source, and there needs to be liability on gun-makers to make their guns difficult for children to use. The Brady Campaign argues that in the eighteen American states which have passed child access protection laws – which make gun owners criminally liable if children access their unsecured weapons – accidental deaths of children from firearms decreased by 23 percent.[21]

What makes children kill is a complex issue, not yet fully understood. Why do so many kids feel the need to take guns to school – and what makes a scant few, normal kids like James Sheets and John Jason McLaughlin, pull those guns out and start to shoot? Until we get closer to understanding these issues, it seems the least we can do is keep the guns out of children's hands. Perhaps the choice isn't between legislation on the one hand and greater personal responsibility on the other. Perhaps all sides have to agree to give up a few freedoms to prevent more school tragedies. It seems like most Americans want it – and it doesn't seem like a heavy price to pay.

There are at least 300,000 prisoners of conscience in the world

Wherever in the world you live, it can take courage to stand up for what you believe in. But in some countries, the simple act of declaring your beliefs, practicing your religion or expressing your pride in your ancestry can be considered a subversive and dangerous act, and the punishment can be severe. In 2002, some 35 countries were detaining confirmed or possible prisoners of conscience.[1] These people are often held in appalling conditions, sometimes tortured, and yet have committed no crime. They have done nothing more than peacefully express their own beliefs. And yet, in some countries, that is considered the worst crime of all.

It's estimated that there are some 300,000 prisoners of conscience currently detained in the world today. Many are political prisoners, detained without charge or trial, or held under "administrative detention." Their governments do this in direct violation of human rights laws. Their stories are all different, of course, but they all speak of a terrible repression, an attempt to deprive people of their right to be heard.

Take the case of gospel singer Helen Berhane, one of around 2,000 people arrested in Eritrea for being members of evangelical churches banned by the government. Her arrest came as the Eritrean authorities launched a crackdown; police and soldiers would break into religious services or weddings being held in private homes, arresting men, women and children. Shortly after releasing an album of Christian music, Helen Berhane was arrested and held without charge or trial for two-and-a-half years. Most of that time she spent locked up in a metal shipping container. She was tortured and beaten in attempts to make her renounce her faith. Released in October

2006, she was hospitalized after further beatings left her confined to a wheelchair.[2]

In some countries, there are activists who have spent most of their lives in some form of detention. Reporters Sans Frontières highlights the shameful case of Nguyen Dinh Huy, a Vietnamese journalist and pro-democracy activist who has spent only 21 months outside prison since the fall of Saigon in 1975. His last arrest came in November 1993 after he requested permission to hold a conference on democracy in Ho Chi Minh City. He was released in February 2005 but the 75-year-old remains under constant police surveillance, with all his telephone calls monitored and two policemen permanently stationed in his home.[3]

The former First Secretary of Syria's Communist Party Political Bureau Riad al-Turk was released in June 1998 after spending eighteen years in solitary confinement. For thirteen of those years, his wife said she did not know for sure where he was and was not allowed to see him. He told Amnesty International that he survived by forgetting about the outside world. He would pick tiny stones out of the lentil soup he was served daily and use them to form intricate shapes on the floor of his cell. "[You have to] find ways to kill time otherwise time will kill you." In 2001, he was detained again: President Bashar Al-Assad had encouraged political debate in the country for a time, but the arrests soon resumed, and al-Turk served another fifteen months in jail. At 76, he remains determined to fight for freedom and democracy.[4]

You might think that arrests on the ground of conscience might never happen in Western Europe, but you'd be wrong. In 2002 both Finland and Switzerland were reported to have detained people who had refused to take part in compulsory military service. Finns are required by law to serve six months in the armed forces. There is an option to do "alternative service," but it's more than twice as long as the military equivalent – hardly a fair option. Young men who refuse to do either form of service are frequently imprisoned and may spend up to 197 days in jail.[5] In Switzerland, Marino Keckeis served a five-month prison sentence after his request for conscientious objection was turned down.[6]

Many of the 35 countries that held prisoners of conscience in 2002 are signatories to the International Covenant on Civil and Political Rights (CCPR). States which have signed the CCPR promise to safeguard people's rights to freedom of thought, conscience and religion, to hold opinions without interference and to express themselves through any medium of their choice. But even if governments have not signed the CCPR or any other human rights instrument, the Universal Declaration of Human Rights powerfully states the case for those freedoms. The Universal Declaration is not a legally binding document, but it sets a "common standard of achievement for all states and all nations."[7] Although all UN members should do what they can to abide by the Declaration, it seems that some are falling far short.

The international community does have the ability to put pressure on states which are not respecting these most basic freedoms. Apart from the usual threats of sanctions and other diplomatic processes, the UN Commission on Human Rights has the ability to pass resolutions on key issues. The body meets once a year in Geneva and spends six weeks debating the human rights standards in various countries. But there are concerns that the Commission has been hijacked by a bloc of governments whose human rights records are less than exemplary. Human Rights Watch called these governments an "abusers' club": Algeria, Libya, Sudan, Syria and Zimbabwe joined forces with China, Cuba and Russia to oppose several important country initiatives. African governments joined forces to block condemnation of abuses in Zimbabwe and Sudan, and governments were even less outspoken in criticizing the worst violators.[8] In January 2003 the Commission elected Libya as its chair, despite a human rights record described as "appalling."[9] Although the 2003 Commission meeting did pass resolutions condemning abuses in North Korea and Turkmenistan for the first time, there are still concerns about its credibility and ability to properly address the world's most serious human rights problems.

Non-governmental groups continue to pressure governments to release prisoners of conscience and reform their human rights standards. Amnesty International is probably the best-known group, founded in 1961 when British civil rights lawyer Peter Benenson published an article in the *Observer* newspaper about people imprisoned due to their beliefs. Amnesty has since evolved to cover a broad spectrum of human rights issues, but it still places great emphasis on the huge achievements that can come from individual action. Writing to prisoners to let them know they are not forgotten, writing to governments to pressure them to let people walk free – a single letter may not achieve much on its own, but when they come in their thousands, things start to happen. In the words of Christine Anyanwu, a Nigerian journalist convicted of treason after a grossly unfair trial by military tribunal, "It is impossible to paint an accurate picture of the actions and reactions as I sat in that tiny cell, the floor carpeted with cards and envelopes. It was deeply touching, greatly encouraging and strengthening. Thereafter, I knew that I was not alone."[10]

In contrast to Amnesty's approach, Human Rights Watch seeks to "name and shame," highlighting repressive regimes by generating press coverage and enlisting governments into exerting diplomatic and economic pressure. There are a host of other human rights groups working in specific countries and even focusing on particular prisoners of conscience. The London-based Prisoners of Conscience Appeal Fund makes grants to prisoners of conscience and their families, helping them to rebuild their lives after they are released.[11]

As we marvel at the bravery of people who carry on their struggle in the face of repressive regimes, we should condemn the cowardly governments who think it is acceptable to lock up those who don't agree with their dictates. A strong and confident government may not like its critics, but it should be able to withstand a robust public debate. The right to be who you are and express what you feel is one of the most fundamental of human existence, and governments who lock up dissenters are showing contempt for all their citizens.

Get involved by writing a letter, raising money for a human rights group, voting for a government that will be strong on human rights issues. Freedom of belief and freedom of expression are far from universal. But, in the words of the Declaration of Human Rights, they are "the highest aspiration of the common people."

Two million girls and women are subjected to female genital mutilation each year

"Our parents told us it was an obligation, so we went. We fought back; we really thought we were going to die because of the pain. You have one woman holding your mouth so you won't scream, two holding your chest and the other two holding your legs. After we were infibulated, we had rope tied across our legs so it was like we had to learn to walk again ... the memory and the pain never really goes."[1]

This is 22-year-old Zainab's recollection of the day she underwent female genital mutilation (FGM). It's an extremely painful process that causes irreparable physical and psychological harm. It's a fundamental violation of the victim's human rights. And yet the World Health Organization (WHO) estimates that every year 2 million girls and women are subjected to it.

FGM takes many forms, but all of them involve cutting away some or all of a girl's genitalia. The most severe form is known as "infibulation" – part or all of a girl's clitoris and labia are cut away, and the vulval opening is joined with thorns or sewn up. A small opening is left so that urine and menstrual blood may pass out. Infibulation accounts for around 15 percent of all FGM. The most common form of FGM involves cutting away the clitoris and labia minora, and this constitutes up to 80 percent of FGM cases.[2]

FGM is practiced by followers of all religious beliefs. It is most routinely practised in Africa – 28 countries there are reported to carry out FGM – but it is also common among some groups in Asia and the Middle East, and in immigrant communities in Europe, Australia, Canada and the USA.[3] It is usually performed by a traditional practitioner using crude instruments and without anaesthetic. Sometimes the event is characterized as a rite of passage: the girls will be given gifts, and they will be told that after the procedure is complete they will have become women.

Families who have performed FGM on their daughters cite a variety of reasons for their decision. Some societies believe in limiting women's sexual desires in order to maintain chastity before marriage and fidelity after it. It can be seen as part of a group's cultural heritage, a ritual, a ceremony. Some believe it enhances fertility, while others cite reasons of hygiene and aesthetics – uncircumcised genitals are seen as "dirty" or "ugly" and a girl who is not circumcised will be considered unfit for marriage. She may be excluded from society, not regarded as a woman in some eyes, even barred from touching food or crops. Then, there are religious considerations. A minority of Muslims believe that their faith requires girls to be circumcised – though the process was established well before the birth of Islam and is not part of the faith.[4]

Due to the secrecy surrounding the practice in many countries and the reluctance of many women to discuss it, it is hard to tell how many women die as a result of FGM. It's hard even to get clear figures on how many have undergone the procedure, though the WHO estimates that between 100 and 140 million women have had some form of FGM.[5] But what is clear is that every single woman will have faced grave health risks in undergoing the procedure, and there are substantial long-term problems associated with it.

At the time the procedure is carried out, a girl suffers severe pain and risks shock, hemorrhage or blood poisoning. FGM is often performed in unsanitary environments with equipment that has been used on other girls, resulting in infections and possible HIV/AIDS transmission. In the long term, the woman may find sex painful and unpleasant. She may suffer scarring and pelvic infections. Where a woman has been infibulated, the retention of urine or menstrual blood can lead to chronic infection. When she first attempts inter-course with her husband, she may need to be "cut," and further operations may be needed before she can give birth.[6] And this is to say nothing of the psychological scars that FGM can leave.

There is no doubt about it: cutting the genitals of girls and women is a barbaric practice which must be stopped. The complexity of the problem and the secrecy surrounding it call for a careful approach, though. It is easy to demonize people and societies that practice FGM; it is much harder to effect the kind of change in attitudes that will see those societies reject it for themselves. But if we are serious about stopping FGM, that's what we must do.

A number of brave women are daring to speak out against FGM in new and unusual ways. When Genet Girma married Addisie Abosie in her home of Kembatta, Ethiopia, in January 2003, she made her stand on circumcision clear – and public. The bride and groom accessorized their outfits with placards around their necks. Genet's read: "I am not circumcised. Learn from me." Addisie's sign declared: "I am very happy to be marrying an uncircumcised woman." The wedding was broadcast on Ethiopian television, and though the families did not attend because they objected to Genet's uncircumcised status, some 2,000 friends showed their support. Genet was the first "uncut" girl from the region to marry. Bogaletch Gebre of the Kembatta Women's Self-Help Center said that it had opened up a debate in the country. "In the area that [Genet and Addisie] come from young girls do not even say the words "female circumcision," it is simply known as "removing the dirt" ... now young men and women are really listening. There has been an amazing ripple effect ... it has opened doors of courage."[7]

For Beatrice and Edna Kandie, the law proved an instrument of protection. With the help of human rights activist Ken Wafula, the sisters from the Rift Valley Province in Kenya secured a permanent injunction against their father Pius Kandie, preventing him from circumcising his daughters. Kenya's President, Daniel Arap Moi, declared the practice of FGM illegal in 2001, although he said that for girls over sixteen it was "their choice." The practice is still wide-spread, though, and by January 2003 Wafula said he had helped seventeen other girls obtain their own injunctions against their parents. The Kandie sisters now tour schools, telling girls their story and educating them about FGM.

Groups like Equality Now believe that FGM needs to be treated as a human rights issue. It needs to be viewed just as any other form of violence against women would be: as a fundamental assault on personal dignity and as an attempt to stifle women's voices and power.[8] The concept of women's equality, integrity and representation is not a Western construct, and viewed in this context, it's easier to deal with arguments that the West is imposing its views on other cultures. As a joint WHO and UN statement puts it, "Culture is not static but it is in constant flux, adapting and reforming. People will change their behavior when they understand the hazards and indignity of harmful practices and when they realize that it is possible to give up harmful practices without giving up meaningful aspects of their culture."[9]

Legislating against FGM is crucial, but states also need to make sure that their laws are enforced. In Tanzania, for example, mass circumcisions still occur despite legal prohibition, and there are reports that the government has refused to press charges even when girls have bled to death after FGM.[10] It is also thought that criminalization can drive the process underground, particularly in countries where FGM occurs among immigrant communities. Legislation must go hand-in-hand with community-based education programs aimed at raising awareness of the practice and the arguments against it.

Community activists are best placed to determine how best to raise such a difficult issue and encourage discussion. Even in relatively educated Western societies it can be difficult and embarrassing to talk about sex; imagine the difficulties in communities where sexual taboos are strong and women may not know how (or to whom) they can talk about their bodies. In Mali, local pop stars were encouraged to write songs about FGM, while in Tanzania children took to the streets to demonstrate against it. Non-governmental organizations have engaged health workers and religious leaders in the discussion, as well as training people who perform FGM in other skills so their livelihoods will not be lost.[11]

There are signs that these campaigns are starting to have an effect. Activists in Eritrea point to national health surveys which show that prevalence of FGM fell from 95 percent in 1995 to 89 percent in 2002. Among the youngest group surveyed – fifteen to nineteen year olds – 78 percent were circumcised, and 60 percent believed the practice should be stopped.[12] In Togo, officials claim that FGM rates have fallen since the government enacted legislation against it in 1998,[13] while in several countries women's groups are encouraging new forms of "rites of passage" celebrations which don't involve any kind of cutting.

In 1997, the WHO, UNICEF and the UN Population Fund unveiled a joint plan to completely eradicate the practice of FGM in three generations. Campaigners are still optimistic that this can be achieved. The most important task is to change attitudes and convince people that they can dispense with FGM without harming their culture. Bogaletch Gebre sums it up: "We are each other's keepers. We must be each other's supporters, for whenever one of us is hurt or violated, all of us are violated."[14]

There are 300,000 child soldiers fighting in conflicts around the world

"Early on when my brothers and I were captured, the Lord's Resistance Army (LRA) explained to us that all five brothers couldn't serve in the LRA because we would not perform well. So they tied up my two younger brothers and invited us to watch. Then they beat them with sticks until the two of them died. They told us it would give us strength to fight. My youngest brother was nine years old."[1]

Imagine the life of a typical eight-year-old in an affluent Western country: going to school, making friends, playing in team sports, maybe learning a musical instrument. Then imagine the life of an eight-year-old child soldier. Abducted, barred from seeing family and friends, brutalized and forced into a life of active combat: this is the reality for more than 300,000 children who fight either for rebel forces or for government armies.

Children under eighteen are fighting in almost every region of the world; they have participated in on-going or recent conflicts in some 33 countries,[2] and child combatants are thought to have been involved in three-quarters of the world's wars.

For unscrupulous armies, child soldiers are a potent resource. Often poor, displaced or separated from their families, children whose communities are involved in violent conflict are easy prey for recruiters. Armies will try to manipulate children, promising them food or shelter or respect, drawing them into conflicts which they are too young to understand.

A small child may start as a porter, perhaps a spy. As soon as they are old enough to carry a gun, the children will be deployed in the conflict. The massive proliferation of small arms means that children can be turned into a lethal force. Human Rights Watch reports that many child soldiers will be forced to the front lines or sent into minefields ahead of adults. They may be forced to commit atrocities against their own families or villages, ensuring they are never able to return – a disgraceful way of buying loyalty.[3] Both boys and girls are recruited. It's hard to accurately calculate the number of young girl soldiers, but many armed groups are thought to be increasing their recruitment of young girls. The Coalition to Stop the Use of Child Soldiers reports that in Sri Lanka, the opposition Liberation Tigers of Tamil Eelam (LTTE) systematically recruit young Tamil girls (especially orphans) to fight against government forces in the civil war. The girls are named "Birds of Freedom" by their colleagues, and government sources claim that the girls are deliberately trained as suicide bombers because they are more likely to evade security forces.[4] Girls may also be given to military commanders as "wives."

Burma is believed to have more child soldiers than any other country in the world.[5] More than a fifth of its 350,000-strong national army are believed to be under eighteen, and children as young as eleven have been forcibly recruited. Boys are frequently apprehended at bus and railway stations, markets and vehicle checkpoints and given a stark choice: join the army or go to jail. Soldiers who bring in new recruits are given cash and rice as a reward, so more and more are turning to the business of finding new blood. Banned from contacting their families, these child recruits are subjected to a humiliating and brutalizing training process, after which they are made to engage in combat. Boys who try to escape are frequently beaten to death.[6]

What these children are made to see is horrific, stomach-churning even to read about, absolutely impossible to imagine in the flesh. One boy told Human Rights Watch about an army massacre he witnessed: "We captured about fifteen women and children ... three babies and four others who were under eighteen. They took the babies away from their mothers. We gathered them in one place and sent a report to headquarters by radio ... the order that came over the radio was to kill them all. Then six of the corporals loaded their guns and shot them ... the soldiers were holding the babies and the babies were crying. Two of them were less than a year old, maybe nine or ten months ... after the mothers were killed, they killed the babies. Three of the privates killed them. They swung them by their legs and smashed them against a rock. I saw it." Khin Maung Than was aged thirteen at the time.[7]

Children are used as an expendable commodity, less valuable perhaps than more highly trained adults, more likely to venture headlong into dangerous situations because they're just too young to understand the risks. One armed group commander in the Democratic Republic of Congo says children make good fighters "because they're young and want to show off. They think it's all a game, so they're fearless."[8]

In the DRC, tens of thousands of children have fought in the bloody conflict which has claimed more than 3 million lives since 1998. Despite the appointment of a power-sharing government in July 2003 and a planned transition to peace, Amnesty International reports that recruitment of children has in fact increased in some areas in the east.[9] Even though the international community and non-governmental organizations have made efforts to demobilize some child soldiers, it is a difficult task and the massive impact on the country's infrastructure means that schools have been destroyed and jobs are scarce. Brutalized communities may be unable to cope with the returning fighters, and many are drawn back into the conflict.

Even if suitable opportunities are available, the psychological scars can take years to heal. At the age of just fifteen, Kalami had spent six years of his life fighting in different armed groups. After a particularly disturbing battle where he and his colleagues burned people alive in their homes and were forced to kill and eat a family, he decided to escape, and was eventually demobilized. "Today, I am afraid. I don't know how to read, I don't know where my family is, I have no future. The worst is during the day when I think about my future. My life is lost. I have nothing to live for. At night I can no longer sleep – I keep thinking of those horrible things I have seen and done when I was a soldier."[10]

As the nature of modern war changes and the large military powers increasingly find themselves confronted with small militia groups working to destabilize tense situations, it is becoming more and more likely that children will be deployed against highly equipped soldiers from the West. It was reported that the first American serviceman to die in combat during Operation Enduring Freedom in Afghanistan was killed by a fourteen-year-old boy,[11] and one senior American general called confrontations with child soldiers "about as tough an issue as we can deal with."[12]

Clearly, the issue of child soldiers is one that the international community must solve, and soon. Groups working with child soldiers emphasize the importance of international law in trying to discourage both states and non-state armed groups from recruiting children. Earlier statutes, like the additional protocols to the Geneva Convention, had set a minimum age limit of fifteen – but the most recent instrument, the Optional Protocol to the Convention on the Rights of the Child on the Involvement of Children in Armed Conflict (which we will refer to here, for the sake of brevity, as the Optional Protocol), sets a minimum age limit of eighteen for compulsory recruitment, and requires that states who have signed the convention take all feasible measures to ensure that those under eighteen do not take a direct part in hostilities. It also proscribes any recruitment – voluntary or otherwise – of under-eighteens by non-state armed groups.

At the time of writing, 115 states had signed the Optional Protocol and 66 had ratified it. Groups campaigning against the use of child soldiers are calling for governments to go one step further and establish a minimum age of eighteen for all recruitment.

Getting non-state actors to comply with international law can be difficult, but as many of these groups are seeking international legitimacy for their causes, they may be more open to suggestions that they comply. Jo Becker of Human Rights Watch notes that a lot of the commitments to stop recruiting child soldiers have not been implemented: "It's sometimes a problem of political will and sometimes practical resources. Some groups are cynical and think that their commitment will get good press but they have no intention to implement it – like the FARC group in Colombia, or the Tamil Tigers in Sri Lanka. There are other groups who want to make these commitments but don't have the ability. We spoke to a general in the Karenni army in Burma and he said that his group would like to abide by the international protocol but it is hard to get support because no one recognizes them as a legal organization."[13]

The UN is clear that all parties to a conflict must be involved in the dialogue: in January 2003 the UN Security Council adopted a new resolution on children in armed conflict, including an explicit list of 23 groups in five conflict situations which it intended to target. As well as these five conflicts – Afghanistan, Burundi, the DRC, Liberia and Somalia – the resolution called for progress reports from a number of other conflicts. Human Rights Watch applauded the move but said that dialogue needs to be systematic, and the UN needs to make clear the consequences if groups fail to make progress.[14]

UN Secretary-General Kofi Annan noted that children in conflict zones are already at risk – from displacement, landmines, deprivation of education and essential healthcare, from use as forced labor and sexual exploitation. "These outrages continue to be perpetrated against children in far too many places in defiance of the international community," he told the Security Council. "The time has come to ensure that the hard-won gains in crafting a protection regime for children are applied and put into practice on the ground."[15]

For every one of the 300,000 child soldiers currently fighting, a childhood has been lost. Those who are lucky will escape with their lives, left with a legacy of guilt and shame, faced with a monumental task of rebuilding their lives and trying to make up for the lost years. We must continue to name and shame governments and armed groups recruiting children, and keep up the pressure on our countries to sign and ratify the Optional Protocol. Support non-governmental organizations working to end child involvement in war, and write letters to governments urging them to do what they can.

A fifteen-year-old girl who had escaped from the Lord's Resistance Army in Uganda told researchers that she wanted to give them a message. "Please do your best to tell the world what is happening to us, the children. So that other children don't have to pass through this violence."[16] Let's not fail her.

Nearly 26 million people voted in the 2001 British General Election. More than 32 million votes were cast in the first season of *Pop Idol*

In the final week of the first season of the British reality TV program *Pop Idol*, the field of young hopefuls had been ruthlessly culled to just two pretenders to the throne of pop. Will Young, a clean-cut politics graduate, was up against Gareth Gates, a former cathedral chorister, and the debate over who would win provided Britain with water-cooler conversation material for days. The two young men took to the streets of Britain wearing election-style rosettes, encouraging their supporters to "Vote Will" or "Vote Gareth." Young emerged the eventual victor, in a frenzied night when nearly 9 million people cast their votes in just over three hours, bringing Britain's telephone system to near-collapse. Had he not won the competition, Young had reportedly said he would like to go into politics.

The irony of this faux-electioneering was particularly bitter for those who would like to see Britain's young people show similar enthusiasm for real politics. During *Pop Idol*'s twenty-week run, more than 32 million votes were cast.[1] According to Britain's Electoral Commission, 25.9 million people voted in the 2001 General Election – the turnout of just below 60 percent was the lowest since 1918.[2] Now, it's important to remember that each voter in a general election is allowed to place just one vote, while in *Pop Idol* people could place as many votes as they liked (or as their phone bill would allow). But it does show one very important fact:

when people are interested in the outcome of a vote, they'll make sure they have their say.

In 1950, 84 percent of Britons turned out to vote – but since then, the number of people choosing to vote in elections has steadily declined. Young people are among the least likely to turn out on election day. The polling organization MORI estimated that in the 2001 election, just 39 percent of 18–24 year olds voted, compared with 70 percent of 65 year olds.[3] It's a trend that is reflected across the world: young people are not voting. In the US Presidential Election of 2000 – one of the closest races in history – just 29 percent of eligible voters aged 18–24 voted, compared with a turnout rate of 55 percent overall.[4] Japan's 2003 House of Representatives election returned the second-lowest turnout ever, and just over a half of people under 30 regularly vote in elections. In the words of one 29-year-old man, "Voting is a waste of time. I am sick of politicians who never change anything in Japan for the better."[5]

In the June 2004 European Parliament elections, less than a third of voters aged between 18 and 24 actually did so[6] – although, to be fair, the electoral turnout for all ages across the EU was so low that European officials called it "pathetically low" and a "disaster."[7] Only 8 percent of young voters said they were "close" to a political group and a worrying 30 percent said they never voted.[8] And this was despite a bizarre array of tactics by political parties across the EU. In Estonia, a political party served coffee at bus stops, British political parties printed their message on beer-mats ("I drink, therefore I vote"), and a daily newspaper in Brussels attempted to explain the inner workings of the parliament in comic-strip form.[9]

Even in South Africa, where a little more than a decade ago many were still fighting and dying for their right to vote, young people do not feel the political process is worth their time. Low rates of voter registration shocked the country's Independent Electoral Commission, but on the streets of Soweto, there was little surprise. Twenty-year-old Tumi Phana does not trust politicians: he says they forget the promises they have made, especially to provide jobs and health-care, and when they get into power they ask people to work for nothing. "There is no honesty. How could you volunteer on an empty stomach? I will not vote; I will not fall for their schemes."[10]

In Britain, the poor turnout among young voters has alarmed the political establishment. MORI's poll for the Electoral Commission showed that a high proportion of young people professed to have no interest in politics at all, while in a BBC poll of non-voters in 2001, 77 percent said there was no point voting because "it would not change a thing."[11] The Electoral Commission quoted arguments that politics is no longer about fundamental ideological differences, but about technical points like entry into the European single currency and the way public transport is owned and funded. Some say that young people's distrust of politicians relates more to the conduct of party politics than the issues at stake; others suggest that voting and participation in politics are no longer seen as a duty.[12]

In the run-up to the 2004 American presidential election, politicians on both sides of the race actively tried to woo young voters. The music channel MTV supported campaigns like Rock the Vote and Choose or Lose, aiming to get young people to register to vote. Musicians like P Diddy reached out to the hip-hop generation, while actress Cameron Diaz fronted commercials aimed at the Latino population.

On election day, though, young people voted in their millions. More than 20 million cast a ballot for president, an increase of 4.6 million on the 2000 election. In fact, turnout was increased across the board: more than 120 million Americans voted in 2004, compared with 105 million in the 2000 election. MTV reported that young voters now believe that their voices can make a difference.[13]

This feeling about a single vote actually being a powerful force for change could be the solution to apathy in young voters. Before the 2004 election, the US-based Center for Information and Research on Civic Learning and Engagement (CIRCLE) published research about how young people participate in the broader political spectrum.

The July 2003 survey found that most young Americans have never contacted a public official (80.9 percent), written to a newspaper or magazine (82 percent) or taken part in a protest or demonstration (84.4 percent). But just over half of people aged 15–25 said they had boycotted a product or brand because of "conditions under which the product is made," and 40 percent said they had taken part in events to raise money for charitable causes.[14]

The CIRCLE research noted that young people are choosing to express their views in ways that they feel will have a real effect: "Mass activities such as the 'Race For The Cure' or the 'AIDS ride' place participants in large groups of like-minded people where participants can "see" themselves making a difference."[15] And perhaps for the first time, young voters in the 2004 election felt that their vote counted.

So what can the rest of the world learn from the American experience? If young people feel they have a stake in the outcome of an election – whether it's deciding who leads the country, or who will have a practically inescapable hit record – they will vote. The challenge is to make politics seem relevant and worthwhile.

Among the reforms being considered by the British government is lowering the voting age to sixteen. Government sources believe that a lower voting age could help build on citizenship and politics lessons at school.[16] A survey by the Nestlé Family Monitor showed that more than half of young people would like the voting age to be lowered, but in the same survey 45 percent said they were not interested in learning about how the political system works.[17]

Some countries are trialling alternative means of voting – using mobile phones to send text messages, voting by phone, through digital television or online. The Electoral Commission cites research that shows young people would be particularly likely to favor changes that made voting more convenient.[18] The first binding Internet voting system was used in Democratic primaries in Arizona, and turnout jumped by more than 600 percent – though only 41 percent of those voting did so through the Internet.[19] Several local councils in the UK experimented with different voting methods in the May 2003 local elections, and the government has set a target of an "e-enabled" general election some time after 2006.

Young people's concerns that politicians are untrustworthy or don't speak to their generation may be harder to address. Many politicians are already using the internet to reach out to younger voters: at the time of writing, the candidates for the 2008 Democratic presidential nomination are taking their battle to the YouTube video-sharing website. One video, featuring Senator Hillary Rodham Clinton singing the US national anthem in less-than-tuneful style, has received over a million hits, while a search for Barack Obama yields more than 1,600 videos. In the UK, Conservative party leader David Cameron has launched his "webcameron," featuring a day-in-the-life-style blog and a video segment called "Ask David."

But it's not just a question of creating pages on MySpace and making party political broadcasts look like music videos. Political parties need to make sure the young voters in their electorates receive all the information they need to understand the issues, perhaps fielding a few younger candidates, thinking about ways in which old-style politics can adapt to a new-style generation – rather than the other way round.

Preaching at young people about the need to honor hard-won freedoms won't work, and nor will making them feel bad about not playing a part in society. Rather than seeking to drive them back to the ballot box, the ballot box could come to them – offering them a chance to have their say on real, vital issues in a way that is convenient for them. Politics isn't boring; the challenge is for politicians to make the announcement of the budget as relevant to everyday life as who'll grab the Christmas number one.

One in six English teenagers believe that reality television will make them famous

There's some debate about who invented reality television: some say it started in the late 1940s with *Candid Camera*, in which members of the public would become involved in pranks staged by the TV crew; others believe that the late-80s American show *COPS* was the first to introduce the television viewing audience to real life in all its griminess, filmed on a hand-held camera.[1] But for most people, it feels like reality television began with *Big Brother*. The show, which first aired in the UK in 2000, has since been duplicated in more than 70 countries.

Big Brother's format – a number of strangers living in a communal house where they are under constant surveillance, and where the public are invited to evict contestants until an eventual winner is found – proved a commercial stroke of genius for the show's creator John de Mol. The show made him a billionaire and catapulted him into the *Forbes* list of the world's richest people. And some of the show's contestants haven't done too badly either, securing lucrative jobs as television presenters.

In January 2006, England's Learning and Skills Council released a survey that showed how hungry English teenagers are for this kind of fame. More than one in ten young people said they would drop out of school to be on television, and more than one in six believed that they would actually become famous on a reality TV show. When asked why they were so keen – despite the odds of actually winning *Big Brother* and becoming successful being around one in 300 million – one in ten teen respondents said they thought fame was a great way to earn money without getting any skills and qualifications.[2]

At the time, an aspirant reality TV star could have sought no better role model than Jade Goody. The former dental nurse from London was a contestant on the third series of *Big Brother* UK. She didn't win, but in the course of the competition managed to secure a place in viewers' hearts as an entertaining young woman who thought Rio de Janeiro was a football player and Saddam Hussein was a boxer. A procession of TV shows, tabloid interviews, fitness DVDs, an autobiography and even a bestselling perfume later, Goody had amassed a personal wealth estimated at some £8 million.[3]

Of course, in January 2007, Goody's celebrity currency imploded on the *Celebrity Big Brother* show, when she was accused of racist bullying of another contestant, Bollywood actress Shilpa Shetty. And the truth is that very few reality television contestants have managed to build lasting careers out of their brush with fame. All the same, for a teenager who's not sure what they want to do with their life, the existence of a modern celebrity looks good. You don't have to be good at sports, or clever, or a good singer – you are just famous because you're famous. Abigail Clancy, a contestant on *Britain's Next Top Model*, seemed to sum it up when she told the show's producers that her ambition was to "marry a footballer, get pregnant and then shop and have fun for the rest of her life."[4]

Why would an attractive, intelligent young woman decide that her aim in life was to become one of the WAGs – the tabloid collective term for the wives and girlfriends of the England football squad? Why would so many young people trade in their education for a chance at a very limited sort of fame? It might just be because they suspect this is their best chance at getting the things that they crave: wealth, acceptance and financial security. Because for a lot of kids, these things seem well out of reach.

In early 2007, UNICEF released a league table of 21 industrialized countries which aimed to look at child well-being. The study looked at a huge variety of indicators: from literacy rates to teenage pregnancy, from the number of times families sit down together to eat dinner to teens smoking and drinking. The UK came bottom out of all 21 countries, prompting the Children's Society head Bob

Reitemeier to say that the UK was failing its young people.[5] The Children's Commissioner for England, Professor Sir Al Aynsley-Green, said that this generation of young people are "unhappy, unhealthy, engaging in risky behaviour, have poor relationships with their family and their peers, low expectations and don't feel safe."[6] One of the authors of the report pointed to decades of under-investment in Britain's children and a "dog-eat-dog" society. Professor Jonathan Bradshaw of York University pointed out that Britain's society is very unequal, with high levels of poverty (albeit poverty defined in relative terms) – and that this fed into children's perceptions of their lives.[7]

As we've seen elsewhere in this book, child poverty in Britain is falling – but one in three children still live in poverty, and the government will struggle to hit its target of halving the number of children in poverty by 2010. Economists also note that social mobility in Britain is slowing, and is likely to slow further.

A child born in 1970 in the UK is less likely to have escaped their class origins than a child born twelve years earlier.[8] Roughly three-quarters of working-class boys born in the middle of the 20th century were likely to have found themselves in a higher class by the age of 35. This was largely because of the huge changes in British society after the end of the Second World War. The business and finance sectors expanded enormously, creating a wealth of white-collar and clerical jobs; farming, mining and manufacturing – once huge employers of working-class people – declined, and continue to do so. It's unlikely that such massive social upheaval will occur again.[9] And with this slowing in mobility comes a sense that it is harder and harder for young working-class people to escape their origins. No wonder so many kids want a comparatively easy route to fame and fortune.

In the US, where matters of class are traditionally thought to be harder to define, things aren't much better. Inequality is growing there too: America's top 1 percent of earners now receive 16 percent of all income, twice what they did in 1980.[10] It's generally thought that

Americans will accept inequality if they think it goes hand-in-hand with opportunity – this, in fact, is probably the foundation of the famous American Dream. But a study by three prominent US economists found that those opportunities are getting harder and harder to come by. At all levels of society, the researchers found that sons retained the same levels of income and occupational prestige as their fathers. One of the study's authors, Professor Robert Perrucci, sums it up: "What has happened in the last 25 years is that a large segment of American society has become more vulnerable. Twenty years ago, going to college was enough. Now, it has to be an elite school. The American dream is being sorely tested." One-fifth of Americans are privileged, with job security, high wages and strong skills; the other 80 percent belong to a "new working class," Perruci believes, that lacks any security.[11]

Given all this, it's easy to see why celebrity seems to be such a feasible short-cut to riches. But it's much harder to figure out what we can do about this, and how we can encourage our young people to find different kinds of role models. As the Learning and Skills Council pointed out when releasing their survey, getting good exam results and securing a place in some kind of training or university program is far more likely than a reality TV role to lead to a decent salary and long-term financial success.[12]

In November 2005, the government's Social Exclusion Unit estimated that there were 1.1 million people between the ages of 16 and 24 who were not in any kind of education or training and were not in a job.[13] The Education Secretary Alan Johnson has said it is "repellent" that sixteen-year-olds might be in this situation, adding that he regretted not staying on at school himself and that "when I left school there were loads of jobs you could walk into without qualifications. That's not going to be the case in the future."[14]

How to get kids to realize that good grades, rather than a good agent, are the thing to aim for? Britain has introduced the Education Maintenance Allowance which pays children over sixteen from low-income families to stay in education or training. The EMA can be worth up to £30 a week, and students who do well in their studies can earn bonuses.[15] Other programs reward students with days out, music downloads or free computer games: Manchester's Motiv scheme rewards students who have a 100 percent school attendance record.[16]

In the US, sports teams like the NBA's Los Angeles Clippers run programs encouraging kids to stay in education by offering college scholarships,[17] while Dell Computers' Techknow project gives students a free computer when they complete a 40-hour IT course. One school area director says that it's helped kids realize the value of staying at school and achieving success in an area they might have thought was beyond their reach.[18]

Schools and education administrators need to take these ideas and be inspired to come up with more. Mentoring schemes and work experience programs – in which kids can go out into the community and learn about career choices first-hand – are important. Schools could build better contacts with employers and colleges in the community and encourage promising students to take on extra projects in areas that interest them. There's also a need to teach subjects like entrepreneurship at school level; it's currently common to have courses like this at university business schools, but all students could benefit from learning that business can lead to the same riches and acclaim as showbusiness.

Despite their dreams of reality television fame, Britain's young people do select some more heartening role models. The Learning and Skills Council asked their young respondents who they most aspire to be like. Their top choice was the entrepreneur Sir Richard Branson – second in line was the Harry Potter author J.K. Rowling. And almost one in twenty said they'd like to be like former British Prime Minister Tony Blair. Their responses about whether they'd like to emulate the then Chancellor of the Exchequer, Gordon Brown, were not recorded. But the man widely thought of as the prime-minister-in-waiting has already expressed his views on modern celebrity culture; he believes its time is up.

In April 2007 Mr. Brown told reporters that he thinks Britain is "moving from this period when, if you like, celebrity matters, when people have become famous for being famous ... people are moving away from that to what lies behind the character and the personality."[19]

As with all politicians, there may be an element of self-serving in this statement; Mr. Brown used this argument to hit back at critics who jibed at his rather dour and serious public image. But perhaps there's more in this than trying to persuade voters that our next prime minister might enjoy a joke. Modern Britain seems to be more about style than substance – it might just be time for the pendulum to swing back the other way.

In 2005, the US spent $554 billion on its military. This is 29 times the combined military spending of the six "rogue states"

Forget hunger, forget poverty, forget disease. If we can determine the true values of humankind through purely financial means, the most important issue in our modern world is defence. The world spends an unthinkable amount of money on its armies, navies and air forces. The Stockholm International Peace Research Institute (SIPRI) estimated that in 2005, world military expenditure was $1.118 billion – up 3.4 percent in real terms from 2004.[1] That's $173 for every person on Earth. Look at it another way: every hour of every day, the world spends more than $127 million on its military.

By far the biggest military spender is the USA. In the 2005 fiscal year, the US military budget request was $554 billion. For 2007, $626.1 billion was requested How can we make sense of such enormous figures? Let's try a few comparisons. Global Issues tracks worldwide military spending. According to its estimates, the US spends over seven times more than China, which is number two on the military expenditure list. In fact, the US spends more than the next fourteen countries combined. When considered together with its NATO partners, and Australia, Japan and South Korea, the US and its close allies spend far more than the rest of the world put together – more than two-thirds of all military spending. And compared with the six "rogue states," the US might is dazzling. America's military expenditure is more than 29 times the combined budgets of Cuba, Iran, Libya, North Korea, Sudan and Syria.[2]

From these figures alone, it's easy to see why so many now

consider the world to have just one global superpower. The US military is lavishly funded, hugely capable.

In 1985, at the height of the Cold War, the world spent $1.2 trillion on defense.[3] Through the late 1980s and 90s, spending slowly declined – but since September 11, 2001, that trend has reversed. And as the global "war on terrorism" shows no sign of being won, it's likely that spending will continue to increase.[4] The US administration plans to spend $2.7 trillion on the military over the next six years.[5]

How is the US's vast spending allocated? The Center for Arms Control and Non-Proliferation breaks it down: $98.6 billion will be spent on personnel (including pay increases); $117 billion on operations and maintenance; and a massive $135 billion on research and procurement – which covers inventing and purchasing new weapons. Christopher Hellman of the CDI points out that the costs of military operations in Afghanistan and Iraq are not included in the defence budget, and nor, for the most part, is homeland security.[6]

In fact, at a time when the US economy faces huge budget deficits, many are arguing that the US defense budget could be better spent. As President Bush signed the National Defense Authorization Act for Fiscal Year 2004 into law, he declared: "The bill I sign today ... [will] prepare our military for all that lies ahead. We will do whatever it takes to keep our nation strong, to keep the peace, and to keep the American people secure."[7] At the same time, Senator John McCain told reporters that the military were still trying to "rip off taxpayers" and that "this incestuous relationship between the contractors and the Pentagon and the lawmakers is just the worst." Senator McCain pointed out that $9.1 billion was being poured into missile defense programmes that were still not operational.[8] One analyst said that the military was still thinking in a Cold War mindset: "The vast majority of the funding is going to traditional programs, rather than transformational ones."[9]

The military think tank, the Center for Defense Information, argues that really, there is no need for the US to develop such advanced new weapons systems – because no other nation is currently developing weapons that are as sophisticated.[10] In fact, the Pentagon has given its permission for arms developers to sell their newest technology overseas almost as soon as it is off the production line. This export of high-tech weaponry has pushed the US into what is effectively an arms race with itself. The Council for a Livable World points out that the export of top-line combat equipment decreases the US's relative military strength, and this in turn leads "politicians, the military and the defense industry to press for higher military spending to procure increasingly sophisticated equipment superior to weapons shipped overseas. This latest technology is again offered to foreign customers, and the cycle begins anew."[11]

This faux arms race encourages smaller nations to invest in high-tech military equipment that they can ill afford. The Amnesty International and Oxfam International "Shattered Lives" report reveals that nearly half of the countries with the highest defense burden have low indicators of human development: Eritrea spends nearly 20 percent of its GDP on the military. Sometimes, this investment may prove to be a waste of money. Tanzania spent $40 million on a joint civil-military air traffic control system in 2001–2 which was reportedly overpriced and inappropriate for its use.[12]

As military spending looks certain to increase, we would do well to consider how the US's massive military might is affecting the global balance of power. At the time of writing the situation in Iraq was fragile, with armed insurgent groups launching terrorist-style attacks on allied forces and international institutions. These tactics point to a new type of war – strategies which experts term "asymmetric threats." Rather than two roughly equivalent fighting forces meeting head to head along front lines, the wars of the future will most likely pit small organized groups against large nations. These groups will identify weaknesses in the established armies and ruthlessly pursue them.

It remains to be seen whether the new technology that the US military seeks to develop will be any use against possible aggressors in an asymmetric-style war. The International Institute of Strategic Studies (IISS) points out that since the US effectively deprived

Al-Qaeda of its Afghanistan base, the military aspect to counter-terrorism operations has decreased. Now, terrorist groups are more likely to be dispersed across numbers of countries and thus there are few traditional targets for the military to strike at. The IISS predicts that "the true transformation of the US military is not just a question of obtaining more advanced weapon systems, but also changing the culture of the armed forces, the way they think and their battlefield operations."[13]

Some argue that if the US really wants more money to be diverted towards researching and building new weaponry, it need not ask for more from the American taxpayer: it could save money by reducing its overseas presence, and by not feeling obliged to intervene in so many other countries.[14] The prospect of a hugely armed sole superpower could have grave consequences for arms control. Nations will seek to build up their military power to become less dependent upon the US, and better able to cope with the regional instability that results.[15] It was ever thus: the bigger your gun, the louder your voice. And the guns being purchased with President Bush's $554 billion are very big indeed.

If the world continues to make military spending its biggest priority, then the money has to come from somewhere. Many groups are concerned that health, education and the environment will suffer, and many poorer nations will continue to put the wellbeing of their armies at a higher priority than the development of their people. It's tempting to think about what we could do with that $1.118 billion. It would cost $15 billion a year to provide basic primary healthcare to all the world's people, about $2 billion to fund famine relief and sustainable agriculture programs and about $5 billion to provide a basic education for all.[16]

It's not hard to conceive of a world where development and wellbeing are made a bigger priority than developing new weapons whose sole purpose is to intimidate, maim and kill. It just requires a new way of thinking: looking again at our preconceptions of what weapons are necessary to guarantee security and how best to combat the enemies who are likely to attack us. Increasingly, the military are meeting opponents who are not intimidated by their staggering arsenals – instead, they view them as an affront and a challenge. By addressing some of the causes of their anger – the perception of Western superiority in the face of their own poverty and deprivation – we may find the greatest weapon of peace.

There are 27 million slaves in the world today

"A man came to the [refugee] camp and chose us; I was taken in a car with five other girls to a house in a place called Khartoum. He would not let us out. We had to work all day. One by one the girls were taken away ... One day a woman came and took me away. I had to do very hard work, I had to do everything: clean the house and big yard, wash clothes by hand and look after her children; [over time] there were five ... I started to play with the children ... I liked to play, I was still a child; they took my childhood. Before, I was in school, now I am not ... I was beaten for every single thing."[1]

Mende was twelve when she was forced to flee her village in Sudan because of the civil war. Recruited from a refugee camp, she spent the next six or seven years as a slave. Eventually, brought to London to work for her mistress, she escaped. This sounds like a story from the late 19th century, but sadly, it isn't. Slavery is happening right now in Sudan, a country ravaged by civil war, where slave traders prey on vulnerable, displaced people. Mende is one of an estimated 14,000 people who have been forced into slavery in Sudan since 1986.[2]

The word "slave" speaks of something barbaric, something shameful in the history of humankind. It seems to be as old as society itself. In ancient cultures, slaves were often prisoners of war. Much of the wealth of classical Athens came from silver mines worked by slaves. In pre-Islamic Arabia, slaves would boast specialized skills: eunuchs, concubines, artists. In medieval Europe, serfs would work land for their masters.

Slavery in Africa was widespread, and the traffic of African slaves to other countries began before the Middle Ages. It reached a peak in the late 18th century, when slaves from West Africa were transported in huge numbers to the New World colonies. It is estimated that some 13 million people were shipped as slaves from Africa.[3]

Slavery was finally abolished in Britain in 1838, and in the US in 1865 (by the Thirteenth Amendment to the US Constitution). The 1926 Slavery Convention outlawed slavery around the world. Article 2 made the position very clear: all parties undertake "to prevent and suppress the slave trade ... [and] to bring about, progressively and as soon as possible, the complete abolition of slavery in all its forms." Then, in 1956, the United Nations passed the Supplementary Convention on the Abolition of Slavery, the Slave Trade, and Institutions and Practices Similar to Slavery. This called on all countries to bring an end to debt bondage, serfdom, sale of women into marriage and child servitude.

You would think that all of this legislation, all of this shameful history, would have ensured an end to slavery in the modern world. It hasn't. There are more slaves in the world today than there have been at any other time in history. Anti-slavery groups estimate that there are some 27 million slaves, on every continent except Antarctica, producing goods that we in the Western World use every day.[4]

The 1926 Convention defined slavery as "the status or condition of a person over whom any or all of the powers attaching to the right of ownership are exercised." Anti-Slavery International's modern definition identifies a few characteristics that set slavery apart from other human rights violations. A slave is forced to work through threats, and is owned or controlled by an employer. Slaves are dehumanized, treated as commodities, bought and sold like property. And they are physically constrained, or not allowed to move freely.

How can so many people in our world be denied such fundamental rights? And how can something that we thought was consigned to the darker parts of human history still be so active – and so invisible?

The traditional or "chattel" form of slavery – where human beings are bought and sold like pieces of property – still exists today. Sudanese armed militia groups use slavery to raise money, abducting women and children and selling them. In Mauritania, slavery was outlawed just twenty years ago, and yet the government has taken little action to further criminalize the practice and take action against those involved.[5]

Bonded labor is now the most common form of slavery, affecting some 20 million people around the world.[6] Bonded laborers have often been forced or tricked into taking out a loan. Their own labor is the only collateral they have, so to repay their debt, they have to work. The terms of their repayment are so harsh and the value given to their work so minimal that they may never manage to pay it off. Loans can be passed down through generations, condemning future children to a life of servitude.

The typical bonded worker lives in South Asia and will be employed in an industry that feeds the local economy: agriculture and brick making are the two most common. One such worker is Kesro, a boy who works for a notoriously harsh landlord in Sanghar, a village in Pakistan. At the time he spoke to Anti-Slavery International, he was twelve years old. Kesro's master keeps hundreds of men, women and children in chains around the clock, beating them if they do not work hard. Kesro's brother and sister died because they were ill, and they did not have medicines. "I still remember the faces of my dying brother and sister. They died because my father didn't have money to buy medicine and was not allowed to take them to the doctor." Kesro's family were bought by their present landlord from another master – who would beat his employees and sexually abuse and rape the women. When asked if he would like to go to school, Kesro answered, "Yes, but who will allow me? Who will do my work?"[7]

Another form of slavery is forced labor: people are lured to major cities or other countries by the promise of good, well-paid work, and instead find themselves enslaved. This form of human traffic is a booming and lucrative trade for criminal gangs, who keep up a steady flow of human beings into Western countries. The US State Department estimates that nearly a million people are trafficked across borders every year.[8]

Irshad was trafficked from Bangladesh to the United Arab Emirates by a friend of his father's. He was just four years old. Irshad was then given to a master to be trained as a camel jockey. Camel racing is exceptionally dangerous: boys are tied to the camels, which are more than six feet tall, and can run at 38 miles an hour. To keep their weight down, boys are given very little food or water. Irshad's parents finally tracked him down in Dubai, but the man who had abducted Irshad told police that *he* was the boy's father – and all three were handed over to the police. Irshad's father was deported. It was not until some time later, when a visiting Bangladeshi government official recognized Irshad, that he was freed and reunited with his family.[9] Tens of millions of children work in hazardous or dangerous conditions around the world, and still others become victims of sexual exploitation, forced into prostitution or pornography.

This new slavery is even more dehumanizing than the slavery of old, and the enslaved person may be in an even worse position. In the past, the relationship between slave and owner was a long-term one. Although their very status was still an abuse of human rights, the slave was more likely to be treated humanely by their owner – one would get little valuable work out of a slave who was hungry or ill, after all. In the modern era, though, the slave is perceived to be a disposable asset, bought and sold cheaply, eminently replaceable.[10] The average slave in the American South cost $40,000 in today's money. Today, a slave costs an average of just $90.[11]

It's this disposability that makes action against slavery so difficult. While boycotts may seem like an easy answer, they don't actually help the slaves. For example, in cocoa plantations in Western Africa, the low commodity prices helped to create the forced labor problem; the only way employers could make a profit was to find a way to make people work for free. Boycotts make the price fall even further, and the situation fails to improve.

As anti-slavery campaigner Kevin Bales points out, the legal battle against slavery is already won.[12] For many other human rights issues, a first step is getting the international community to make a clear statement that a particular practice – say, female genital mutilation – is wrong, and must be stopped. But for slavery, that hard work has already been done, by the campaigners who brought an end to slavery in the 19th and 20th centuries. Laws against slavery exist in every country.

Bales identifies three things that need to happen. Firstly, there has to be public agreement that it is time to end slavery for good – and we must tell our politicians that. Secondly, we will need to spend money – but, as Bales says, "not nearly as much as you might think." And thirdly, governments must enforce their own anti-slavery laws, and understand that if they don't, they will face serious pressure from the international community.[13]

Groups of activists around the world are working to change things. They report some successes – both in freeing individual slaves and helping them rebuild their lives, and in getting governments to face up to their responsibilities. We can all play a part in this. Get involved in action campaigns, donate to anti-slavery groups, write to your government and get them to take action against slavery, trafficking and child labor – and put pressure on other countries who don't do the same. Because, as an Indian anti-slavery campaigner points out, nobody is free until everybody is free.

Americans discard 2.5 million plastic bottles every hour. That's enough bottles to reach all the way to the moon every three weeks

If you bought your lunch today from a high-street retailer, chances are you'll have purchased a whole load of plastic along with your sandwich. There's a bottle or can for your drink, a plastic wrapping for the egg and cress on white, a plastic bag of chips, maybe a piece of cake in another plastic box. When you factor in the cup from your morning coffee, a few disposable plastic cups from the water cooler, maybe another can of soft-drink to give you a mid-afternoon sugar burst – that's quite a·lot of packaging. And chances are, you threw all of it in the garbage can.

Human beings consume, and in consuming we make waste. Archaeologists regularly uncover garbage dating back thousands of years, and what our early ancestors chose to throw away is often as revealing as any monuments they constructed. In the late 19th century, America started to express concern about the way rubbish was disposed of: a health officer's report from 1889 noted that "appropriate places for [refuse] are becoming scarcer year by year, and the question as to some other method of disposal must soon confront us." And those words were uttered before the invention of the disposable razor (1895), the paper towel (1907) or the paper cup for drinking water (1908).[1]

It's hard to imagine what that health officer would have made of our rubbish today. The world's population has exploded, the industrialized world has become far richer, and the rise in disposable income has led to a rise in disposable culture.

Every hour, British households throw away enough rubbish to fill

227

the Royal Albert Hall. In a year, each person disposes of 1,100 pounds of detritus. There is an estimated 25 million tons of litter scattered along Britain's streets and grass verges – much of it, one often feels, in one's own borough.[2] The mountains of waste are growing by 3 percent every year, and 81 percent of the rubbish produced goes straight into landfills.

In the US, the figures are even more staggering. Almost a third of the waste produced is made up of product packaging. Every year, America produces enough plastic wrap to cling-film the state of Texas. Each Christmas, an additional 5 million tons of rubbish is generated – 4 million of that is wrapping paper and shopping bags (presumably that leaves a million tons of unwanted presents). Offices use enough paper each year to build a thirteen-foot-high wall between Los Angeles and New York. And every three months, Americans throw away enough aluminium cans to rebuild the country's entire commercial air fleet.[3] Now of course the US is a far larger country than Britain, in terms of both population and physical size. But in both countries, people are becoming aware that we consume and throw away far too much.

The problem is worst in the developed world, but the developing world is quickly catching up. China produces and discards more than 45 billion pairs of disposable chopsticks every year, and cuts down 25 million trees to do it.[4] In the Bangladeshi capital Dhaka, more than 10 million plastic bags are dumped every day, clogging the city's drains. When flooding comes, the plastic bags make matters far worse.

Rubbish damages the environment. It can cause serious health problems – experts say Britain's rat population has increased 29 percent between 1998 and 2001 and now stands at a staggering 60 million.[5] Some studies show a link between living near incineration or landfill sites and increased cancer risk. And environmental groups warn that we are in serious risk of drowning in our own rubbish.

It's said there are only two man-made structures that can be seen from outer space: the Great Wall of China, and the Fresh Kills landfill near New York. Whether that's true or not, it's clear that big cities need big spaces to house their waste, and many are running out of room. A landfill closes in the US every day, and industry research suggests that the country has eighteen years of landfill capacity left.[6] In the UK, the managing director of London Waste admits that all of the capital's landfill sites were filled "years ago" and that rubbish is now shipped 50 miles away to sites in Cambridgeshire.[7] A recent report revealed that a third of all food that Britons buy ends up being thrown away – resulting in 6.7 million tons of waste.[8] According to the World Wildlife Fund, if everyone in the world consumed as much as the average Westerner (and emitted carbon dioxide at the same rate) we would need at least another two Earths to cope with all the waste.

Burying our waste isn't the only answer, of course – we could incinerate it, but that creates even more pollution. There is the question of shipping it elsewhere, but where? Developing countries, as we've already seen, have their own issues, and the thought of dumping rubbish in unpopulated areas like the center of Australia or the frozen north of Russia or Canada is horrifying.

The best hope for a solution – best, at least, for the environment, if not for marketers and compulsive shoppers – is to buy and consume less, recycle and reuse more. The US recycles about a tenth of household rubbish, while Britain is only fractionally better, with 11 percent. Both look very sloppy next to Britain's neighbors in Europe. Swiss households recycle some 56 percent of their waste, and if you live in Geneva and dare to dispose of bottles or paper along with the rest of your rubbish you can face a fine of 100 Swiss francs.[9] Austria, Germany and the Netherlands all boast recycling rates of over 45 percent. All of these countries have managed to make recycling a habit for their citizens by initiating curbside recycling schemes – and imposing fines on those who don't make use of them.

It's not just about the familiar mantra of paper, bottles and cans. Environmental groups are starting to express concerns about electronic waste – the millions of televisions, computers and other once-high-tech items that become obsolete every year. The US Environmental Protection Agency (EPA) estimates that 250 million computers will become obsolete and 130 million mobile phones are discarded every year. The components in electronic goods are often valuable in their own right – precious metals, steel, glass – or labor- and energy-intensive to produce. And if they're thrown away, they can be harmful to the environment: one cadmium battery could pollute 600,000 liters of water.

"E-cycling" may be a self-consciously cute name, but the initiative is serious business. Unwanted machines are either reconditioned for sale to developing countries, or dismantled to get at the valuable materials. A number of manufacturers in the US are starting to offer incentives for e-cycling, and Britain's five main mobile phone operators are now participating in a scheme whereby unwanted handsets can be recycled.

One of the biggest problems faced by the environmental movement is making people see that even their smallest actions have a consequence. Reducing the thermostat on your central heating or turning off a light in a room once you leave it has a tiny effect on the amount of fossil fuels burned to generate electricity, but when millions of people do it, the effects aren't so tiny. Environmentalists realize that in order to get people to change their behavior, it has to be as easy and painless as possible.

Curbside recycling is the most effective step a local council can take to reduce waste volumes. Once recycling becomes a habit, it's then important to promote the benefits of "closing the circle" – providing a market for those recycled products. From a business perspective, recycling can only compete with more traditional forms of waste management if the end products can be sold on. So it's important to lobby the business community to use a greater range of recycled products (and become involved in recycling waste from the manufacturing process) as well as pressing consumers to purchase "greener" products.

Quite apart from the prospect of choking in its own rubbish, Britain has another reason to lift its game. By 2010, the EU has directed that its member states should recycle 30 percent of household rubbish, rising to 35 percent by 2015. If those targets are missed, the EU has the power to levy large fines on errant governments. Many European countries already reach those targets effortlessly – in Britain, there's work to do.

Most people want to do the right thing by the environment, and businesses need to realize that. Some campaigners suggest picking up litter in the street and mailing it to supermarket bosses. I'm not sure I could bring myself to do that. But when you're next out shopping, think about how you're going to use what you're buying, and how you're going to dispose of it. Buy concentrated products if you can. Avoid the flashy plastic trays in the fruit and vegetable section. Look for recycled loo paper and bin bags, and if you can't find them, request that your local shop stocks them. But don't stop there: join opt-out lists for junk mail, read your newspaper online, take your old clothes to a garage sale and make a few dollars rather than throwing them out. Once you get started on your own mission to save the planet, it can be pretty hard to stop.

The average urban Briton is caught on camera up to 300 times a day

As you go about your daily business in any town or city in Britain, you're being watched. Some 4.2 million closed circuit television (CCTV) cameras are monitoring the UK, sending images to flickering screens. With 10 percent of the world's CCTV cameras, British people are the most watched in the world. But who's watching, why are they watching – and should we be worried?

Researchers estimate that in a single day, a citizen of London could expect to be filmed by more than 300 cameras on more than 30 separate CCTV systems.[1] There are thousands of cameras watching underground train lines, and Waterloo station alone is estimated to have 250 cameras.[2] The surveillance industry has become a multi-million-pound business. A 2006 report by a group of academics called the Surveillance Studies Network says that Britons are the most-surveilled people in the Western world.[3]

Privacy International is one of a growing number of groups concerned about the ever-expanding surveillance in Britain. It notes that the limits of CCTV are constantly being extended. What was at first a strategy to deter terrorist attacks and property crime has been extended into a system to monitor anti-social behavior, like graffiti, littering, urinating in public and obstruction.[4] The Home Office claims that CCTV is a solution for problems like vandalism, drug use, public drunkenness, racial and sexual violence and disorderly behavior.[5]

The culture of surveillance doesn't end when you close your front door behind you, either. A basic home CCTV kit costs around $200, and it's a simple matter to install a wireless camera. You can train it on your car in your driveway, to see who's vandalizing it; or set it to watch what goes on in your home when you're not there. The latest accessory for the busy working parent is a "nanny-cam" – a CCTV camera hidden inside a soft toy or ornament that will monitor the hired help.

CCTV is thought of as a "feel-good" technology. It's perceived to provide an easy and relatively cost-effective answer to some of our most pressing social problems: street crime, vandalism, anti-social behavior. But the trouble is, many experts doubt that the cameras actually reduce crime by any significant amount. The crime reduction group Nacro suggested that surveillance cameras were most effective in reducing property crime – say, in car parks or areas prone to vandalism. But the impact on personal crime was much less clear-cut.[6] In fact, the brighter street lighting needed to operate the CCTV systems is thought to be more effective in reducing crime than the cameras themselves.

Much of the research suggests that video surveillance just acts to displace crime – moving it to other areas where there are no cameras. And even if the cameras are switched on and being monitored, that doesn't necessarily mean that crime will be picked up before it happens. A US Department of Justice report concluded that getting a live person to monitor video cameras is unrealistic, as the task of watching a number of video screens is "both boring and mesmerizing ... after only about 20 minutes of watching and evaluating monitor screens, the attention of most individuals has degenerated to well below acceptable levels."[7]

Thus bored with the task of watching the screens, the watchers may be tempted to abuse their all-seeing eyes. There are anecdotal reports of operators using cameras to spy on women, and the human rights group Liberty suggests that it's "highly likely" cameras are being used for illicit reasons. Of course, we could employ technology to do the monitoring for us – using face recognition software that would allow computers to match images on cameras against pictures of wanted criminals – but so far it hasn't been particularly helpful. The police department in Tampa, Florida, decided in August 2003 to abandon a two-year trial of face recognition technology because it had failed to produce a single identification or arrest.[8]

Britain's piecemeal and outdated privacy legislation is not coping well with the barrage of new technologies designed to keep watch over its citizens. The use of CCTV is still not well regulated – and there are few more poignant examples of that than the Geoffrey Peck case.

In 1995, Peck was severely depressed after losing his job and finding out his partner was terminally ill. He was filmed by CCTV on Brentwood High Street in Essex, holding a kitchen knife, about to slash his wrists. Police rushed to the scene and led him away – he was not charged with any crime. But the local council gave the footage to two local newspapers and two television networks, wanting to boast about the success of CCTV in stopping crime. Peck was easily identifiable in the pictures. He took the council to court and had little success: the courts found that the council was not prevented by law from releasing the footage. Eventually, the European Court of Human Rights ruled that Peck's right to privacy had been violated.

Far from seeking to protect privacy, the British government has been expanding the ways in which it can watch its citizens. The Regulation of Investigatory Powers Act 2000 (RIPA) gave the Home Secretary power to issue warrants for the interception of communications, and public authorities were given the power to access communications data without a warrant. Legislation dubbed the "snoopers' charter" will give a huge variety of public bodies – from fire authorities and job centers to the Gaming Board and the Charity Commission – the power to use surveillance to investigate crime. Some groups will be given automatic access to phone and Internet data. The government also wants to oblige companies to keep personal data just in case it proves useful. Privacy International warns that through various international treaties, this information will eventually become available to investigators in most other European countries.[8]

In the aftermath of September 11, Internet and communications surveillance have reached all-time highs. Governments have used the excuse of additional security risks to implement wide-ranging new policies. In the US, the "Patriot Act" authorized the use of telephone wire-taps and Internet monitoring software, granted the power to conduct "sneak and peek" searches without letting the target know, and required libraries, bookstores and other organizations to provide records of their customers. Internet service providers can give the government access to any user's communications if they believe "in good faith" that there is an emergency.[9]

So, in the hope of protecting us from terrorist attacks, our governments are deploying surveillance as never before. Proponents of this increased watching argue that if you have nothing to hide, you have nothing to fear. But we need to start thinking about the balance between security and privacy – and how much we are prepared to concede. If we seek to prevent terrorism, how does blanket retention of information about the whole of Britain help that? And how might we soon see data shared – so that, say, the news that you've spent a day surfing the Internet to look up articles on heart disease might reach your insurance company? It's the stuff of conspiracy-theorist nightmares. With 3.1 million Britons now captured on the national DNA database – at more than 5 percent of the population, this is the biggest in the world[11] – and the British government's decision to press ahead with iris recognition schemes, it is possible that we may never be anonymous. We will be able to be identified no matter where we go.

There is a danger that we may be modelling our society in the image of something we once feared – the controlling and all-seeing State, monitoring our every move. As Barry Hugill of Liberty puts it, "When the Berlin Wall fell and the Soviet regime fell there was a lot in the press about the oppression in these countries, particularly East Germany, and a lot was written about the files kept by the Stasi. Everyone had a file and everything was always noted, and people said that's why the Cold War was won, to prevent that kind of thing. But we're moving ourselves towards that – the government now wants ID cards for everyone, and you now have the compilation or the holding of information on people for no obvious reason other than wanting to have the information."[12]

There are a few things you can do to protect your privacy. Your Internet surfing will be less easily tracked if you do it at an Internet café or use an anonymous web browser. You can also use encryption software to make sure your e-mails can't be read, and buy a pay-as-you-go mobile phone. But even those aren't foolproof. Under the RIPA, Britons can be required to hand over encrypted communications in plain-text format or even hand over encryption keys, while mobile phone companies are able to look at "friendship networks" and figure out your new phone number very quickly.

Simon Davies of Privacy International points out that the biggest danger is perhaps not the individual technologies, but the overall idea that the surveillance culture is unavoidable and even in our best interests. "We need to make the case about why this is important. By and large the technologies become normalized and regulated, and you find fewer and fewer abuses, so people start to accept it. But if you get people thinking about why privacy is important, they will find their own means of resistance."[13]

Privacy and dignity is a fundamental human right, but we're in danger of having it removed by a surveillance culture that claims to have our best interests at heart. Let's not allow our governments to dispense with our right to a private life.

Some 120,000 women and girls are trafficked into Western Europe every year

"I paid a man 350 German marks to go to Greece since I had no papers. Instead, he brought me to Greece and sold me to a bar. He told me he would kill me if I left. We could not leave the house. There were twelve women, all of us from fifteen to twenty years old. We slept with a lot of men, ten men a day. We were beaten if we tried to leave. I was beaten with a belt ... the police came and arrested all of us women and brought us to a small prison. I stayed for four months in prison. After that I went to court. Because I did not have papers, the court gave me three months [suspended sentence and immediate deportation] and told me I could not return to Greece for five years."[1]

This is the human reality of the trafficking of women and girls. It's a shocking trade that destroys the lives of its victims. But it's a massive source of revenue for the traffickers, and they have been quick to exploit women in poorer countries. They promise jobs with decent money, a better life, a chance to send money home to feed their families. They deliver a "career" in the sex industry, where women are virtually enslaved – their passports taken away, their earnings confiscated to "pay" for their passage. The women may be bought and sold many times. If they are caught, they are often put in prison or sent home, where they will face rejection and shame from their communities.

The International Organization for Migration (IOM) estimates that some 120,000 women and children are trafficked every year into Western Europe.[2] Many come from Eastern Europe – Moldova, Romania and the Ukraine are the three most common starting points – but others are from Africa, Asia, South America. Traffickers set up elaborate networks of accomplices, "from false-front employment agencies to passport forgers, truckers in human cargo, new-girl display rooms and "warehouses," Internet distributors and, last, houses of prostitution in the West."[3] The United Nations estimates that the trade is worth some $7 billion a year.[4] Within Europe, there are several trafficking routes, thought to be dominated by organized crime groups. Bosses pay recruiters about $500 for each new girl – and if recruiters are clever about it, it's money easily made.

Traffickers prey upon the vulnerable, the poverty-stricken, and they offer tempting rewards: a chance to travel overseas to a good job in a rich country. Some are told they will work in the sex industry but in good conditions, others are promised work as waitresses, cleaners, secretaries. The huge economic and social upheaval in former Soviet Union countries has led to widespread poverty and unemployment. Legal migration is nearly impossible, so it's easy to understand the lure of the recruiters, offering seemingly legitimate passage to a wealthier country and a good job at the end of it.

The trafficking industry seeks to exploit the inequalities existing between the developed and developing worlds, and the basic human desire to make our own situation better. And it's happening all over the world. US government figures suggest that as many as 900,000 people are trafficked across international borders every year.[5] Girls from villages in Nepal and Bangladesh are sold to brothels in India. Young women from the Philippines travel to Japan to work as "entertainers," but find themselves virtually enslaved by their employers. Mexican girls are taken on dates by wealthy men who promise them new lives in the United States, only to be smuggled in as illegal immigrants and forced to work as prostitutes.

Like any business – legal or illegal – trafficking is a matter of supply and demand. So where the traffickers perceive a new demand, they're quick to move.

In March 2002 Fox News conducted an undercover report documenting the US military's participation in the commercial sex industry in South Korea. A few months later, the American magazine *Military Times* featured the story of "Lana," a young Kyrgyz woman lured by a newspaper advertisement looking for women to dance in nightclubs frequented by American servicemen in South Korea. Lana's fate was all too familiar: her employer took away her passport and forced her to become a prostitute. US troops stationed in South Korea are not formally permitted to visit brothels, but the Fox investigation reported that Courtesy Patrol officers would facilitate visits for the servicemen. The NGO Equality Now reports that almost everywhere US troops are stationed, there is a resulting growth of the local sex industry: in 1999, when US forces returned to the Philippines, the number of registered "entertainers" in one city nearly doubled.[6]

There is also concern that legalized prostitution, rather than providing a safer and more regulated environment for sex workers, may encourage traffickers to increase their efforts in new markets. In the Netherlands, where prostitution is legal, one study reported that 80 percent of women working in brothels had been trafficked from other countries.[7] Germany took the first steps towards legalizing prostitution in 1993, and it's estimated that up to 85 percent of women in the industry are from other countries. NGOs believe most of these women have been trafficked, since it is almost impossible for women from poorer countries to pay for their own travel and set themselves up in "business."[8] In November 2003 Thai sex workers told a public forum that they strongly opposed the legalization of the sex industry. Looking at the European experience, academic Weerada Somsawasdi told the forum that legalization would be "like handing human traffickers a gift."[9]

There is an urgent need for all countries to decisively address the trafficking problem. The relatively low risk of being caught provides a huge incentive for traffickers to carry on their trade – particularly when there is such a lot of money to be made. That needs to change. In the words of former UN High Commissioner for Human Rights Mary Robinson, "this is more than a labor rights issue or an issue of unequal development. It is a basic human rights issue because it involves such a massive and harmful form of discrimination."[10] The Universal Declaration of Human Rights is clear: not only should all people be "born free and equal in dignity and rights," but the slave trade in all its forms "shall be prohibited."

Fortunately, many countries are starting to respond. The UN Protocol to Prevent, Suppress and Punish Trafficking in Persons, Especially Women and Children adds to the existing UN Convention against Transnational Organized Crime, and calls on states to enact legislation to criminalize trafficking and all associated corruption. It came into force on December 25, 2003, and at the time of writing 117 states had signed it.

At the same time, the US has embarked on its own anti-trafficking initiative. In 2000, Congress enacted the Trafficking Victims Protection Act, which provides for an annual State Department report on trafficking to monitor progress around the world. The report classifies countries according to three tiers: tier one countries fully comply with the minimum standards, tier two states are judged to be "making significant efforts," and tier three are falling short (and may be subject to sanctions). In September 2003 President George W. Bush announced sanctions against Burma, Cuba and North Korea; he said the US "will not provide funding for participation by officials or employees of these governments in educational and cultural exchange programs until such government complies with the Act's minimum standard."[11] While human rights groups criticized the State Department for not being tough enough on some countries, the report has the potential to act as a powerful tool to bring governments into line with international norms.[12]

As well as requiring states to enact laws criminalizing human trafficking, the UN Protocol calls on states to take action to protect victims of trafficking. It suggests that they should consider providing appropriate housing, medical and psychological treatment, counselling and legal advice. Too often victims of trafficking are treated as illegal aliens and deported summarily. Not only does this fail to recognize the hugely traumatic and dehumanizing experience of these women, but it means that valuable evidence which could help punish their employers is gone. Once back in their villages, victims of trafficking may find themselves rejected by their former neighbors, and they will once again be vulnerable to traffickers. Many states have changed their laws: Italy established a witness protection program which included a six-month visa and counselling for the women, which has seen prosecutions increase fourfold,[13] while the US has unveiled a temporary "T-visa" which allows victims to stay and assist in legal proceedings.

As long as there are inequalities in the world, and people who are unscrupulous enough to exploit them, it's hard to see that trafficking will end completely. But governments can do much to increase the chances that traffickers will be caught – and, by helping their victims, make sure that they are convicted. To do that, they need to enact legislation that criminalizes traffickers, not victims, and make sure that it is enforced properly. There also needs to be cooperation on an international level to enable networks to be properly dismantled. The trade in human lives is one of the biggest assaults to human dignity in the world today. It must not be allowed to continue.

A kiwi fruit flown from New Zealand to Britain emits five times its own weight in greenhouse gases

A modern supermarket is a thing of wonder. Even if it's snowing outside and summer is a distant memory, you can buy strawberries, peaches or grapes. If you want root vegetables in the middle of a heatwave, you can have them. Ex-pat Americans can have their Oreo cookies, while homesick New Zealanders can console themselves with wine and kiwi fruit. Within days of being picked off the vines, the fruit is in your shopping cart, tasting of spring as the leaves are falling outside.

It's all great until you start contemplating the vast mileage sitting in your shopping basket. Those kiwi fruits have travelled nearly 20,000 kilometers – or 12,000 miles. They've flown in a plane and travelled by road. By the time they reach the supermarket, they're responsible for five times their own weight in greenhouse gases being pumped into the atmosphere.[1] Increasingly, our food is coming from further and further away, and we're becoming more and more dependent on the fuel it takes to get them to us.

This dependence was illustrated very clearly during the September 2000 fuel price protests in Britain. Inspired by similar actions in France, a group of farmers and truck drivers decided to blockade the Stanlow oil refinery in Cheshire. The protest quickly snowballed, and gas tankers were unable to leave refineries. Panic buying saw more than 90 percent of gas stations run dry. And with supplies unable to get through, supermarket shelves quickly emptied.

It's estimated that food now accounts for as much as 40 percent of all UK road freight, and the international food trade is increasing faster than the world's population and food production.[2] In other words, food is moving around more than ever, and the environmental impact could be huge.

Despite the UK's cool climate being perfectly suited for growing apples, nearly three-quarters of the apples eaten in the UK are imported, and more than 60 percent of Britain's apple orchards have been destroyed in the past 30 years.[3] We're now putting more energy into transporting some crops than we get out of eating them. For every calorie of lettuce imported to the UK from America's west coast, 127 calories of fuel are used.[4] Put it another way: flying over a kilogram of Californian lettuce uses enough energy to keep a 100-watt light bulb glowing for eight days.

Some countries are now in the remarkable situation of effectively "swapping food." Countries export large amounts of a product while importing a similar amount of the same thing – a bizarre and hugely wasteful practice. The milk trade provides a particularly clear example. In 2001 the UK exported 149,000 tons of fresh milk and imported 110,000 tons.[5] Forty years ago most people would have drunk milk produced by local farmers, but between 1961 and 1999 milk exports increased by 500 percent.[6] Forget milk coming straight from the cow – the stuff you pour on your cereal comes straight from the tanker, probably after travelling thousands of miles.

While this well-travelled food may look as fresh as the locally grown equivalent, it's unlikely to pack the same nutritional punch. Research has shown that the further food travels, the more the vitamin and mineral content deteriorates.[7]

But that loss of nutrients is a small concern compared with the very serious health issues raised by the transport of animals and their feed. Britain exported some 800,000 live lambs and sheep every year before the foot and mouth crisis of 2001, some of them travelling as far away as Italy and Greece. Even within the UK, the increasing centralization and specialization of meat processors means that animals may be reared on one farm but fattened on another – then sent to a large central abattoir for slaughtering, and another processor for cutting and packing. These long journeys, combined with uncontrolled contact with other consignments of animals, are thought to have contributed to the spread of foot and mouth and BSE, the degenerative condition known as "mad cow disease." With such a complex web of animal transport, tracing the source of outbreaks is made far more difficult.

Campaigners claim that transported animals are tightly packed into containers without adequate food or water – not only does this harm and often kill the animals, but when they are eventually slaughtered, the resulting meat may be bruised or dry – a poorer-quality product delivered in a cruel process.[8] In July 2003 the European Commission approved proposals to overhaul animal transport laws. These toughened up on some aspects of transport such as breaks, access to water and temperature controls, but they did not prescribe a maximum journey length – so that 90-hour journeys to Greece would still be permissible.[9]

Short of the total depletion of the world's oil stocks – which is a looming deadline, though still relatively distant – there seems to be little incentive to change. The Kyoto Protocol, which seeks to limit the world's emission of greenhouse gases, does not include emissions from international sea and air freight. The search for an endless culinary summer may be seriously damaging our planet, and as we consumers get used to buying tropical fruit in the middle of winter, it's hard to see what will make us change our habits.

But we must. With climate change no longer a threat but a reality, it's clear that our food production and transport methods are a major contributor. Supermarkets claim financial necessity – customers want cheap food and convenience, and that means sourcing cheap products. But analyzing the real cost of importing produce may lead to some different conclusions. A survey conducted by South West Local Food Partnership concluded that products sold at farmers' markets were on average 30–40 percent cheaper than those sold at supermarkets.[10]

We can't just adopt "buy local" as a mantra, though. It's a question of working out which foods use the fewest resources on their way to our dinner table. For example, it's more energy-efficient for Swedish shoppers to buy Spanish tomatoes than locally grown ones – the Swedish tomatoes are grown in greenhouses warmed by fossil fuels.[11]

The realities of a British climate mean the UK will always have to import some food from other countries. But there are still good choices and bad choices. Air freighting food is a costly and environmentally damaging option – transporting produce by boat emits just one-60th of the greenhouse gas. In the US, there are moves to introduce "eco-labels" for food that indicate how much energy it took to produce and transport that product.[12]

When you're next in the supermarket, have a good look at the labels on your food, particularly the fresh produce – and think about how far that package of chillies or prawns has flown. If you see a pallid-looking tomato that's hard to the touch, think about what it will taste like. Summer and sunshine – or early picking followed by a long journey in a refrigerated transporter?

The growing movement in praise of "slow food" – casting aside convenience and speed in favor of taste and enjoyment – may be on to something here. Who wants *mange-tout* in the middle of winter, anyway? Take time to buy proper seasonal produce and rediscover a more leisurely way of cooking it, and your tastebuds will certainly thank you. And so, in time, will the environment.

The US owes the United Nations more than $1 billion in unpaid dues

In late 2002 and early 2003, while the world deliberated whether to go to war in Iraq, all eyes were on the United Nations. How far would the Security Council go towards authorizing military action? How much would the UN be expected to contribute to nation-building and peacekeeping? And when all was said and done, did it really matter? Many, many inches of newspaper coverage were dedicated to discussions about the UN's continued relevance.

Few people would dispute the importance of some kind of world body where nations can come together to pursue common aims. The UN and all its agencies and funds operate on a budget of around $20 billion a year – that's about $3 for every human being on the planet.[1] It's what the world spends on its military every five days. That seems like value for money, right? But in the eyes of many governments, paying UN contributions is a very low priority. For more than a decade, the UN has suffered from a crippling financial crisis, as member states cut back on their voluntary commitments and lag behind on paying their "regular assessments" – which go towards the day-to-day running of the UN. As of December 31, 2006, the UN's total arrears stood at $2.34 billion. By far the biggest debtor is the US: on that day, it owed the UN $1.01 billion.[2]

How did it get this way? How on earth can UN Under-Secretary-General Catherine Bertini be forced to tell the General Assembly that "the financial stability of the organization is under pressure"?[3] And what could be the consequences of such massive under-funding?

The structure and operation of the United Nations was forged in the closing stages of the Second World War. One of the main aims at that time was to ensure that such a global catastrophe never happened again. After a series of meetings in Washington, DC during 1944, the US, the UK, Russia and China agreed on the aims, structure and functions of a world organization. On June 26, 1945, delegates of 50 nations attended a ceremonial signing of the UN's Charter in the Veterans' War Memorial in San Francisco. After he signed the Charter, US Secretary of State Edward Stettinius said that it was "a compact, born of suffering and of war; with it now rests our hope for a good and a lasting peace."[4]

At first, optimism ran high. The first General Assembly was held in London in January 1946, adopting its first resolution on the peaceful use of atomic energy and the elimination of weapons of mass destruction. Its first observer mission was established in Palestine in 1948. That same year, the Universal Declaration of Human Rights was adopted, and in 1949 a UN envoy secured a ceasefire between the new state of Israel and Arab states.[5]

The first serious financial problems arose over the UN's early attempts at peacekeeping.[6] In 1956, the UN's first major peacekeeping initiative in the Sinai started an argument about who should pay. A number of states refused to cough up, saying that those who were responsible should bear the cost. A similar dispute arose in 1960 over contributions to a peacekeeping mission in the Congo, where policy differences led to some countries refusing to pay their contributions.

During this time, the US was prompt with its payments, especially in comparison with the Soviet Union. But under the presidency of Ronald Reagan, things started to change. Advisers began to cast the UN as a pro-Soviet body, fomenting radical beliefs in the developing world. In 1983, an amendment to the US's UN Appropriations Bill denied US funds to UN programs that supported the Palestinian Liberation Organization (PLO) or Namibia's independence movement. In 1985, the US withdrew from the UN's Educational, Scientific and Cultural Organization (UNESCO), claiming it was badly managed and too politicized. The arrears began to mount. While the UN was forced to slash budgets, the US began delaying the payment of its regular contributions: due at the beginning of the year, they were often paid many months late. Those delays in payment have continued to this day.

In the late 1980s and early 90s, the economic upheaval in the former Soviet Union and other Eastern European countries saw other nations begin to rack up large debts. At the same time, the US began to increase its military focus, considering interventions in conflicts around the world. Although the Clinton administration had initially considered an expanding role for the UN in peacekeeping, it continued the same hard-line approach to the budget. By September 1994, the UN's arrears had soared to $3.5 billion, of which $1.5 billion was owed by the US.

Congress has not hesitated to block funding for particular UN bodies where it has concerns about their mandates. Since 2002 the Bush administration has withheld US funding for the UN Population Fund, because it was believed to have links with groups promoting forced abortions in China. The funding block continued despite a US-led investigation which found no evidence that the fund had supported any such operation.[7]

In 1999 the US passed legislation which agreed to pay back a substantial part of the arrears to the UN. The "Helms-Biden" agreement – named after its sponsors – provided a plan for three large installments of money to be paid to the UN. Under the plan, a total of $926 million was paid to the UN and its specialized agencies, with $712 million going towards the regular operating budget. But the legislation came with conditions, giving the US the right to withhold further payments if budgetary and reform targets were not met. The US also asked for permanent reductions in its share of the UN's regular budget as well as its payments to the World Health Organization, the Food and Agriculture Organization and the International Labor Organization.[8]

But substantial as it was, the Helms-Biden legislation only went part-way towards paying the total amount of arrears owed by the US. According to UN figures, as of August 31, 2003, the US still owed

$1.22 billion in both past and current obligations – more than half the monies outstanding to the UN.[9]

Of course, the US is not the only debtor. By the end of 2003, two-thirds of the member states had not paid their contributions in full and as of November 2004, $695 million of the UN's regular 2004 budget remained unpaid. Of the fifteen biggest contributors, the US, Brazil and Mexico had not paid their annual dues in full.[10]

This unpredictability, combined with the large amount of money owed, is having serious repercussions for the UN. Payments for the international tribunals for the former Yugoslavia and Rwanda are so far in arrears – there was a $96 million shortfall for 2003 alone – that officials were forced to borrow $41 million from the UN peace-keeping accounts. This borrowing came despite the fact that the UN's peacekeeping fund was already more than $1.1 billion in the red.[11] In late October, the "Group of 77" developing nations warned that the UN was taking too long to reimburse contributors to peace-keeping missions and complained about the practice of dipping into other funds. But Under-Secretary-General Bertini told them that if all countries paid their assessments in full, it wouldn't happen.[12]

It seems such a simple solution: all governments, particularly wealthy and powerful ones, should make sure they pay their UN dues in full and on time. To do otherwise puts the UN's future in jeopardy. US payments have been out of sync for so long that they're now a habit, and it has encouraged other countries like Japan to adopt the practice of late payment. The US Congress has already voiced its concern: the Fiscal Year 2003 State Department Authorization Bill stated that "late payment of US dues forces the United Nations and other international organizations to engage in budgetary practices that are neither sound nor responsible."[13] The House of Representatives recently called for a report on the ramifi-cations of late payment, and directed the President to create a plan to resume paying UN dues at the beginning of each calendar year.

Even the American public appears to support a more responsible attitude towards the UN's finances: in one survey, more than 60 percent said the US should pay its UN arrears in full,[14] and when Americans were informed that the US contribution was determined by its share in the world economy, 56 percent felt it was a fair amount to pay.[15]

There is no doubt that the repayments made under the Helms-Biden legislation did much to help the UN's financial situation. But more needs to be done. As the world's major economic player and (some say) sole superpower, it is only right that the US should make the biggest contribution. But it needs to make its payments on time and in full, and stop using delays as a means of forcing reforms or changes in policy.

The money required is a small fraction of what the US is spending on fighting its war against terrorism. But through its humanitarian programs, international legal instruments and multilateralist approach to world events, the UN might just be the best front-line fighter the US has. The American people believe that UN contributions are money well spent – now all they have to do is convince their leaders.

Children living in poverty are three times more likely to suffer a mental illness than children from wealthy families

It's a fact that should make Britain feel ashamed: it is the world's fourth-largest economy, and yet it has one of the highest rates of child poverty in the industrialized world. Nearly 4 million British children – one in every three – live in poverty.[1] That's three times the number below the poverty line in 1970. More than half of inner-London children live in poverty, in a city that has the highest income per head in Europe and the greatest number of millionaires.[2]

Poverty in the West is defined differently from poverty in the developing world. Rather than looking at a pure income threshold – the $1 a day level often used by aid agencies, for example – poverty in Europe is defined using relative standards. Researchers look at a minimum acceptable standard of living, looking at all a person's resources – material, cultural and social. If they fall short of this standard, that person is living in poverty.

The effects of this social exclusion can be extreme. Children born into poverty are more likely to die in the first year of life, are more likely to die from childhood accidents, and will live shorter lives than children born to wealthier families.[3] They are more likely to live in cramped homes with damp problems and lack of heating; in the UK, 750,000 families with children live in poor housing.[4] Poor children are much more likely to be excluded from social activities like school trips and leisure services.[5] And young people living in persistent and severe poverty are more likely to have strained relationships with their parents, and are less likely to be happy with their appearance and their lives as a whole.[6]

It's little wonder, then, that children in the lowest income groups are three times more likely than children from the wealthiest families to suffer some kind of psychiatric problem. The British Office for National Statistics reports that 16 percent of children living in families with a weekly income of less than £100 have mental health problems, compared with around 6 percent of children in families earning over £500 a week.[7]

Neera Sharma, senior policy officer at the children's charity Barnardo's, explains how Britain's inequalities impact on children's mental health. "There are lots of children who take for granted things like days out, holidays, trips to Pizza Hut and that kind of thing. But there are lots of kids who don't have these things, which really makes them feel socially excluded. Many of these children often care for a disabled parent or a parent that may have a mental illness. These things can lead to bullying at school, which makes kids feel excluded or different, and that has an impact on their mental health."[8]

If children are diagnosed with a mental illness, chances are the care they receive will not be adequate. According to government-funded research reported by the BBC, up to a quarter of British teenagers with mental health problems are getting care deemed "inappropriate" by their own doctors.[9] Total spending on child and adolescent mental health in the UK is about £240 million – just 7 percent of the adult mental health budget.[10] Just over a quarter of children with psychiatric problems are in touch with specialist services – a number that desperately needs to increase.[11]

As well as essentials like warm clothing and a healthy diet, children born into poverty may be deprived of opportunities to work their way towards a better life. One father on a south-London council estate told the *Observer* newspaper that when he left school, he went on a scheme to become a welder and found work within months; his boys go on schemes but there's never a job at the end of them. Another man points to the lack of expectation: "The Thatcher government took our working-class life away from us but they didn't replace it with anything. The reason our children have fewer life opportunities isn't because they can't go to university, it's because they can't go to work."[12]

Poor children are likely to grow up to be poor adults. They are at a greater risk of unemployment and low pay when they grow up. If they leave school without qualifications, they are three times less likely to receive job-related training.[13] If they have fallen prey to a mental disorder, they are ten times more likely to have been in trouble with the police, and more likely to continue to have problems in later life: up to half of all adult mental disorder is first diagnosed in childhood.[14]

The director of the Child Poverty Action Group, Martin Barnes, points out that many people still believe that poverty is not a problem in Britain – and that makes the problem still harder to address. "The poverty of today is often forced behind closed doors, driven there by stigma, isolation and embarrassment. The personal and economic costs are real and increasing, but instead of outrage and urgency, there is widespread indifference and complacency."[15] Poverty in Britain exists not because it is a poor country, but because it is an unequal country. And dealing with that inequality poses a complex problem to any government brave enough to attempt it.

Britain is now twice as unequal as it was in 1977,[16] and the gap between rich and poor grew markedly over the 1990s. The country's Gini coefficient – which measures inequality in societies – has grown steadily over the past 30 years and is now at an all-time high. The bottom 10 percent of the population get just 3 percent of the income, while the top 10 percent get more than a quarter.[17] Britain's rich now get more of the nation's post-tax income than at any time in history, while the poor are suffering.

The British government has acknowledged that child poverty is a massive problem, and in 1999, Prime Minister Tony Blair committed to eradicating it within a generation. Chancellor Gordon Brown called the problem "a scar on the soul of Britain" and talked about children trapped in a no-win situation: "poor when young, unemployed when older."[18] Brown said the government planned to eradicate child poverty completely in twenty years – and to halve it by 2010. Unfortunately, it looks as though that goal may not be met. The 2005/2006 Households Below Average Income survey showed that the number of children in poverty had increased by 100,000. The End Child Poverty Campaign said this raised "serious doubts" about whether the 2010 target could be reached – in order to do so, that would mean 200,000 children must be lifted out of poverty every year.[19] Changes to the UK's tax and benefit system have provided some answers, as has the effort to get people who want to work off benefits and into jobs. But there is a limit to how much initiatives like this can achieve. The government should address the issue of low pay and job retention as a matter of urgency. To meet the Council of Europe's "decency threshold," the minimum wage in Britain should be set at £7.32 an hour. It is currently £4.85.

Increasing income is one important factor to solving the poverty problem – access to good-quality public services like transport, education and social services is also vital. It's also important that the benefits system is addressed so that those who cannot work are not disadvantaged. Barnardo's also stresses that resources need to be directed towards particularly vulnerable children – those who are disabled, from ethnic minorities, or in severe and persistent poverty. A one-size-fits-all system will not help these kids.

The Labor government has acknowledged that merely getting poorer people into jobs is not enough to address the inequalities in British society, and that a redistribution of wealth, opportunity and power is necessary. Indeed, if the government managed to achieve this, the results could be dramatic. One study noted that if Britain's inequality were restored to 1983 levels, some 7,500 deaths of people younger than 65 could be prevented – and if child poverty were eradicated, an estimated 1,400 lives per year would be saved among children under fifteen.[20]

Reducing inequality is an incredibly difficult task. Raising taxes to improve public services is always seen as electoral suicide in Britain

– and yet a 2001 poll conducted by MORI suggested that nearly two-thirds of Britons would support this.[21] But whether they would support any perceived redistribution of wealth is less clear; another poll showed that just 6 percent of Britons considered poverty and inequality to be an important issue facing the country.[22]

The British government is starting to tackle the problem of child poverty, although clearly there is a lot more it can do. Perhaps, then, the major shift needs to be in our thinking. Britain may be a wealthy country, able to give millions of pounds in overseas aid, able to wage costly wars to save people from poverty and oppression overseas. But its economic might has come at the expense of vulnerable people at home. Until it recognizes the scope and the urgency of the child poverty problem, Britain is failing.

Sources for the 50 Facts

The average Japanese woman can expect to live to be 84. The average Botswanan will reach just 39.
news.bbc.co.uk/1/hi/health/1977733.stm; US Census Bureau, quoted in www.usaid.gov/press/releases/2002/pr020708.html.
A third of the world's obese people live in the developing world.
http://www.who.int/nutrition/topics/obesity/en/
If you stand at the junction of Oxford Street and Regent Street in central London, there are 161 branches of Starbucks within a five-mile radius.
http://www.starbucks.com/retail/locator/
China has 44 million missing women.
Amartya Sen, "Many Faces of Gender Inequality," *The Hindu*, October 27, 2001.
Brazil has more Avon ladies than members of its armed services.
http://www.br.avon.com/PRSuite/info/aboutHistory.jsp
http://www.nationmaster.com/country/br-brazil/mil-military
Ninety-four percent of the world's executions in 2005 took place in just four countries: China, Iran, Saudi Arabia and the USA.
http://web.amnesty.org/pages/deathpenalty-sentences-eng.
British supermarkets know more about their customers than the British government does.
Author's interview with customer forecaster for a British supermarket, September 30, 2003.
Every cow in the European Union is subsidised by $2.50 a day. That's more than what 75 percent of Africans have to live on.
"Cows Can Fly Upper Class on Common Agricultural Fare," *Guardian*, September 25, 2002.
In more than 70 countries, same-sex relationships are illegal. In nine countries, the penalty is death.
www.ilga.org/Information/Legal_survey/ilga_world_legal_survey%20introduction.htm.
One in five of the world's people lives on less than $1 a day.
UN Human Development Report (UNHDR) 2005, www.undp.org/ hdr2005.
More than 12,000 women are killed each year in Russia as a result of domestic violence.
"Russia: Domestic Violence Persists," Radio Free Europe/Radio Liberty, March 2001, www.rferl.org/nca/features/2001/03/07032001120749.asp.
In 2006, 16 million Americans had some form of plastic surgery.
http://www.plasticsurgery.org/media/press_releases/2006-Stats-Overall-Release.cfm
Landmines kill or maim at least one person every hour.
www.landmines.org.uk/6.
There are 44 million child laborers in India.
International Labour Organization, quoted at www.globalmarch.org/ worstformsreport/world/india.html.

People in industrialized countries eat between fourteen and fifteen pounds of food additives every year.
Erik Millstone and Tim Lang, *The Atlas of Food* (London: Earthscan, 2003). Figures have been converted from the imperial figures (between thirteen and fifteen pounds).

David Beckham's deal with the LA Galaxy football team will earn him $100 every minute.
http://www.telegraph.co.uk/sport/main.jhtml?xml=/sport/2007/01/12/sfnfron12.xml.

Seven million American women and 1 million American men suffer from an eating disorder.
National Association of Anorexia Nervosa and Associated Disorders, www.anad.org/site/anadweb/content.php?type=1&id=6982.

Nearly half of British fifteen year olds have tried illegal drugs and nearly a quarter are regular cigarette smokers.
"Smoking, Drinking and Drug Use Among Young People in England in 2002," survey carried out on behalf of the Department of Health, 2002, www.doh.gov.uk/public/sddsurvey02.htm.

One million people become new mobile phone subscribers every day. Some 85 percent of them live in emerging markets.
Figures from the GSMA, http://www.gsmworld.com, quoted at http://news.bbc.co.uk/1/hi/business/6339671.stm

Cars kill two people every minute.
World Road Association/Global Road Safety Partnership/Department for International Development, "Keep Death Off Your Roads," April 2003.

Since 1977, there have been more than 90,000 acts of violence and disruption at abortion clinics in North America.
National Abortion Federation Violence and Disruption Statistics, at www.prochoice.org, count 128,466 incidents in the period 1977–December 2006. It is noted that these are reported incidents only – the actual number of incidents is likely to be "much higher."

Global warming already kills 150,000 people every year.
http://www.nature.com/nature/journal/v438/n7066/abs/nature04188.html
http://www.who.int/mediacentre/factsheets/fs266/en/

In Kenya, bribery payments make up a third of the average household budget.
Transparency International, Kenyan Urban Bribery Index, January 2001, www.transparency.org/cpi.

The world's trade in illegal drugs is estimated to be worth around $400 billion – about the same as the world's legal pharmaceutical industry.
UN Office on Drugs and Crime, figures quoted by Kofi Annan at www.un.org/ News/Press/docs/1998/19980608.gasm45.html. www.worldpharmaceuticals.net/marketresearch.html estimates the industry grew to $406 billion in 2002.

A third of Americans believe aliens have landed on Earth.
National Science Foundation, "Science and Engineering Indicators 2002," Chapter 7.
More than 150 countries use torture.
Amnesty International, "Combating Torture: A Manual for Action," www.amnesty.org/library/Index/ENGACT400012003?open&of=ENG-313.
Every day, one in five of the world's population – some 800 million people – go hungry.
UN World Food Program, January 2001, www.wfp.org/index.asp?section=1.
Black men born in the US today stand a one in three chance of going to jail.
Bureau of Justice Statistics, "Prevalence of Imprisonment in the US Population, 1974–2001," August 2003.
A third of the world's population is at war.
Armed Conflict Report 2002, Project Ploughshares, www.ploughshares.ca/content/ACR/acr.html.
The world's oil reserves could be exhausted by 2040.
Colin Campbell and Jean Laherrere, "The End of Cheap Oil," *Scientific American*, March 1998.
Eighty-two percent of the world's smokers live in developing countries.
Worldwatch Institute, Vital Signs 2003.
Britons buy 3 billion items of clothing every year – an average of 50 pieces each. Most of it ends up being thrown away.
"Well Dressed?: The Present and Future Sustainability of Clothing and Textiles in the United Kingdom," University of Cambridge Institute for Manufacturing, 2006, www.ifm.eng.cam.ac.uk.
A quarter of the world's armed conflicts of recent years have involved a struggle for natural resources.
Worldwatch Institute, Vital Signs 2003.
Some 30 million people in Africa are HIV-positive.
www.worldbank.org/afr/aids.
Ten languages die out every year.
portal.unesco.org/culture/en/ev.php@URL_ID=8270&URL_DO=DO=TOPIC&URL_SECTION=201.html.
More people die each year from suicide than in all the world's armed conflicts.
www.who.int/mental_health/prevention/suicide/suicideprevent/en/.
Every week, an average of 54 children are expelled from American schools for bringing a gun to class.
Brady Campaign to Prevent Gun Violence, http://www.bradycampaign.org. The most recent figures that the US Department of Education has published refer to the school year 2002–03, and that year 2,143 children were expelled – in a 40-week school year, that averages 54 expulsions. http://nces.ed.gov/fastfacts/display.asp?id=54.

There are at least 300,000 prisoners of conscience in the world.
Author's conversation with Neil Durkin of Amnesty International.
Two million girls and women are subjected to female genital mutilation each year.
WHO, "Female Genital Mutilation Fact Sheet," June 2000.
There are 300,000 child soldiers fighting in conflicts around the world.
Human Rights Watch, hrw.org/campaigns/crp/index.htm.
Nearly 26 million people voted in the 2001 British General Election. More than 32 million votes were cast in the first season of *Pop Idol*.
According to iTouch UK, the communication company that handled the votes for Thames: http://www.itouch.co.uk/news/index.php?body=20030806a
Electoral Commission, "Voter Engagement and Young People," August 2002
<http://www.electoralcommission.org.uk/templates/search/document.cfm/
6188>http://www.electoralcommission.org.uk/templates/search/document.
cfm/6188
One in six English teenagers believe that reality television will make them famous.
http://readingroom.lsc.gov.uk/lsc/2006/externalrelations/press/kids-
seeking-reality-tv-fame.pdf.
In 2005, the US spent $554 billion on its military. This is 29 times the combined military spending of the six "rogue states."
World Military Spending, Global Issues, February 2007; http://www.
globalissues.org/Geopolitics/ArmsTrade/Spending.asp
There are 27 million slaves in the world today.
www.antislavery.org/archive/press/pressRelease2002-festivalofflight.htm.
Americans discard 2.5 million plastic bottles every hour. That's enough bottles to reach all the way to the moon every three weeks.
http://www.eco-action.net/id87.htm.
The average urban Briton is caught on camera up to 300 times a day.
Michael McCahill and Clive Norris, "CCTV in London," Working Paper no. 6, Urban Eye project, June 2002.
Some 120,000 women and girls are trafficked into Western Europe every year.
IOM, "Victims of Trafficking in the Balkans," January 2002.
A kiwi fruit flown from New Zealand to Britain emits five times its own weight in greenhouse gases.
"A Free Ride for Freight," Financial Times, 21 November 2000.
The US owes the United Nations more than $1 billion in unpaid dues.
http://www.globalpolicy.org/finance/tables/core/un-us-06.htm.
Children living in poverty are three times more likely to suffer a mental illness than children from wealthy families.
Social Survey Division of the Office for National Statistics, "The Mental Health of Children and Adolescents in Great Britain," 1999.

Notes

The average Japanese woman can expect to live to be 84. The average Botswanan will reach just 39.

1 Population Reference Bureau (PRB), "Human Population: Fundamentals of Growth," www.prb.org/Content/NavigationMenu/PRB/Educators/Human_Population/Human_Population_Fundamentals_of_Growth_and_Change.htm.

2 Jim Oeppen and James Vaupel, "Broken Limits to Life Expectancy," *Science*, May 2002, quoted at news.bbc.co.uk/1/hi/health/1977733.stm.

3 US Census Bureau, quoted at www.usaid.gov/press/releases/2002/pr020708.html.

4 PRB, "Human Population: Fundamentals of Growth," op. cit.

5 World Bank DepWeb, "Life Expectancy," www.worldbank.org/depweb/english/modules/social/life.html.

6 The Global Fund, "Partners in Impact: Results Report 2007," February 2007.

A third of the world's obese people live in the developing world.

1 Worldwatch Institute, "Chronic Hunger and Obesity Epidemic Eroding Global Progress," March 2000.

2 "FAO/WHO Launch Expert Report on Diet, Nutrition and Prevention of Chronic Diseases," press release, April 23, 2003.

3 WHO figures, quoted in "Clustering in Cities, Asians Are Becoming Obese," *New York Times*, March 13, 2003.

4 "US Lifestyles Blamed for Obesity Epidemic Sweeping Mexico," *Guardian*, 11 August 2003.

5 WHO, "Globalization, Diet and Health: An Example from Tonga," 2001.

6 Quoted by Aziz Choudry, "Killing Me Softly," ZNet Commentary, August 3, 2003.

7 Fijian government press release, March 15, 2001, www.fiji.gov.fj./press/2001_03/2001_03_15-01.shtml.

8 Letter from the Sugar Association to Gro Harlem Brundtland, WHO Director-General, quoted in *Guardian*, "Sugar Industry Threatens to Scupper WHO," March 21, 2003.

9 WHO, "Globalization, Diet and Health: An Example from Tonga," op. cit.

If you stand at the junction of Oxford Street and Regent Street in central London, there are 161 branches of Starbucks within a five-mile radius.

1 http://www.nationmaster.com/graph/foo_cof_con-food-coffee-consumption.

2 http://www.realcoffee.co.uk/Article.asp?Cat=Trivia&Page=1.

3 http://www.starbucks.com/retail/locator/, setting the distance to two miles.

4 http://www.beveragedaily.com/news/ng.asp?n=64001-starbucks-coffee-russia, November 18, 2005.

5 http://www.starbucks.com/aboutus/company_factsheet.pdf, February 2007.

6 http://www.time.com/time/magazine/printout/0,8816,1568488,00.html.

7 http://news.bbc.co.uk/1/hi/business/6319525.stm.

8 http://www.guardian.co.uk/china/story/0,,1993358,00.html.

50 FACTS...

9 http://politics.guardian.co.uk/development/story/0,,2001039,00.html.
10 Find out more at http://www.blackgoldmovie.com.
11 http://www.starbucks.com/aboutus/pressdesc.asp?id=713.
12 http://www.oxfam.org.uk/press/releases/starbucks261006.htm.
13 Douglas B. Holt, "Is Starbucks Coffee That Cares?," Oxford Said Business School, January 25, 2007; http://www.sbs.ox.ac.uk/starbucks/Is+Starbucks+Coffee+That+Cares.htm.
14 http://www.oxfam.org.uk/applications/blogs/pressoffice/2007/03/oxfam_urges_starbucks_to_honou.html.
15 "Clone Town Britain: the loss of identity on the nation's high streets," New Economics Foundation, September 2004.
16 Evening Standard, November 1, 2001 – quoted in the NEF report, ibid.
17 "Starbucks' Schultz Steams," Forbes magazine, February 23, 2007: http://www.forbes.com/markets/2007/02/23/starbucks-howard-schultz-face-cx_mk_0223autofacescan03.html.

China has 44 million missing women.

1 Shanghai Star, October 30, 2002, quoted at www.china.com.cn/english/life/47238.htm.
2 news.bbc.co.uk/1/hi/world/south_asia/736466.stm, dated May 4, 2000.
3 "More female fetuses being aborted in India, UNICEF says," International Herald Tribune, December 12, 2006.
4 "China's Missing Girls," Shanghai Star, October 24, 2002, www.shanghaistar.com.cn/2002/1024/fo5-1.html.
5 International Herald Tribune, op. cit.
6 Radha Venkatesar, "Female Infanticide: Old Reasons, New Techniques," The Hindu, July 24, 2001.
7 Research for the British Medical Journal, quoted in news.bbc.co.uk/1/low/world/south_asia/3076727.stm.
8 Elisabeth Rosenthal, "China's Widely Flouted One-Child Policy Undercuts its Census," New York Times, April 14, 2000.
9 The Society for the Prevention of Infanticide, www.infanticide.org/history.htm.
10 Quoted at www.aidindia.org/nodowry/index.shtml.
11 Quoted at www.indiatogether.org/2003/jul/wom-girls.htm.
12 Demographer Minja Kim Choe from the East–West Center in Honolulu, quoted in "Modern Asia's Anomaly: The Girls Who Don't Get Born," New York Times, June 5, 2001.

Brazil has more Avon ladies than members of its armed services.

1 www.brazil.org.uk/page.php?pid=94.
2 pr.avon.com.br/PRSuite/selling/benefits.jsp.
3 Goldman Sachs figures, quoted in Economist, May 24, 2003.
4 Study by London Guildhall University, quoted at news.bbc.co.uk/1/hi/uk/1038531.stm.
5 David Buss, quoted in transcript of radio programme, The Descent of Man, available at www.abc.net.au/science/descent/trans2.htm.
6 Reuters, February 9, 2003.
7 "Brazil set to be world's third largest beauty market by 2007," cosmeticsmontior.

com; posted May 23, 2006, accessed March 16, 2007 at: http://www.
cosmeticsdesign.com/news/ng.asp?id=67870-abihpec-brazil-cosmetics-
growth
8 "An Army of Underemployed Goes Door-to-Door in Brazil," *Wall Street Journal*, February 19, 2003.
9 Roberto DaMatta, quoted ibid.
10 Ibid.
11 "Demand for Quality: Consumer Products Focusing on Cosmetics," *Inside Brazil* magazine, August 20,1996.
12 "Avon Lady Calls on the Girl Power Generation," *The Times*, October 5, 2002.
13 www.the-infoshop.com/study/eo15474_direct.html.

Ninety-four percent of the world's executions in 2005 took place in just four countries: China, Iran, Saudi Arabia and the USA.
1 Texas Department of Criminal Justice, www.tdcj.state.tx.uk/stat/beazley napoleonlast.htm.
2 "Napoleon's Last Stand," *Texas Monthly* magazine, July 2002.
3 "Bush Defends Executions," CBS News.com, May 26, 2000.
4 www.gallup.com/poll/releases/pr030519.asp.
5 Amnesty International, "Facts and Figures on the Death Penalty," web.amnesty.org/pages/deathpenalty_facts_eng.
6 http://web.amnesty.org/pages/deathpenalty-sentences-eng. Amnesty estimates that a further 20,000 people are currently condemned to death or awaiting execution (ibid.).
7 Amnesty International, "China: Striking Harder Than Ever Before," January 9, 2003.
8 For example, see news.bbc.co.uk/1/hi/world/asia-pacific/627293.stm.
9 *Beijing Today* report, quoted in "China Uses Mobile Death Vans to Execute Prisoners," *The Wire*, Amnesty International, May 2003.
10 Hands Off Cain 2004 Report, available at www.handsoffcain.org.
11 www.hrw.org/wr2k3/mideast3.html.
12 Quoted in news.bbc.co.uk/1/hi/world/middle_east/2287381.stm.
13 http://web.amnesty.org/library/Index/ENGMDE130102007?open&of=ENG-IRN
14 Amnesty International, "Facts and Figures on the Death Penalty," op. cit.
15 web.amnesty.org/library/print/engamr510032002.
16 Ibid.
17 Statement by the President, July 12, 2002, at www.whitehouse.gov/news/releases/2002/07/20020712-9.htm.
18 Human Rights Watch World Report 2003, www.hrw.org/wr2k3.
19 Interview with *BBC HardTalk*, April 25, 2002.
20 Associated Press, March 12, 2007.
21 Quoted at www.cbsnews.com/stories/2003/01/11/national/main536143.shtml.
22 www.whitehouse.gov/news/releases/2003/01/20030113-6.html.

British supermarkets know more about their customers than the British government does.

1 Author's interview with customer forecaster for a British supermarket, September 30, 2003.
2 "What Wal-Mart Knows About Customers' Habits," *New York Times*, November 14, 2004.
3 "The Card up their Sleeve," *Guardian*, July 19, 2003.
4 "Buying Trouble," *Village Voice*, July 24–30, 2002.
5 Ibid.
6 "Claim: RFID Will Stop Terrorists," *Wired* magazine, August 8, 2003, www.wired.com/news/privacy/0,1848,59624,00.html.
7 "UK Trial Addresses Privacy Issue," *Rfidjournal*, October 23, 2003.
8 http://news.bbc.co.uk/1/hi/technology/6389581.stm
9 http://www.theregister.com/2007/04/11/cybercrime_trends_mcafee/
10 "Smart Cards Track Commuters," BBC News Online, September 25, 2003.
11 Author's conversation with Barry Hugill of Liberty, November 27, 2003.

Every cow in the European Union is subsidised by $2.50 a day. That's more than what 75 percent of Africans have to live on.

1 Quoted in "Cows Can Fly Upper Class on Common Agricultural Fare," *Guardian*, September 25, 2002.
2 World Bank President James Wolfensohn, quoted in *Christian Science Monitor*, June 13, 2003.
3 europa.eu.int/pol/agr/overview_en.html.
4 Quoted in "EU pays the price for farm subsidies," *International Herald Tribune*, June 26, 2002.
5 Ibid.
6 http://news.bbc.co.uk/1/hi/business/6180363.stm
7 "EU pays the price for farm subsidies," *International Herald Tribune*, June 26, 2002.
8 Zac Goldsmith, "When common sense is a crime," *New Statesman*, June 30, 2003.
9 "Stop the Dumping! How EU Agricultural Subsidies are Damaging Livelihoods in the Developing World," Oxfam briefing paper October 31, 2002.
10 Ibid.
11 http://news.bbc.co.uk/1/hi/business/4466388.stm
12 Quoted in "Cutting Agricultural Subsidies," November 20, 2002, web.worldbank.org/wbsite/external/news/.
13 "Uncle Sam's teat," *Economist*, September 7, 2006.
14 "Questions and Answers – US Farm Bill," May 2002, europa.eu.int/comm/agriculture/external/wto/press/usfarmbill.pdf.
15 http://news.bbc.co.uk/1/hi/business/5216080.stm

In more than 70 countries, same-sex relationships are illegal. In nine countries, the penalty is death.

1 "Saudis Beheaded for Sodomy," *The Washington Blade*, January 4, 2002.
2 web.amnesty.org/pages/deathpenalty-developments-eng.
3 Surah VII (Araf), verses 80–81, quoted in www.al-fatiha.net/pamphlet.html.
4 Ibid.

5 web.amnesty.org/library/Index/ENGACT530032002?open&of=ENG-392.
6 Quoted in "Campaigning for Gay and Lesbian Human Rights," Amnesty International, September 1999, web.amnesty.org/library/Index/ENGACT 790022001?open&of=ENG-347.
7 Ibid.
8 Ibid.
9 Amnesty International, "Crimes of Hate, Conspiracy of Silence," 2001.
10 Ibid.
11 www.aclu.org/lesbiangayrights/lesbiangayrightsmain.cfm.

One in five of the world's people lives on less than $1 a day.

1 Jeffrey Sachs and Sakiko Fukuda-Parr, "If We Cared To, We Could Defeat World Poverty," *LA Times*, July 9, 2003.
2 World Bank World Development Report 2000/2001.
3 Sachs and Fukuda-Parr, "If We Cared To, We Could Defeat World Poverty," op. cit.
4 OECD DAC Development Co-operation Report 2006, www.oecd.org/dac.
5 UN Human Development Report (UNHDR) 2003.
6 Ibid.
7 Ibid.
8 Ibid. Using the Gini coefficient − a measure whereby 0 stands for perfect equality and 1 stands for complete inequality − Brazil measures 0.61, while the world measures 0.66.
9 World Bank World Development Report 2000/2001.
10 UNHDR, 2003.
11 Ibid.
12 Jubilee Research, "Inequality and Poverty − a Spiral of Despair," www.jubilee2000uk.org.
13 Jeffrey Sachs and Sakiko Fukuda-Parr, "If We Cared To, We Could Defeat World Poverty," op. cit.
14 Report for OECD Round Table on Sustainable Development, January 2003.
15 Oxfam, "Rigged Rules and Double Standards," www.maketradefair.org/stylesheet.asp?file=03042002121618&cat=2&subcat=6&select=1.
16 "Debt cancellation and the Millennium Development Goals," Oxfam briefing paper 78, September 2005; Oxfam.org.uk.
17 UNHDR, 2003.
18 www.heifer.org.
19 "Drugs Are Just the Start," *Guardian*, August 28, 2003.

More than 12,000 women are killed each year in Russia as a result of domestic violence.

1 Quoted in *Human Rights Watch*, "Uzbekistan Turns its Back on Battered Women," July 2001.
2 The Commonwealth Fund, "Health Concerns Across a Woman's Lifespan: 1998 Survey of Women's Health," May 1999, quoted at www.endabuse.org.
3 Lori Heise, Mary Ellsberg and Megan Gottemoeller, "Ending violence against women," Population Reports series L, no. 11, December 1999, quoted at www.endabuse.org.
4 Quoted in "Russia: Domestic Violence Persists," Radio Free Europe/Radio

Liberty, March 2001, www.rferl.org/nca/features/2001/03/07032001120749. asp.

5 Ibid.
6 Zero Tolerance Charitable Trust, "Young People's Attitudes Towards Violence, Sex and Relationships," 1998, quoted by the Women's Aid Federation of England, www.womensaid.org.uk.
7 William Blackstone, Commentaries on the Laws of England (1765–9), Book 1, Chapter 15.
8 Human Rights Watch, "What Will It Take? Stopping Violence Against Women," June 2000.
9 US Department of Justice, "Violence by Intimates: Analysis of Data on Crimes by Current or Former Spouses, Boyfriends or Girlfriends," March 1998, quoted at www.endabuse.org.
10 Bureau of Justice Statistics Crime Data Brief, "Intimate Partner Violence 1993–2001," February 2003, quoted at endabuse.org.

In 2006, 16 million Americans had some form of plastic surgery.

1 Profiles at www.plasticsurgery.org/public_education/patient_profiles.cfm.
2 Ibid.
3 "Pots of Promise," Economist, May 24, 2003.
4 www.plasticsurgery.org/history.cfm.
5 John Orlando Roe, 19th-century American plastic surgeon, quoted at www. plastic surgery.org/history.cfm.
6 www.cosmeticscanada.com/cosmetic_surgery_popular.html.
7 "Pots of Promise," Economist, op. cit.
8 Ibid.
9 Quoted in Alissa Quart, Branded (Boulder, CO: Perseus, 2003), p. 162.
10 "'Extreme Makeover' Gave Local Man New Face, New Life," Seattle Post-Intelligencer, September 20, 2003.
11 "Saving Face," Observer, March 16, 2003.

Landmines kill or maim at least one person every hour.

1 International Committee of the Red Cross, "Basic Facts: The Human Cost of Landmines," January 1995.
2 Profiles from www.landminesurvivors.org.
3 Human Rights Watch, "Global Progress on Banning Landmines: United States Gets Mixed Reviews," September 2003.
4 The World Federation of Public Health Associations Resolution on Landmines, May 1994, viewed at www.apha.org/wfpha/landmines.htm.
5 www.icbl.org/resources/problem.html.
6 N. Dentico, "Landmines: The Silent Sentinels of Death," IDOC Internazionale 1, 1995.
7 International Campaign to Ban Landmines, Landmine Monitor Report 2003.
8 http://www.icbl.org/lm/2006/findings.html.
9 Quoted in Human Rights Watch, "Exposing the Source: US Companies and the Production of Anti-personnel Mines," April 1997.
10 Quoted at www.oneworld.org/guides/landmines/.

There are 44 million child laborers in India.
1 "Marked for Life," *New Internationalist* magazine, July 1997.
2 Global March against Child Labor, www.globalmarch.org.
3 US Department of Labor, "By the Sweat and Toil of Children," 1998.
4 Anti-Slavery International Annual Report, www.anti-slavery.org.
5 Human Rights Watch, "Promises Broken," December 1999.
6 "Child labor crackdown," BBC News Online, April 24, 2002.
7 "American Working Teens Fact Sheet," www.nclnet.org/workingteens.htm.
8 UNICEF Voices of Youth, "Children and Work," www.unicef.org/foy/meeting/lab/farcase1.htm.
9 Human Rights Watch, "Promises Broken," op. cit.
10 "Thank You, Mr Harkin, Sir," *New Internationalist*, July 1997.
11 "Child workers face uncertain future," BBC News Online, October 9, 2006: http://news.bbc.co.uk/1/hi/world/south_asia/6034203.stm.
12 www.enda.sn.
13 www.rugmark.org.
14 "Marked for Life," *New Internationalist* magazine, op. cit.

People in industrialized countries eat between fourteen and fifteen pounds of food additives every year.
1 Federation of European Food Additives and Food Enzyme Industries, "Additives: Ingredients with a Purpose," www.elc-eu.org/addit-d.htm.
2 Erik Millstone and Tim Lang, *The Atlas of Food* (London: Earthscan, 2003).
3 www.faia.org.uk/honey.htm.
4 www.foodcomm.org.uk/additives_sweets2_98.htm.
5 Erik Millstone and Tim Lang, *The Atlas of Food*, op. cit.
6 David Rall, retired Assistant Surgeon General, US Public Health Service, quoted at www.cspinet.org/foodsafety/additives_acesulfame.html.
7 www.cspinet.org/reports/chemcuisine.htm.
8 Erik Millstone and Tim Lang, *The Atlas of Food*, op. cit.

David Beckham's deal with the LA Galaxy football team will earn him $100 every minute.
1 http://news.bbc.co.uk/sport1/hi/football/1795385.stm.
2 http://sportsillustrated.cnn.com/2007/writers/grant_wahl/01/17/beckham.qa/?cnn=yes.
3 Ibid.
4 http://www.forbes.com/2006/06/12/06celebrities_money-power-celebrities-list_land.html.
5 http://www.pga.com/tournaments/money-leaders/pga_money_leaders.cfm.
6 "Mining Woods For Gold," *Sports Illustrated* Online, September 20, 2000.
7 Quoted at www.golftoday.co.uk/news/yeartodate/news00/woods56.html.
8 "Mining Woods for Gold," op. cit.
9 news.bbc.co.uk/sport1/hi/golf/1024896.stm.
10 http://www.indystar.com/apps/pbcs.dll/article?AID=/20070201/LOCAL/702010431/.
11 http://www.leagueoffans.org/fieldadsvictory.html.
12 http://football.guardian.co.uk/News_Story/0,,2020869,00.html.
13 http://football.guardian.co.uk/News_Story/0,1563,1334980,00.html.

14 http://sportsillustrated.cnn.com/2007/writers/grant_wahl/01/17/beckham. qa/?cnn=yes.
15 http://www.washingtonpost.com/wp-srv/sports/mls/longterm/2006/mls. salaries.html.
16 http://news.bbc.co.uk/sport1/hi/football/6248835.stm.

Seven million American women and 1 million American men suffer from an eating disorder.

1 Eating Disorders Coalition, www.eatingdisorderscoalition.org/reports/ statistics.html.
2 Mayo Clinic study, quoted at www.pbs.org/wgbh/nova/transcripts/2715thin. html.
3 "TV Brings Eating Disorders to Fiji," news.bbc.co.uk/1/hi/health/347637.stm.
4 "Ultra-thin Magazine Models Found to Have Little Negative Effect on Adolescent Girls," www.apa.org/monitor/oct99/nb9.html.
5 "Elson Wins Battle with Anorexia," Vogue Online, August 9, 2002.
6 www.anred.com/causes.html.
7 Dying to be Thin, PBS Nova documentary, December 12, 2000, www.pbs. org/wgbh/nova/transcripts/2715thin.html.

Nearly half of British fifteen year olds have tried illegal drugs and nearly a quarter are regular cigarette smokers.

1 "Smoking, Drinking and Drug Use Among Young People in England in 2002," survey carried out on behalf of the Department of Health, 2002.
2 European Monitoring Centre on Drugs and Drug Abuse, annual report, 2003.
3 Pride Survey 2002–2003, released September 2003, www.pridesurveys. com.
4 "Smoking, Drinking and Drug Use Among Young People in England in 2002," op. cit.
5 Ibid.
6 American Lung Association, "Adolescent Smoking Statistics," November 2003, www.lungusa.org.
7 National Institute on Drug Abuse, "Monitoring the Future," 2002.
8 "Reducing Underage Drinking: A Collective Responsibility," Institute of Medicine at the National Academy of Science, September 2003.
9 www.teenpregnancy.org.
10 "Smoking, Drinking and Drug Use Among Young People in England in 2002," op. cit.
11 European Monitoring Centre on Drugs and Drug Abuse, annual report, 2003.
12 American Lung Association, "Adolescent Smoking Statistics," op. cit.
13 "Teenage Drug Use," British Medical Journal, 1996, 313:375.
14 "Tobacco Giant's Secret Papers Revealed," Observer, September 7, 2003.
15 Schools Health Education Unit study, October 2003, quoted at news.bbc. co.uk/1/hi/education/3171254.stm.
16 www.theantidrug.com/steerclear/factsheet.asp; www.nida.nih.gov/Marij Broch/parent pg9-10N.html.

...THAT SHOULD CHANGE THE WORLD

One million people become new mobile phone subscribers every day. Some 85 percent of them live in emerging markets.
1 "A New Calling," *Forbes* magazine, April 16, 2007, http://www.forbes.com/free_forbes/2007/0416/174.html.
2 Figures from the GSM Association, http://www.gsmworld.com, quoted at http://news.bbc.co.uk/1/hi/business/6339671.stm.
3 http://www.economist.com/business/displaystory.cfm?story_id=E1_RPRTJRS.
4 Ibid.
5 A developing country with an extra ten phones per 100 people between 1996 and 2003 would have had GDP growth 0.59 percent higher than an otherwise identical country. Study by the Centre for Economic Policy Research; Waverman, Meschi and Fuss, *The Impact of Telecoms on Economic Growth in Developing Countries, Africa: The Impact of Mobile Phones*, Vodafone Policy Paper Series 2 (March 2005), detailed at http://www.vodafone.com/start/responsibility/our_social___economic/socio-economic_impact/impact_of_mobile_phones.html.
6 Willams, *The Relationship between Mobile Telecommunications Infrastructure and FDI in Africa* (February 2005), quoted by Vodafone, ibid.
7 Ibid.
8 http://news.bbc.co.uk/1/hi/technology/6241603.stm.
9 "The digital universe," report by EMC Corporation, March 2007, http://www.emc.com/about/destination/digital_universe/, quoted at http://technology.guardian.co.uk/news/story/0,,2027327,00.html.
10 http://www.internetworldstats.com/stats.htm.
11 For more information, go to www.tradenet.biz
12 World Bank figures quoted in Hernandez-Coss, "The Impact of Remittances: Observations in Remitting and Receiving Countries," discussion paper, Intergovernmental Group of September 24, 2006, accessed at www.g24.org.
13 http://www.economist.com/opinion/displaystory.cfm?story_id=E1_SJQQPVJ.
14 For more information, visit the Internet Freedom of Expression Exchange at www.ifex.org.
15 "Mobiles, protests and pundits," *Economist*, October 26, 2006.

Cars kill two people every minute.
1 Details from the UK's RoadPeace charity, www.roadpeace.org/articles/WorldFirst Death.html.
2 Department for Transport, www.dft.gov.uk.
3 World Road Association/Global Road Safety Partnership/Department for International Development, "Keep Death Off Your Roads," April 2003.
4 Bureau of Transportation Statistics, www.bts.gov.
5 WHO, "Road Traffic Injury Prevention," www.who.int/violence_injury_prevention/unintentional_injuries/road_traffic/rtip1/en/. 6 WHO press release, www.epha.org/a/754.
7 World Bank, www.worldbank.org/html/fpd/transport/roads/saf_docs/graph1.xls.
8 OECD Newsroom, "Road Deaths Cost OECD Economies the Equivalent of

2% of GDP," July 30, 1999.

9 Department for Transport, "Transport Statistics for Great Britain 2004 Edition," available at www.dft.gov.uk.

10 G.D. Jacobs and Amy Aeron-Thomas, "A Review of Global Accident Fatalities," RoSPA Road Safety Congress, March 2000, accessed at DFID, www.transport-links.org.

11 Quoted in Vinand Nantulya and Michael Reich, "The Neglected Epidemic," British Medical Journal, 2002, vol. 324.

12 Speech by Prime Minister Laisenia Qarase to Road Safety Forum, February 2002, quoted at www.fiji.gov.fj./speeches_features/S2002_02/S2002_02_25-01.shtml.

13 "Keep Death Off Your Roads," op. cit.

14 GRSP annual report, July 2003.

15 Nelson Mandela, The Long Walk To Freedom, quoted in "Keep Death Off Your Roads," op. cit.

Since 1977, there have been more than 90,000 acts of violence and disruption at abortion clinics in North America.

1 news.bbc.co.uk/1/hi/world/americas/3077040.stm.

2 www.agi-usa.org/pubs/archives/nr_011503.html.

3 National Abortion Federation Violence and Disruption Statistics, at www.prochoice.org, count 128,466 incidents in the period 1977–December 2006. It is noted that these are reported incidents only – the actual number of incidents is likely to be "much higher."

4 Essay by Horsley, quoted at www.christiangallery.com/aog.html, accessed 12 October 2003.

5 NOW's "The Truth About George" website, www.thetruthaboutgeorge.com/women/index.html. The comparison between abortion and terrorism came when President Bush decided to declare the 29th anniversary of Roe v. Wade, January 22, 2002, as "National Sanctity of Human Life Day." Bush's proclamation: "On September 11, we saw clearly that evil exists in this world, and that it does not value life ... now we are engaged in a fight against evil and tyranny to preserve and protect life."

6 National Organization for Women, "Anti-Abortion Leader Loses Two Court Fights," July 3, 2002.

Global warming already kills 150,000 people every year.

1 http://www.earth-policy.org/Updates/2006/Update56.htm, July 28, 2006.

2 Ibid.

3 http://www.telegraph.co.uk/news/main.jhtml?xml=/news/2005/09/22/wheat22.xml.

4 UN Environment Programme, "Impacts of summer 2003 heatwave in Europe," Environmental Alert Bulletin, March 2004.

5 Ibid.

6 http://www.guardian.co.uk/italy/story/0,,1983891,00.html.

7 Dr Paul Epstein of the Center for Health and Global Environment, Massachusetts, quoted at http://www.twnside.org.sg/title/twr125g.htm.

8 http://www.bmj.com/cgi/content/full/315/7111/805

9 http://www.who.int/mediacentre/factsheets/fs266/en/

10 http://www.guardian.co.uk/guardianweekly/story/0,,2007802,00.html
11 Access the full report at http://www.hm-treasury.gov.uk/independent_
   reviews/stern_review_economics_climate_change/stern_review_report.cfm.
12 http://news.bbc.co.uk/1/hi/business/6096084.stm.
13 http://news.bbc.co.uk/1/hi/sci/tech/6524325.stm.
14 http://www.greenpeace.org/international/campaigns/climate-change/take_
   action/12_steps.
15 The list of links is currently at this page: http://www.defra.gov.uk/environment/
   climatechange/uk/carbonoffset/links.htm

In Kenya, bribery payments make up a third of the average household budget.
1 Kevin Omindo, quoted in "Country of Bribes," www.worldpress.org/africa/359.
   cfm.
2 Conversation with the author, October 16, 2003.
3 Transparency International Corruption Perceptions Index 2003.
4 "Wolfensohn in Kenya Addresses Corruption," web.worldbank.org, August
   13, 2003.
5 "Lesotho fines second dam firm," BBC News Online, August 27, 2003.
6 "Swiss join oil bribery enquiry," *Guardian*, May 7, 2003.
7 2006 Transparency International Progress Report on OECD Convention
   Enforcement, www.transparency.org.
8 Transparency International, Bribe Payers Index 2002, May 2002.
9 "Fine words but corruption soars," BBC News Online, January 2, 2006, http://
   news.bbc.co.uk/1/hi/world/africa/4511746.stm.
10 Conversation with the author, op. cit.
11 "Kibaki and 30 MPs Declare their Riches," *Daily Nation*, September 30, 2003.

The world's trade in illegal drugs is estimated to be worth around $400 billion – about the same as the world's legal pharmaceutical industry.
1 Quoted in Edward Brecher, "The Consumers Union Report on Licit and Illicit
   Drugs," 1972, at www.druglibrary.org.
2 National Drug Control Strategy, FY 2008 Budget Fact Sheet, February 2007;
   http://www.whitehousedrugpolicy.gov.
3 Quoted at www.drugpolicy.org/library/factsheets/economiccons/fact_
   economic.cfm.
4 UN Office on Drugs and Crime, www.unodc.org.
5 www.worldpharmaceuticals.net/marketresearch.html estimates the industry
   grew to $406 billion in 2002.
6 "Just Say No: Government's War on Drugs Failure," John Stossel, ABC
   News, July 30, 2002.
7 Cleveland Report, quoted in *Observer*, December 9, 2001.
8 www.drugpolicy.org/global/terrorism.
9 Ibid.
10 UN Office for Drug Control and Crime Prevention, op. cit.
11 Cleveland Report, op. cit.
12 National Household Survey on Drug Abuse, 2001.
13 University of Amsterdam Centre for Drug Research, 1997, quoted in www.
   drugwar facts.org.

14 "Just Say No," ABC News, op. cit.

A third of Americans believe aliens have landed on Earth.
1 National Science Foundation, "Science and Engineering Indicators 2002," Chapter 7.
2 Poll by media consortium Roar, quoted in *London Evening Standard*, December 17, 1999.
3 See "Close Encounters," *Time* magazine, September 29, 2003.
4 edition.cnn.com/us/9706/15/ufo.poll.
5 Josef Allen Hynek, quoted in Popular Mechanics magazine, popularmechanics. com/science/space/1998/7/6_ufo_sightings.html.
6 Floyd Rudmin, "Conspiracy Theory as Naïve Deconstructive History," April 2003, newdemocracyworld.org/conspiracy.htm.
7 Seth Shostak, quoted at www.space.com/searchforlife/seti_shostak_visit_020627.html, June 2002.
8 www.setileague.org/general/drake.htm.
9 www.setileague.org.

More than 150 countries use torture.
1 Quoted at web.amnesty.org/pages/stoptorture-manual-index-eng.
2 "US decries abuse but defends interrogations," *Washington Post*, December 26, 2002.
3 Joint hearing of the House and Senate Intelligence Committees, September 26, 2002.
4 For more, see Human Rights Watch, www.hrw.org/us/usdom.php?theme= Torture/Mistreatment.
5 news.bbc.co.uk/1/hi/world/americas/3182346.html.
6 Amnesty International, "Human Dignity Denied: Torture and Accountability in the 'War on Terror'," October 2004.
7 Quoted at edition.cnn.com/2003/law/03/03/cnna.dershowitz.
8 Basil Fernando, Executive Director of the Asian Human Rights Commission, quoted at www.omct.org/displaydocument.asp?DocType=Appeal&Index= 2810&Language=EN.
9 Cesare Beccaria, Of Crimes and Punishments, 1764, Chapter 16. 10 Conversation with the author, October 24, 2003.

Every day, one in five of the world's population – some 800 million people – go hungry.
1 WHO, "Nutrition for Health and Development: A Global Agenda for Combating Malnutrition," 2000.
2 Erik Millstone and Tim Lang, *The Atlas of Food* (London: Earthscan, 2003).
3 "Why Half the Planet is Hungry," *Observer*, June 16, 2002.
4 "Why Famine Stalks Africa," BBC News Online, November 12, 2002.
5 www.fao.org/worldfoodsummit/english/fsheets/food.pdf.
6 "Armed Conflict and Hunger," www.worldhunger.org.
7 Care International, "HIV/Aids and Food Insecurity: Breaking the Vicious Cycle," 2002.
8 "The State of Food and Agriculture 2001," www.fao.org.
9 "Against the Grain," *Guardian*, September 11, 2003.

10 "Food Aid to Save and Improve Lives," www.fao.org/worldfoodsummit/english.fsheets.wfp.pdf.
11 UNESCO figures, quoted by FAO, ibid.
12 World Bank figures, quoted by FAO, ibid.
13 Press release, October 16, 2003.
14 WHO press release, September 3, 2003, www.who.int/nut/nutrition1.htm.

Black men born in the US today stand a one in three chance of going to jail.
1 US Department of Justice, Bureau of Justice Statistics, Corrections, February 2007; http://www.ojp.usdoj.gov/bjs/correct.htm
2 Bureau of Justice Statistics, "Prevalence of Imprisonment in the US Population, 1974–2001," August 2003.
3 Ibid.
4 The Sentencing Project, "Facts About Prisons and Prisoners," www.sentencingproject.org/pdfs/1035.pdf.
5 Bureau of Justice Statistics, Sourcebook of Criminal Justice Statistics, 2001, www.albany.edu/sourcebook.
6 The Sentencing Project, "Facts About Prisons and Prisoners," ibid.
7 Ira Glasser, "American Drug Laws: The New Jim Crow," speech to the 1999 ACLU Biennial Conference, at www.aclu.org/drugpolicy/drugpolicy.cfm?id=5040&c=82.
8 For more, see the excellent discussion at www.jimcrowhistory.org.
9 The Sentencing Project, "Does the Punishment Fit the Crime? Drug Users and Drunk Drivers, Questions of Race and Class," www.sentencingproject.org/ pdfs/9040smy.pdf.
10 ACLU, "Drugs and race," December 17, 2001.
11 Ibid.
12 Center for Constitutional Rights, "CCR Achieves Historic Settlement in Street Crimes Unit Class Action," September 18, 2003, www.ccr-ny.org.
13 The Sentencing Project, "Fact Sheet: Women in Prison," www. sentencing project.org/pdfs/1032.pdf.
14 "Hardest Hit by the Prison Craze," Salon.com, January 12, 2001.
15 The Sentencing Project, "Fact Sheet: Women in Prison," op. cit.
16 Human Rights Watch/The Sentencing Project, "Losing the Vote," 1998.
17 Ira Glasser, "American Drug Laws: The New Jim Crow," op. cit.
18 "One in 100 Black Adults now in Jail," *Observer*, March 30, 2003.
19 Paul Street, "Race, Prison and Poverty," *Z Magazine*, May 2001.
20 Ibid.

A third of the world's population is at war.
1 Visit them at www.ploughshares.ca.
2 Project Ploughshares, Armed Conflict Report 2006; http://www.ploughshares.ca/libraries/ACRText/ACR-TitlePageRev.htm.
3 "Sudan: Displaced Caught in the Crossfire," IRINnews.org, 2002, www.irinnews.org/webspecials/idp/rSudan.asp.
4 Ibid.
5 International Rescue Committee, DR Congo Mortality Survey 2002.
6 International Rescue Committee, "IRC staff members talk about 'the biggest humanitarian crisis on the planet'," April 2003.

7 Examples from PBS documentary, *The Environmental Impact of War*, August 29, 1999, produced by the Center for Defense Information.
8 Interview with IRIN, 2003, www.irinnews.org.
9 Report of the Secretary-General to the Security Council on the Protection of Civilians in Armed Conflict, November 26, 2002.
10 President Dwight D. Eisenhower, April 16, 1953.

The world's oil reserves could be exhausted by 2040.

1 www.opec.org.
2 Colin Campbell and Jean Laherrere, "The End of Cheap Oil," *Scientific American*, March 1998.
3 Quoted in the Money Programme, "The Last Oil Shock," October 23, 2001.
4 CIA, "Global Trends 2015: A Dialogue About the Future with Nongovernment Experts," 2000.
5 Renewable Energy Information Sheet, US Department of Energy, www.eia.doe.gov.
6 Motor Equipment and Manufacturers' Association, www.mema.org.
7 "The Big Green Fuel Lie," *Independent*, March 5, 2007.
8 Ibid.
9 "GM Confident Hydrogen Powered Vehicles Will Hit Road from 2010," Asia Pulse, 28 October 2003.

Eighty-two percent of the world's smokers live in developing countries.

1 In 2000, 4.83 million people are estimated to have died from smoking-related conditions. Study published in the *Lancet*, September 2003, cited at www.cbsnews.com.
2 www.who.int/tobacco/health_impact/en/.
3 Worldwatch Institute, Vital Signs 2003.
4 National Center for Chronic Disease Prevention and Health Promotion, "Smoking Prevalence Among US Adults," October 2003.
5 National Statistics, "Living in Britain 2001."
6 Spokesman for Rothmans, 1992, quoted in WHO, The Tobacco Atlas, www.who.int/tobacco/statistics/tobacco_atlas/en.
7 Studies quoted in "Tobacco Explained," prepared for Action on Smoking and Health, adapted for WHO's World No Tobacco Day.
8 World Health Organisation, Regional Office for the Western Pacific, press release, 28 May 2002.
9 WHO, The Tobacco Atlas, op. cit.
10 "From Social Taboo to 'Torch of Freedom': The Marketing of Cigarettes to Women," Tobacco Control, vol. 9, 2000.
11 Ibid.
12 Center for Disease Control, Global Youth Tobacco Survey.
13 Ibid.
14 Action on Smoking and Health, "Tobacco: Global Trends," www.ash.org.uk/html/international/html/globaltrends.html.
15 "In Ex-Soviet Markets, US Brands Took on Role of Capitalist Liberator," *Washington Post*, September 19, 1996.
16 Richard Peto, quoted in "Vast China Market Key to Smoking Disputes," *Washington Post*, 20 November 1996.
17 World Bank, "Economics of Tobacco Control," www1.worldbank.org/tobacco.

18 "Tobacco Ruling Makes Japan Laughingstock," Yomiuri Shimbun, October 22, 2003.

19 Vendhan Gajalakshmi, Richard Peto, Thanjavur Santhanakrishna Kanaka and Prabhat Jha, "Smoking and Mortality from Tuberculosis and Other Diseases in India," Lancet, vol. 362, issue 9383, August 2003.

20 www.aidsmap.org/treatments/ixdata/english/10838483-5ca4-46a3-aea3ffc 8fbd88667.htm.

21 World Bank, "Economics of Tobacco Control," ibid.

22 See the WHO inquiry of tobacco industry influence, available at www.who. int/tobacco/policy/industry_conduct/en/index.html.

23 Speech to BAT annual general meeting, April 29,1999.

24 Study published in the Canadian Medical Association Journal 2002, quoted in Worldwatch Institute, Vital Signs 2003.

Britons buy 3 billion items of clothing every year – an average of 50 pieces each. Most of it ends up being thrown away.

1 "Clothing & Footwear Industry Market Review 2006," www.marketresearch. com, quoted in "Well Dressed?: The Present and Future Sustainability of Clothing and Textiles in the United Kingdom," University of Cambridge Institute for Manufacturing, 2006; www.ifm.eng.cam.ac.uk.

2 http://www.dailymail.co.uk/pages/live/femail/article.html?in_article_ id=447541&in_page_id=1879&in_page_id=1879.

3 Downloadthefullreportathttp://www.waronwant.org/Fashion+Victims+13593. twl.

4 "Let's Clean Up Fashion: The State of Pay Behind the British High Street," Labor Behind The Label, September 2006; http://www.labourbehindthelabel. org/content/view/126/53/.

5 "Redressing a Global Imbalance: The Case for Fairtrade Certified Cotton," Fairtrade Foundation Briefing Paper, November 29, 2005; http://www.fairtrade. org.uk/products_cotton.htm.

6 The World Bank, February 2003, "Irrigation in Central Asia: Social, Economic and Environmental Considerations," quoted in "Well Dressed?," op. cit.

7 http://www.soilassociation.org/web/sa/saweb.nsf/848d689047cb466780256 a6b00298980/3d9ba1c2e564145280256ef50041bf72!OpenDocument.

8 http://www.sixwise.com/newsletters/05/12/21/the_6+_synthetic_fabrics_ you_most_want_to_avoid_and_why.htm.

9 "Well Dressed?," op. cit.

10 Ibid.

11 http://www.dailymail.co.uk/pages/live/femail/article.html?in_article_ id=447541&in_page_id=1879&in_page_id=1879.

12 http://www.cleanupfashion.co.uk.

13 "M&S set to launch Fair Trade range," BBC News, January 30, 2006; http:// news.bbc.co.uk/1/hi/business/4660410.stm.

A quarter of the world's armed conflicts of recent years have involved a struggle for natural resources.

1 Worldwatch Institute, Vital Signs 2003.

2 International Rescue Committee, DR Congo Mortality Survey 2002.

3 Final Report of the Panel of Experts on the Illegal Exploitation of Natural

Resources and Other Forms of Wealth of the Democratic Republic of Congo, report to the UN Security Council, October 16, 2002.
4 "Vital Ore Funds Congo's War," *Washington Post*, March 19, 2001.
5 Report to the Security Council, October 28, 2003.
6 Council on Foreign Relations, www.terrorismanswers.com/groups/farc.html.
7 Quoted in "Middle East Water – Critical Resource," National Geographic, May 1993.
8 www.fao.org.
9 CGIAR press release, November 2, 2003, www.waterforfood.org.
10 UN IRIN service, published at www.scienceinafrica.co.za/2003/may/ nile. htm.
11 southasia.oneworld.net/article/view/69335/1.
12 "Water Hotspots," BBC News Online, news.bbc.co.uk/1/shared/spl/hi/world/ 03/world_forum/water/html/default.stm.
13 "'Real Conflicts' Over the World's Water," BBC News Online, 20 March 2003.
14 "Armed forces are put on standby to tackle threat of wars over water," *Independent*, February 28, 2006.

Some 30 million people in Africa are HIV-positive.

1 UNFPA, "State of the World's Population 2003," October 2003.
2 US Census Bureau, quoted in www.usaid.gov/press/releases/2002/ pr020708.html.
3 UNFPA representative to Sierra Leone Dr Mamadou Diallou, quoted in UNFPA press release, July 16, 2002.
4 Lecture at Fort Hare University, quoted in the *Daily Telegraph*, October 27, 2001.
5 Account taken from "The Belated Global Response to AIDS in Africa," *Washington Post*, July 5, 2000.
6 Ibid.
7 Human Rights Watch, "China's Epidemic of Secrecy," October 30, 2003.
8 "Hidden from the World, a Village Dies of AIDS while China Refuses to Face a Growing Crisis," *Guardian*, October 25, 2003.
9 Human Rights Watch, "AIDS in India: Money Won't Solve Crisis," November 13, 2002.
10 "The Impact of HIV and AIDS on Africa," www.avert.org/aidsimpact.htm.
11 Ibid.
12 www.guardian.co.uk/aids/graphic/0,7367,898064,00.html.
13 UNFPA, "HIV/AIDS in Sub-Saharan Africa," www.unfpa.org/africa/hivaids. htm.
14 "Annan Issues Stark AIDS Warning," BBC News Online, September 22, 2003.
15 www.nationmaster.com.

Ten languages die out every year.

1 "Alarm Raised on the World's Disappearing Languages," *Independent*, May 15, 2003.
2 Barbara F. Grimes, "Global Language Viability," www.sil.org/sociolx/ndg-lggrimes_article.html.

3 The database is owned by SIL International (www.sil.org), a service organization working with people who speak the world's lesser-known languages.
4 www.ethnologue.com.
5 Quoted at www.unesco.org/education/educprog/wtd_99/english/mother.htm.
6 www.nzhistory.net.nz/gallery/tereo/history.htm.
7 www.tpk.govt.nz/maori/language/educationmi.asp.
8 www.unesco.org/courier/2000_04/uk/doss21.htm.

More people die each year from suicide than in all the world's armed conflicts.

1 Center for Disease Control (CDC), "Suicide in the United States," www.cdc.gov/ncipc/factsheets.suifacts.htm.
2 Office of National Statistics, "Non-fatal Suicidal Behavior Among Adults Aged 16 to 74," March 2002, quoted in Guardian, March 25, 2002.
3 WHO, Suicide Prevention Program, www.who.int/mental_health/ prevention/suicide/suicideprevent/en/.
4 American Association of Suicidology, "The Links between Depression and Suicide," www.suicidology.org.
5 Quoted in Matthews, "How did Pre-Twentieth Century Theories of the Aetiology of Depression Develop?," www.priory.com/homol/dephist.htm.
6 World Vision, "Intervention Proves Effective in Treating Depression in Africa," www.worldvision.org.
7 N. Husain, F. Creed and B. Tomenson, "Depression and Social Stress in Pakistan" (2000), Psychological Medicine, 30:395–402.
8 www.nimh.nih.gov/publicat/depression.cfm.
9 "Lifestyle Causing Huge Rise in Suicide by Men," The Times, September 29, 2003.
10 Office of National Statistics, "Social Trends 31," 2001.
11 CDC, "Suicide in the United States," op. cit.
12 www.nimh.nih.gov/publicat/depression.cfm.
13 www.suicidology.org.
14 Ibid.
15 Ibid.
16 Quoted in "Stigma Ties," Guardian, September 11, 2002.
17 www.who.int/mental_health/management/depression/definition/en.
18 WHO, "Suicidal behavior in Europe," 1998.
19 Albert Camus, The Myth of Sisyphus, 1943.
20 Figures quoted in the Economist, "Might As Well Live," October 30, 2004.
21 Quoted in Andrew Solomon, The Noonday Demon (London: Chatto and Windus, 2001).
22 Our Healthier Nation, www.ohn.gov.uk
23 Quoted in Andrew Solomon, The Noonday Demon, op. cit.

Every week, an average of 54 children are expelled from American schools for bringing a gun to class.

1 Account from "Red Lion Reeling from Two Deaths," York Daily Record, April 25, 2003.
2 www.wsvn/news/articles/C27361/.

3 Quoted in "Bullies, Bullied: Armed and Dangerous," CBS News Online, April 15, 2003.
4 Quoted in "Our Kids Have Guns, Now What do We do About it?," *Time*, April 2, 2001.
5 National Gun Policy Survey of the National Opinion Research Center, December 2001, quoted in The HELP Network, "Guns and Gun Attitudes in America," www.helpnetwork.org/frames/resources_factsheets_gunsinus.pdf.
6 National Institute of Justice, Research in Brief, May 1997, quoted in The HELP Network, "Guns and Gun Attitudes in America," op. cit.
7 US Secret Service National Threat Assessment Center and the US Department of Education, "Safe School Initiative," May 2002, quoted at www. kidsandguns.org.
8 Center for Disease Control, "Rates of Homicide, Suicide and Firearm-related Death Among Children – 26 Industrialized Countries," Morbidity and Mortality Weekly Report, February 7, 1997.
9 Author's conversation with Neil Durkin of Amnesty International UK, October 24, 2003.
10 National Institute of Justice, Guns in America: National Survey on Private Ownership and Use of Firearms, May 1997.
11 Amnesty International and Oxfam International, "Shattered Lives," 2003.
12 Quoted in "The Myth of the Second Amendment," Brady Campaign to Prevent Gun Violence, www.bradycampaign.org/facts/issues/?page=second.
13 Quoted at nrawinningteam.com/0105/fortune.html, May 18, 2001.
14 "The NRA's Enormous Political Clout," CNN.com, April 29, 2003.
15 Quoted in "Senate Leaders Scuttle Gun Bill Over Changes," *New York Times*, March 3, 2004.
16 Transcript of the third presidential debate, held on October 13, 2004, accessed at www.pbs.org/newshour/vote2004/debates/3rddebate/part5. html.
17 Peter Hart Research Associates, "Americans' Attitudes on Children's Access to Guns," July 1999.
18 S. Teret et al., "Support for New Policies to Regulate Firearms," *New England Journal of Medicine*, 1998, quoted at www.helpnetwork.org.
19 Quoted in Johns Hopkins University Center for Gun Policy and Research Factsheet, "Firearm Injury and Death in the United States," www.jhsph.edu/gunpolicy.
20 Quoted at news.bbc.co.uk/1/hi/world/americas/332555.stm.
21 *Journal of the American Medical Association*, 1997, quoted in "Kids and Guns in America," www.bradycampaign.org/facts/issues/?page=kids.

There are at least 300,000 prisoners of conscience in the world.

1 Amnesty International World Report 2003.
2 Amnesty International, *The Wire*, March 2006 and February 2007; http://web.amnesty.org/wire/February2007/Eritrea; http://web.amnesty.org/wire/March2006/Eritrea
3 http://www.rsf.org/print.php3?id_article=12455.
4 Amnesty International, "Riad al-Turk Talks to The Wire," *The Wire*, November 2003.
5 See www.hermaja.org.
6 www.wri-irg.org/news/htdocs/27032002b.html.

7 Preamble, Universal Declaration of Human Rights, adopted 10 December 1948.
8 Human Rights Watch, "UN Rights Body in Serious Decline," April 25, 2003.
9 Human Rights Watch, "Libya's Human Rights Record in the Spotlight," January 17, 2003.
10 www.amnestyusa.org/prisoners_of_conscience/.
11 For more information see www.prisonersofconscience.org.

Two million girls and women are subjected to female genital mutilation each year.

1 Quoted in UNFPA, "FAQs About Female Genital Cutting," www.unfpa.org/gender/faq_fgc.htm.
2 WHO, Female Genital Mutilation Fact Sheet, June 2000, www.who.int/inf-fs/en/fact241.html.
3 Ibid.
4 For a further discussion see Muslim Women's League, "Female Genital Mutilation," www.mwlusa.org/publications/position papers/fgm.html.
5 WHO, Female Genital Mutilation Fact Sheet, op. cit.
6 www.fgmnetwork.org.
7 "Couple's Stand Against Female Circumcision," BBC News Online, January 22, 2003.
8 Author's conversation with Jacqui Hunt of Equality Now, November 18, 2003.
9 Joint statement by the World Health Organisation, UNICEF and UN Population Fund, February 1996, quoted in Amnesty International, "Female Genital Mutilation: A Human Rights Information Pack," 1998.
10 Equality Now, "Tanzania: Failing to Enforce the Law Against Female Genital Mutilation," June 2001.
11 Conversation with Jacqui Hunt of Equality Now, op. cit.
12 Samia Mohammed, "Campaigns Against Female Genital Mutilation are Paying off in Eritrea," National Union of Eritrean Youth and Students Awaken magazine, April 2003.
13 "Togolese Anti-FGM Legislation Shows Results," afrol News Online, October 29, 2002.
14 Quoted in "Young Africans Reject Genital Mutilation," Women's e-News, January 10, 2003.

There are 300,000 child soldiers fighting in conflicts around the world.

1 Testimony of Martin P., aged thirteen, abducted in February 2002. Quoted in Human Rights Watch, "Stolen Children: Abduction and Recruitment in Northern Uganda," March 2003.
2 Human Rights Watch, "Facts about Child Soldiers," www.hrw.org/ campaigns/crp/facts.htm.
3 Ibid.
4 Coalition to Stop the Use of Child Soldiers, Child Soldiers Global Report, May 2001.
5 Human Rights Watch, "'My Gun Was as Tall as Me': Child Soldiers in Burma," October 2002.
6 Ibid.

7 Ibid.
8 Coalition to Stop the Use of Child Soldiers, Child Soldiers Global Report, op.cit.
9 Amnesty International, "DR Congo: Children at War," September 2003.
10 Amnesty International, "DR Congo: Child Soldiers Tell their Stories," September 2003.
11 "Tough Calls in Child-soldier Encounters," Christian Science Monitor, June 27, 2002.
12 Brig-Gen. William Catto of the Marine Corps Warfighting Laboratory, quoted in Christian Science Monitor, op. cit.
13 Conversation with the author, November 21, 2003.
14 Ibid.
15 "Secretary-General Provides List to Security Council of those Using Child Soldiers, Says Exposure Means Violators of Protection Norms Can No Longer Act with Impunity," UN press release, January 14, 2003.
16 Quoted at web.amnesty.org/pages/childsoldiers-index-eng.

Nearly 26 million people voted in the 2001 British General Election. More than 32 million votes were cast in the first season of Pop Idol.

1 According to Telescope, the communication company that handled the votes for Thames: www.telescopeuk.com/news_popidols2.html.
2 Electoral Commission, "Voter Engagement and Young People," August 2002.
3 "Survey of Attitudes During the 2001 General Election Campaign," MORI, July 4, 2001.
4 "Candidates Wooing Younger Voters," The News Journal Online, November 9, 2003.
5 "Election Leaves Young Japanese Cold," Asia Times Online, November 7, 2003.
6 European Commission Flash Eurobarometer, Post European Elections Survey, July 2004.
7 "Shellshocked Brussels Seeks Apathy Antidote," BBC News Online, June 15, 2004.
8 European Commission Flash Eurobarometer, op. cit.
9 "Weird and Wonderful Euro Vote Tactics," BBC News Online, June 4, 2004.
10 "Young People are not Interested in Politics," The Star, November 11, 2003.
11 Electoral Commission, "Voter Engagement and Young People," op. cit.
12 Ibid.
13 "For 21 Million Young Voters: What Next?" MTV.com, November 5, 2004.
14 CIRCLE, "How Young People Express their Political Views," July 2003.
15 Ibid.
16 "Ministers Contemplate Cut in Voting Age to 16," Times Online, February 14, 2003.
17 MORI survey for Nestlé Family Monitor, 16 July 2003.
18 Electoral Commission, "Voter Engagement and Young People," op. cit.
19 "Text Message Voting to be Trialled," BBC News Online, February 5, 2002.

One in six English teenagers believe that reality television will make them famous.

1 There is a pretty good analysis of reality television on Wikipedia: http://en.wikipedia.org/wiki/Reality_television.
2 "Kids seeking reality TV fame instead of exam passes," Learning and Skills Council press release, January 13, 2006.
3 http://www.economist.com/world/britain/displaystory.cfm?story_id=E1_RGDDDGP.
4 http://www.thisislondon.co.uk/showbiz/article-23123563-details/Abigail%3A+l%27m+a+WAG+wannabe/article.do.
5 http://news.bbc.co.uk/1/hi/uk/6359363.stm.
6 Ibid.
7 Ibid.
8 http://www.economist.com/world/britain/displaystory.cfm?story_id=E1_QQRJTPT.
9 Ibid.
10 http://www.economist.com/surveys/displaystory.cfm?story_id=E1_SRSRDST.
11 Quoted in "Does Class Count in Today's Land of Opportunity?," *New York Times*, January 18, 2003; http://www.nytimes.com/2003/01/18/arts/18CLAS.html.
12 Learning and Skills Council, op. cit.
13 http://findoutmore.dfes.gov.uk/2007/02/sixteen_and_thi.html.
14 http://news.bbc.co.uk/1/hi/education/6254833.stm.
15 http://www.dfes.gov.uk/financialhelp/ema/.
16 http://www.motiv.org.uk.
17 http://www.nba.com/clippers/community/.
18 http://www.dell.com/content/topics/topic.aspx/global/shared/sitelets/pub_solutions/k12/programs/dell_techknow?c=us&cs=RC957128&l=en&s=k12.
19 "Brown says public tired of trivia," Reuters, April 15, 2007.

In 2005, the US spent $554 billion on its military. This is 29 times the combined military spending of the six "rogue states."

1 Stockholm International Peace Research Institute, SIPRI Yearbook 2006, chapter 8.
2 http://www.globalissues.org/Geopolitics/ArmsTrade/Spending.asp#WorldMilitarySpending.
3 Global Issues, "High Military Expenditure in Some Places," June 11, 2003, www.globalissues.org.
4 Worldwatch Institute, Vital Signs 2003.
5 Center for Arms Control and Non-Proliferation, "FY04 Military Budget."
6 CDI, "The Pentagon Budget: More of the Same. Much, Much More," March 14, 2003, www.cdi.org.
7 Speech transcript, November 24, 2003, www.whitehouse.gov.
8 "Bush Signs $401b Defense Bill," *Boston Globe*, November 25, 2003.
9 Steve Kosiak of the Center for Strategic and Budgetary Assessments, quoted in the *Boston Globe*, op. cit.

10 CDI, "Top Seven Reasons Why We Need to Increase Military Spending (and why they're wrong)," www.cdi.org, May 1998.

11 Council for a Livable World, "Pentagon Allows Export of US Navy's Newest Jet," *Arms Trade Insider*, August 9, 2001.

12 Amnesty International and Oxfam International, "Shattered Lives," 2003.

13 International Institute of Strategic Studies, press statement, "The Military Balance 2003–2004," October 15, 2003.

14 CDI, "Top Seven Reasons," op. cit.

15 For an excellent discussion see "How the Iraq War Will Affect the International System," Project on Defense Alternatives briefing report, May 6, 2003, www.comw.org/pda/0305br15.html.

16 OS Earth Global Simulations, "What the World Wants," www.osearth.com/resources/wwwproject/index.html.

There are 27 million slaves in the world today.

1 As told to Beth Herzfeld, *Anti-Slavery International Reporter* magazine, October 2003.

2 Ibid.

3 Historical summary from www.wikipedia.org.

4 Figures from www.antislavery.org and www.iabolish.org.

5 Amnesty International, "Mauritania: A Future Free from Slavery," November 7, 2002.

6 www.antislavery.org.

7 Anti-Slavery International, "Debt Bondage" December 1998.

8 US State Department Trafficking in Persons Report 2003, www.state.gov/g/tip/rls/tiprpt/2003/.

9 Anti-Slavery International, Action Briefing, "Trafficking to the UAE," August 2003.

10 Amnesty International, "Mauritania: A Future Free from Slavery," op. cit.

11 www.freetheslaves.net.

12 Kevin Bales, "How We Can End Slavery," *National Geographic* Online, September 2003.

13 Ibid.

Americans discard 2.5 million plastic bottles every hour. That's enough bottles to reach all the way to the moon every three weeks.

1 The Rotten Truth About Garbage, "A Garbage Timeline," Association of Science-Technology Centers and the Smithsonian Institution Traveling Exhibition Service, 1998.

2 Tidy Britain campaign, quoted in "Drowning in a Tide of Discarded Packaging," Guardian, March 9, 2002.

3 All figures from Clean Air Council, "Waste Facts and Figures," www.cleanair.org/Waste/wasteFacts.html.

4 "China's Chopsticks Crusade," *Washington Post*, February 6, 2001.

5 National Rodent Survey 2002, www.npta.org.uk.

6 National Solid Wastes Management Association, "Garbage by the Numbers," July 2002.

7 "The State We're In," *Guardian*, October 23, 2003.

8 http://environment.guardian.co.uk/waste/story/0,,2035853,00.html.

9 "Tackling Britain's Waste Mountain," BBC News Online, July 11, 2002.

The average urban Briton is caught on camera up to 300 times a day.
1 Michael McCahill and Clive Norris, "CCTV in London," Working Paper no. 6, Urban Eye project, June 2002.
2 Ibid.
3 "Britain is 'surveillance society'," BBC News Online, November 2, 2006; http://news.bbc.co.uk/1/hi/uk/6108496.stm.
4 Privacy International, FAQ about CCTV, www.privacyinternational.org/issues/cctv/cctv_faq.html.
5 "CCTV: Looking Out for You" brochure, quoted in Privacy International FAQ about CCTV, op. cit.
6 "To CCTV or Not to CCTV?," Nacro research briefing, May 2002, www.nacro.org.uk/data/briefings/nacro-2002062800-csps.pdf.
7 US Department of Justice, "The Appropriate and Effective Use of Security Technologies in US Schools," September 1999.
8 "Tampa Cops Send Face Recognition Code Packing," *The Register*, August 20, 2003.
9 "Security Fears Over UK 'Snooper's Charter'," *The Register*, November 4, 2003.
10 Country summary given in Privacy International and GreenNet Educational Trust, "Silenced: An International Report on Censorship and Control of the Internet," September 2003.
11 Home Office figures, quoted in "Suspect Nation," *Guardian*, October 28, 2006.
12 Conversation with the author, November 27, 2003.
13 Conversation with the author, December 1, 2003.

Some 120,000 women and girls are trafficked into Western Europe every year.
1 Human Rights Watch interview with Bulgarian trafficking victim in Korydallos women's prison, Athens, November 2000, quoted at www.hrw.org/ campaigns/ migrants.
2 IOM, "Victims of Trafficking in the Balkans," January 2002.
3 "Facing Down Traffickers," *Newsweek*, August 25, 2003.
4 "Trafficking of Women and Children in South East Asia," UN Chronicle Online, issue 2, 2003.
5 US Department of State, Trafficking in Persons Report, 2003.
6 Equality Now, "United States: The Role of Military Forces in the Growth of the Commercial Sex Industry," June 2003.
7 Study by the Budapest Group, "The Relationship Between Organized Crime and Trafficking in Aliens," June 1999, quoted in Coalition Against Trafficking in Women International, "Ten Reasons for Not Legalizing Prostitution," www.womenlobby.org/htmldoc/reasons.html.
8 Ibid.
9 "Move to Legalize Prostitution in Bangkok Opposed," AFP, November 28, 2003.
10 UN Department for Public Information backgrounder for the World Conference Against Racism, Durban, "The Race Dimensions of Trafficking in Persons

– Especially Women and Children," August 31, 2001.
11 Presidential determination 2003–35, September 9, 2003.
12 Human Rights Watch, "Letter to Colin Powell on the Trafficking in Persons Report 2003," June 27, 2003.
13 "Facing Down Traffickers," *Newsweek*, op. cit.

A kiwi fruit flown from New Zealand to Britain emits five times its own weight in greenhouse gases.
1 "A Free Ride for Freight," *Financial Times*, November 21, 2000.
2 Sustain/Elm Farm Research Center Report, "Eating Oil – Food in a Changing Climate," December 2001.
3 "Miles and Miles and Miles," *Guardian*, May 10, 2003.
4 Sustain/Elm Farm Research Center Report, "Eating Oil," op. cit.
5 FAO, FAOStat database, 2003.
6 Erik Millstone and Tim Lang, *The Atlas of Food* (London: Earthscan, 2003).
7 Sustain/Elm Farm Research Center Report, "Eating Oil – Food in a Changing Climate" quotes two studies: D.A. Bender and A.E. Bender, *Nutrition Reference Handbook* (Oxford: Oxford University Press, 1997) and MAFF, *Manual of Nutrition* (London: The Stationery Office Books, 1997).
8 news.bbc.co.uk/1/hi/uk_politics/3025927.stm.
9 European Commission press release IP/03/1023, 16 July 2003.
10 "Local Food Costs Less at Farmers' Markets," March 2002, www. southwest foodlinks.org.uk.
11 Rich Pirog of the Leopold Center for Sustainable Agriculture, Iowa State University, quoted in "Local Foods Could Make For Greener Grocers," Science News Online, August 9, 2003.
12 Ibid.

The US owes the United Nations more than $1 billion in unpaid dues.
1 http://www.globalpolicy.org/finance/index.htm.
2 http://www.globalpolicy.org/finance/tables/core/un-us-06.htm.
3 UN press release GA/AB/3578, October 21, 2003.
4 Speech delivered at signing of UN charter, San Francisco, June 26, 1945.
5 Historical events detailed at www.un.org/aboutun/milestones.htm.
6 I am indebted to the analysis from Global Policy Forum, "Background and History of the UN Financial Crisis," www.globalpolicy.org.
7 http://www.americansforunfpa.org/site/c.enKMIRNpEkG/b.933339/k.627E/ US_Defunding_of_UNFPA.htm.
8 United Nations Association of the United States of America, "Status of US Financial Obligations to the United Nations," June 2003, www.una-usa.org.
9 Global Policy Forum, "US vs Total Debt to the UN 2004," op. cit.
10 Ibid.
11 "Peacekeeping Assessments More than $1.1 Million in Arrears, UN Official Says," UN News Service, November 20, 2003.
12 "War Crimes Tribunals Forced to Borrow Cash," *Washington Times*, November 24, 2003.
13 Quoted at www.betterworldfund.org/factsheets/o_21563.shtml.
14 Poll by Zogby International, December 1998.

15 1996 poll conducted by PIPA, quoted at www.americans-world.org/digest/global_issues/un/un3b.cfm.

Children living in poverty are three times more likely to suffer a mental illness than children from wealthy families.
1 End Child Poverty Campaign, www.ecpc.org.uk.
2 Survey for the Greater London Authority, December 28, 2002, reported at www.wsws.org/articles/2002/dec2002/lond-d28.shtml.
3 End Child Poverty Campaign, op. cit.
4 Ibid.
5 Save the Children, "Britain's Poorest Children," 2003.
6 Ibid.
7 Social Survey Division of the Office for National Statistics, "The Mental Health of Children and Adolescents in Great Britain," 1999.
8 Conversation with the author, December 9, 2003.
9 "Teenagers 'get poor mental care'," BBC News Online, May 8, 2002.
10 www.youngminds.org.uk/policy/million_children.php.
11 Ibid.
12 "Council Estate Decline Spawns New Underclass," *Observer*, November 30, 2003.
13 www.poverty.org.uk/summary/key_facts.htm.
14 www.youngminds.org.uk/policy/million_children.php.
15 Quoted in "Report Reveals Britain's 10 Poorest Areas," *Guardian*, February 18, 2002.
16 Conversation with Neera Sharma of Barnardo's, December 15, 2003.
17 Institute for Fiscal Studies, "Inequality and Living Standards in Great Britain: Some Facts," December 2002.
18 news.bbc.co.uk/1/hi/uk_politics/394115.stm.
19 http://www.ecpc.org.uk/index.php?id=63.
20 Policy Press, "Inequalities in Life and Death – What if Britain Were More Equal?," 2000.
21 MORI poll for the GMB union, December 1, 2001.
22 MORI poll for *The Times*, February 22, 2001.

Glossary

CIA The Central Intelligence Agency, the US agency which is responsible for obtaining information about foreign governments, corporations and individuals. It also has a large covert military operation.

EU The European Union is a grouping of European states which is set to expand to 25 countries in 2004. It has five institutions: the European Parliament (to which each member state elects representatives, known as Members of the European Parliament, or MEPs); the European Commission, a group of twenty appointed commissioners which represents the interests of Europe as a whole; the Council of the European Union, which is made up of ministers from the member states (and should not be confused with the Council of Europe, which is a separate international organization of 45 European states); the European Court of Justice; and the European Court of Auditors.

FAO The Food and Agriculture Organization of the United Nations. Its responsibilities include farming, production and distribution of food, nutrition and hunger elimination.

FBI The Federal Bureau of Investigation, the US Department of Justice's principal investigation body which has jurisdiction over federal crimes. It also has authority to protect the US from foreign terrorist threats.

G8 and G21 G8 stands for "the group of eight," a coalition of the eight leading industrialized nations: Britain, France, Germany, Italy, Japan, the US, Canada and Russia. G21 was the name adopted by a coalition of 21 developing nations – led by Brazil, India, South Africa and China – which famously blocked the "subsidy superpowers" at the World Trade Organization talks in Cancún.

GDP Gross domestic product is a measure of the total economic output of a country; it is often expressed as a per capita measure, which calculates the average economic output for each person. GNP, gross national product, is slightly different – it measures all earnings of all people from a particular country, wherever they may be in the world, so it includes overseas earnings.

ILO The International Labor Organization, the UN body which is responsible for labor matters. It promotes labor rights, training and representation, and was the first UN specialized agency.

IMF The International Monetary Fund, which seeks to lower trade barriers between countries by monitoring foreign exchange systems and lending money to developing countries.

IOM The International Organization for Migration, a body which works with displaced persons, refugees and migrants.

NATO The North Atlantic Treaty Organization, a grouping of nineteen countries from North America and Europe. Its main purpose is collective security through political and military means, but in the past fifteen years it has taken a more active role in peacekeeping.

NGO "Non-governmental organization" simply means an international body whose members are individuals and not states. The term spans a massive variety of organizations, from charities to community organizations to lobby groups. They are generally independent of political parties and run on a not-for-profit basis.

NRA The National Rifle Association, a powerful US lobby group that seeks to protect the rights of gun owners.

NSA In the context of armed conflict, the term "non-state actors" refers to armed groups which act autonomously of recognized governments. NSAs may be rebel groups, armed militias or de facto territorial governing bodies, and they pose a particular challenge to groups seeking to enforce international law and help victims of conflict.

OECD The Organization for Economic Cooperation and Development is a grouping of 30 industrialized countries which, according to its website, "share a commitment to democratic government and the market economy."

OPEC The Organization of Petroleum Exporting Countries represents eleven developing countries which rely heavily on oil exports. The cartel sets output levels for its members in an attempt to balance supply and demand of oil.

Perestroika An initiative launched by Russia's President Mikhail Gorbachev in the mid-1980s which sought to move the country towards a more market-oriented economy and opened up trade and economic relations with the West. It hastened the break-up of the former Soviet Union.

PLO The Palestinian Liberation Organization, a grouping of Palestinian political parties and militant bodies. Formerly led by Yasser Arafat, the PLO is generally accepted as the organization of the Palestinian people.

SARS Severe Acute Respiratory Syndrome, a viral outbreak first reported in Asia in February 2003 which spread to twenty countries, killing 774 people.

SEC The US Securities and Exchange Commission regulates public companies, stock exchanges, mutual funds, investment advisors and so on. It requires public companies to disclose meaningful information to help investors make decisions. It also brings civil actions against people and companies that break securities law.

Sharia Sharia, often referred to as Islamic law, is the body of religious law that governs Islamic life – both religious and secular. The enforcement of Sharia in the courts varies widely from country to country.

UN The United Nations is *the* international organization, counting 191 countries among its members as well as a host of "observer" missions like the Holy See (Vatican City State), the Palestinian Authority and the European Community. The General Assembly, made up of all member states, meets once a year. The Security Council, which is responsible for maintaining peace among the UN's membership, has five permanent members – Britain, the US, France, China and Russia – with twenty elected member countries serving two-year terms.

UNAIDS The Joint United Nations Program on HIV/AIDS. It is "co-sponsored" by nine other organizations, including the World Health Organization and the World Bank.

UNESCO The United Nations Educational, Scientific and Cultural Organization encourages collaboration among nations to promote education, diverse culture, science and communication.

UNFPA The UN Population Fund is the world's largest source of funding for population and reproductive health issues. It works to promote safe pregnancy and childbirth and family planning, while preventing the spread of sexually transmitted diseases (including HIV/AIDS) and violence against women.

UNICEF The UN Children's Fund, promoting long-term humanitarian assistance to children: projects include basic education for all children, immunization and child protection.

WHO The World Health Organization's objective is for all people of the world to achieve the highest possible level of health. It is governed by the World Health Assembly, which is made up of the WHO's 192 member states.

World Bank The World Bank aims to provide member countries with finance for development and poverty reduction. It is criticized by anti-globalization campaigners for pursuing trade liberalization policies at the expense of national sovereignty.

WTO The World Trade Organization deals with the global rules of trade between nations. It oversees a series of agreements signed by countries establishing trade guidelines. The WTO believes that open trade based on multilateral agreements is the best way to promote economic growth; its opponents say that the WTO's agreements provide a means for rich industrialized countries to dominate world trade at the expense of smaller developing nations.

Getting involved

If what you've read here makes you want to get active – or even just find out a bit more about some of the facts – here are some organizations that will help you do that. Obviously it's not an exhaustive list. There are many, many hundreds of aid organizations, think tanks and NGOs out there doing great work, and listing them all would take a whole book in itself. Instead, these are some organizations I found very useful when I was writing this book. If you're looking for a place to start, here are a few ideas.

Human rights groups

American Civil Liberties Union (ACLU). Founded in 1920, it claims to "fight violations of civil liberties wherever they occur," and lobbies in Washington to protect civil rights. www.aclu.org.

Amnesty International. Campaigns on a wide variety of human rights issues, and famous for its "direct action" letter-writing campaigns. The main website is www.amnesty.org.

Human Rights Watch. Dedicated to preserving and promoting human rights around the world, HRW aims to name and shame abusers while also building coalitions around specific human rights abuses. www.hrw.org.

Liberty. UK-based human rights group that seeks to secure human rights and freedoms while opposing excessive use of power by governments. www.liberty-human-rights.org.uk.

Think tanks

Center for Responsive Politics. A Washington DC-based group that tracks money in politics and its effects on elections and policy. www.opensecrets.org.

Global Policy Forum. Monitors policy-making at the UN, promotes accountability of global decisions and advocates on issues of peace, justice and citizen involvement. www.globalpolicy.org.

Jubilee Research. Began life as the Jubilee 2000 debt cancellation campaign. Jubilee now describes itself as a "think-and-do" tank. www.jubilee2000uk.org.

Worldwatch Institute. Takes a global and inter-disciplinary approach to environmental and other world issues. Its *Vital Signs* and *State of the World* annual reports are excellent. www.worldwatch.org.

Aid organizations

Actionaid. Works to secure food, water, healthcare and education for people living in poverty and enables them to stand up for their rights. www.actionaid.org.

CAFOD. The overseas development and relief agency of the Catholic

Church, CAFOD promotes poverty reduction and long-term development in more than 60 countries, regardless of race or creed. Its policy briefings on globalization are particularly good. www.cafod.org.uk.

CARE International. A humanitarian and relief organization which also provides emergency food and shelter to survivors of wars, conflicts and natural disasters. www.care.org.

Oxfam. Oxfam GB is a UK-based development, relief and campaigning organization which seeks to end poverty and suffering around the world. There are Oxfam organizations all over the world. The international website is at www.oxfam.org. Also check out its excellent Make Trade Fair campaign at www.maketradefair.com.

Anti-corruption

Transparency International. Claims to be the only international NGO devoted to combating corruption. Its Corruption Perceptions Index is a fascinating look at how people see their governments, and it has branches all over the world. www.transparency.org.

Abortion rights

British Pregnancy Advisory Service. Supports reproductive choice by advocating safe and accessible birth control and abortion. www.bpas.org.

International Planned Parenthood Federation. Links autonomous family planning organizations in more than 180 countries, and advocates for reproductive choice through sex education, contraception and legal abortion. www.ippf.org.

Naral Pro-Choice America. Works both to protect women's rights to legal abortions and to reduce the need for abortions by promoting sex education. www.naral.org.

Women's rights, family violence, female infanticide

Equality Now. Protects and promotes the human rights of women around the world. www.equalitynow.org.

Family Violence Prevention Fund. An international group that works to prevent violence in the home and in the community. Their website, www.endabuse.org, is an excellent source of research on family violence.

National Organization for Women. US-based group which promotes equal rights for women by ending discrimination, securing birth control and reproductive rights and ending violence against women. www.now.org.

Society for the Prevention of Infanticide. Seeks to educate the public on the historical and current practice of infanticide. www.infanticide.org.

Death penalty, criminal justice, discrimination

Al-Fatiha. International organization for Muslims who are lesbian, gay, bisexual or transgender. www.al-fatiha.net.

International Lesbian and Gay Association. Network of groups promoting the equality of lesbians, gay men, bisexuals and transgendered people. Their site gives a great overview of the legal status of homosexuality around the world: www.ilga.org.

Reprieve. UK-based charity which provides humanitarian and legal assistance to prisoners on Death Row in the US. www.reprieve.org.uk.

Sentencing Project. US-based charity which promotes a reduced reliance on imprisonment. It's an excellent source of research into criminal justice policy. www.sentencingproject.org.

Gun control

Brady Campaign to Prevent Gun Violence. A US-based grassroots organization named after Jim Brady, President Ronald Reagan's press secretary, who was badly wounded during an assassination attempt on the President. www.bradycampaign.org.

Control Arms. The world's largest anti-gun campaign, launched in 70 countries in October 2003, and run jointly by Oxfam, Amnesty International and the International Action Network on Small Arms. www.controlarms.org.

Health, nutrition, medical crises

Action on Smoking and Health (ASH). A group that promotes non-smokers' rights by bringing or joining legal actions concerning smoking. www.ash.org.

The Global Fund to Fight AIDS, Tuberculosis and Malaria. Partnership between governments, civil society, the private sector and affected communities to combat three of the world's most devastating diseases. www.theglobalfund.org.

International Committee of the Red Cross. Humanitarian mission established in 1863 to help victims of war and internal violence. The ICRC is at the root of the international Red Cross and Red Crescent movements, and it also promotes international humanitarian law. www.icrc.org.

Médecins sans Frontières. Medical aid agency which provides assistance wherever needed and aims to raise awareness of the plight of the people it helps. www.msf.org.

Slow Food Movement. Aims to protect cultural heritage through celebrating seasonal produce, small local food producers and traditional ways of preparing and eating food. www.slowfood.com.

Sustain. An alliance for better food and farming, which aims to promote animal welfare and protect the environment. www.sustainweb.org.

Worldhunger. Excellent online resource about hunger, its causes and effects, and what is being done. www.worldhunger.org.

Landmines

Adopt-A-Minefield. Raises funds for the campaign to ban mines. www.landmines.org.

International Campaign to Ban Landmines (ICBL). Network of NGOs in 60 countries, pushing for a total ban on anti-personnel mines. Its annual report monitors progress around the world. www.icbl.org.

Conflict

Coalition to Stop the Use of Child Soldiers. Works to monitor and report the use of children in conflict. www.child-soldiers.org.

International Rescue Committee. A group set up in 1933 at the suggestion of Albert Einstein to help the victims of Hitler, the IRC provides assistance to refugees and other people affected by armed conflict. www.theirc.org.

Project Ploughshares. This Canadian group produces an Armed Conflict Report each year which gives an assessment of all the conflicts going on around the world. www.ploughshares.ca/content/acr/acr.html.

Slavery, forced labor, child labor

African Movement for Working Children and Youth. A coalition of hundreds of grass-roots groups working to improve conditions for working children and young people. www.enda.sn/eja.

Anti-Slavery International. Founded in 1839, Anti-Slavery is the world's oldest human rights organization. It is based in London and its excellent website is at www.antislavery.org; its sister organization in the US is Free the Slaves, www.freetheslaves.net.

Fairtrade Foundation. A UK-based group which awards consumer labels – "Fairtrade marks" – to products that have been proved to be fairly and ethically traded. Their website is at www.fairtrade.org.uk, and you can find out about international initiatives at Fairtrade Labelling Organizations International, www.fairtrade.net. Another example of consumer labelling is the **Rugmark** initiative which identifies South Asian carpets made without child labor – check out www.rugmark.org.

Global March Against Child Labor. A worldwide movement based in Delhi which works with a large number of international groups dedicated to ending child labor. www.globalmarch.org.

Climate change

Stop Climate Chaos. A coalition of environmental groups, aid agencies and other campaigning bodies which aims to put pressure on the British government to act on global warming. Their website is www.stopclimatechaos. org and you can join their action campaign, I Count, at www.icount.org.uk. In the US, check out www.climatecrisiscoalition.org; international groups include the **Campaign Against Climate Change** (www.campaigncc.org).

There are many, many NGOs dedicated to the environment – here are just a few to get you started. **Greenpeace** has been campaigning on environmental issues since 1971 – it has nearly 3 million supporters and 41 regional offices. Find out more at www.greenpeace.org. **Friends of the Earth** has a UK website at www.foe.org.uk and its international site is at www.foei.org. And the **World Wildlife Fund** is making climate change one of its major campaigns: they're at www.wwf.org.

Climatecrisis.net is the official website for the film *An Inconvenient Truth* – it has carbon calculators and lots of ideas about ways you can take action.

Ethical clothing

Clean Clothes Campaign aims to educate consumers, lobby government and monitor companies to improve working conditions in the garment industry: www.cleanclothes.org. The UK platform, **Labor Behind The Label**, has reports about major British retailers at www.labourbehindthelabel.org. **Sweatshop Watch** maintains a "Shop With A Conscience" list at www.sweatshopwatch.org (mostly US companies), while Britain's **Soil Association** offers more information about organic clothing and textiles: www.soil association.org/textiles.

For a huge variety of ethical shopping alternatives – not just clothing – check out *Ethical Consumer* magazine at www.ethicalconsumer.org.

Child poverty

Barnardo's. The UK's largest children's charity which works with children and families who are at risk due to poverty, abuse or discrimination. www.barnardos.org.uk.

Child Poverty Action Group. Lobbying and advocacy group for children and families in poverty. www.cpag.org.uk.

End Child Poverty Campaign. Excellent source of facts and figures about the extent of child poverty in Britain. www.ecpc.org.uk.

Save the Children. Has an international perspective on child poverty. www.savethechildren.org.

Surveillance, privacy, information gathering

Caspian. US-based group which campaigns against loyalty cards and other information gathering by retailers. www.nocards.org.

Privacy International. Human rights group that acts as a watchdog on privacy and surveillance issues. Excellent resources and research. www.privacyinternational.org.

Think global, act local

Joining an NGO isn't the only way to start changing the world. Keep in mind the idea of thinking globally, acting locally; some of the biggest changes we can make, particularly in the environmental sphere, start with some very small actions.

One of the most important things you can do is consider how you can lessen the impact you have on the Earth. Environmentalists talk about reducing your footprint – cutting down on the amount of the Earth's resources you use. Recycle as much as you can, and buy recycled products. Encourage your workplace to implement a recycling program, too. Buy "green" cleaning products like Ecover (www.ecover.com) and replace your lightbulbs (or, indeed, all your electrical appliances) with energy-saving models; for some more ideas, check out www.energystar.gov or www. saveenergy.co.uk. Leave your car at home if you can, and take public transportation.

When you're shopping, try looking for Fairtrade products: www.fairtrade. org.uk has lists to help you find them in the supermarket, as well as links to international websites. Get Ethical (www.getethical.com) is a British-based guide to sound shopping, while Responsible Shopper (www.responsible shopper.org) is a US equivalent. Also, think about food miles: instead of costly out-of-season vegetables that have flown half way around the world, try rediscovering good-quality local produce. The Slow Food movement (www.slow-food.com) is a good resource.

Some banks are starting to incorporate ethical investment practices into their business: among others, Britain's Cooperative Bank (www.co-operative-bank.co.uk), the Banca Etica in Italy (www.bancaetica.com) and Canada's Citizens' Bank (www.citizensbank.ca) operate their business along strict ethical guidelines, while the Netherlands-based Triodos Bank (www.triodos.com) offers its clients an opportunity to invest in specific funds, like micro-finance projects in developing countries or projects to develop alternative energy sources. And to make that shopping trip slightly more guilt-free, some banks offer credit cards where, each time you use them, the bank donates to your favorite charity.

These are just a few ideas – you'll probably have plenty of your own. The most important thing is to realize that these small things do make a difference, and if lots of people join in, it'll make a difference you can see. Activism doesn't have to be about big gestures. In fact, it could be that these everyday actions are the movements that will really change the world.

Index

disinformation®